The Excellent Women

Whether ultimately these lectures will develop themselves into genuine local colleges, offering the highest instruction attainable to women, whether they will form an important part of those educational agencies of the future which are to affect not only our women but our men, it is premature to say ... But we do see in these beginnings the germs of something far greater, of something indeed capable of almost indefinite expansion and development.

Elizabeth Wolstenholme-Elmy, *The Education of Girls, its Present and its Future,* 1869.

For their work continueth,
Broad and deep continueth,
Far beyond their knowing.

Inscribed on the plaque originally in
the Entrance Hall of Atholl Crescent
and now located in the north wing of the
main concourse.

Paraphrased from Kipling's *A School Song*

THE
EXCELLENT
WOMEN

THE ORIGINS AND HISTORY OF
QUEEN MARGARET COLLEGE

BY
TOM BEGG

FOREWORD BY PHILIPPA MELLON

JOHN DONALD PUBLISHERS Ltd
EDINBURGH

A catalogue record for this book is available
from the British Library.

ISBN 0 85976 404 4

Phototypeset by ROM-Data Corporation Ltd, Falmouth, Cornwall.
Printed and bound in Great Britain by Bell & Bain Ltd., Glasgow.

Foreword

This book will be read with great enjoyment by all who have been connected with Queen Margaret College through the years. But it will also appeal to the general reader as a description of the struggle for women's education in Britain.

For most of the nineteenth century many intelligent, middle-class girls were forced to lead insipid lives at home, where often they were starved of purpose and direction. Typically there was no possibility for them to develop their talents or to occupy themselves usefully outside the family circle. Women who had no men to provide for them, (spinsters, widows and many working-class women) lived in penury with no hope of obtaining the training necessary to lead independent lives.

Tom Begg describes the poor living conditions in the older parts of Edinburgh at that time. Gradually, improvements were made. An adequate supply of clean, piped water was developed, hospitals were built and there was also heightened public awareness of the need for domestic hygiene and better nutrition.

Such progress gave Christian Guthrie Wright, Louisa Stevenson and their friends the opportunity to organise public lectures and demonstrations on cooking, as well as on matters related to household health. Their efficiency and shrewd judgements demonstrated their business prowess to all the world and they lost no chance to challenge and change public attitudes and to open doors for women. Slowly, it became acceptable for women of all classes to go out into the town on their own without escort, to learn how to become better wives and mothers by producing wholesome meals for their families. Gradually, too, women in domestic service found that they could earn better livings as trained cooks or housekeepers, developing careers which did not conflict with the vested interests of men.

Despite the hostility of many of the men in power, and despite even the objections of some of the female reformers, there was a deep underlying demand for domestic science teaching and, therefore, for appropriate teachers. By dint of persistent effort the door to women's education was levered open the first vital few inches. Domestic science colleges were founded around the country. The school in Edinburgh was one of the first, one of the best, and certainly, one of the most influential. Today it is the only one of its 19th century sister institutions that survives as an independent college of higher education.

The 'Excellent Women' in Scotland were in close contact with other leading pioneers in England. Their influence led, not only to the expansion of vocational training opportunities, but also to the opening up of university education to women. They had to face some vicious opposition.

One of my father's proudest boasts was that he was the only man in a suffragette march down the Strand one day before the First World War. As he carried a banner along with the women marchers, he was pelted with rotten eggs. After the War, he married a fellow-scientist, a second generation Girton girl, my mother. He was a great supporter of women's education and used to quote to my sister and myself what he maintained was a Chinese proverb: 'Educate a man and you educate an individual. Educate a woman and you educate a family.' But his was very much a minority view. Massive prejudice had to be overcome. It was a few determined ladies, supported by the necessary complement of a few enlightened gentlemen, who set in motion the process of equal education for women.

In 1893 the first eight women graduated from the University of Edinburgh. They had been sponsored by the Edinburgh Association for the University Education of Women and their triumph represented the culmination of a twenty-five year struggle waged, on the one side by persistent and determined reason and on the other, by bigoted prejudice and vested interest. On the night of the graduation ceremony a packed meeting of the Association rapturously saluted their Honorary Secretary, Louisa Stevenson, then also Chairman of the Edinburgh School of Cookery and Domestic Economy. For most of the years of the struggle Christian Guthrie Wright had also been deeply involved as Honorary Treasurer and principal fund-raiser ('Chrissie and her wills!'), generating the essential resources needed to sustain the various aspects of the conflict. How fitting, therefore, that exactly one hundred years on this book should have been written to pay tribute to these brave, dauntless women.

This story, however, is more than just an account of the founders. Rather it outlines the life of an institution which has flourished and evolved for more than a century. The Edinburgh School of Cookery became so popular that it gradually took over most of Atholl Crescent and the very street name soon came to be associated around the world with excellent domestic education. But nothing can stand still and in the changing world of modern times it became necessary for a new college to grow from the old. In 1970 the 'rabbit warren' of Atholl Crescent was exchanged for the purpose-built campus of Queen Margaret College at Clermiston. There were then under 500 women students. Over the past twenty years male students have joined the College - they now make up some twenty-five per cent of the student body - and the scope of the courses has been greatly expanded to embrace an impressive range of study. Under the vigorous leadership of Professor Donald Leach the College recently gained the right to validate its own degrees and there are now 2,500 undergraduates as well as others engaged in postgraduate research.

This is an enjoyable and informative book. Tom Begg is to be congratulated on making the narrative so coherent and entertaining and for explaining much of the context in which the College has existed. The reader is never overwhelmed by facts and figures. They are recorded, as is proper, but the human story is what one remembers. The personalities who have featured throughout the history of the College come across vividly. Many fascinating anecdotes are quoted from contemporary letters and diaries. After 118 years Queen Margaret College is surely on the threshold of university status. How delighted those nineteenth century 'Excellent Women' would be with the fine oak which has grown from the acorn they planted.

PHILIPPA MELLON

Acknowledgements

*T*HIS book has been my occasional, but amiable companion over several years, since it had to be researched and written in the odd corners of an otherwise busy life. It could not have been completed without the assistance and co-operation of many people to whom proper acknowledgement is due.

I am grateful to the College Principal, Professor Leach and to his predecessor, Miss Morgan for granting me unrestricted access to the College archives.

Over the 119 years of its existence the College has accumulated a formidable collection of records of one kind or another and my task was made possible by the careful manner in which important material has been preserved by previous generations of College staff. In particular, the scrap books of newspaper and other cuttings, begun in the very earliest days of the College, make up a fine record of activities over the years and I had frequent cause to appreciate the careful manner in which this material had been gathered and stored.

Various past Principals, notably Miss de la Cour and Miss Wingfield, also took the trouble to record their memories of various episodes and their notes (for speeches and so on) made it easier to understand some of the documents. Similarly, to mark the College centenary in 1975, Miss Morgan caused a portfolio to be gathered from which was assembled a short file of records outlining parts of the College history. The main collection saved much time on my part and my thanks go to those unnamed individuals who gathered this material in the 1970s.

I am also grateful to many current members of staff for their invaluable assistance. Penny Aitken, Christine Farish, Anne Marie Warnock and their colleagues in the Library were a constant source of cheerful information and advice and never failed to obtain required works of reference. In addition, past and present members of staff - one or two of whom had been students in the Atholl Crescent days - were always willing to share their memories and to impart nuggets of information. In this context individuals are too numerous to mention, but my gratitude goes to them all.

Much of the photographic material which illustrates this book was prepared with the help of the College photographer, Peter Murray, and I am grateful to him as I am to Elsbeth Talbot who contributed useful art-work and arranged the reproduction of a selection of signatures from the visitors' book. Where it has been possible to identify the copyright holder of original photographs permission has been sought and I acknowledge the help of all who allowed their work to be used.

Finally, I much appreciate the willingness of several friends and colleagues to discuss and debate with me some of the issues dealt with in the text. Thoughtful comment, criticism and encouragement were absolutely invaluable to me, particularly at those times when I was acutely conscious of being a male analysing and describing a movement and institution of major significance to women. Pam Turner, Alison Rankin, Scott Allan, Dick Murray and my wife, Mary, were all helpful in this sense. I am especially grateful to those who read and commented on the draft text, including Miss Morgan and Lady Philippa Mellon. To the latter, of course, goes my warmest thanks for contributing her generous and thoughtful Foreword.

Queen Margaret College,   Tom Begg
Edinburgh

Contents

Preamble

O N 1st September 1992 Queen Margaret College was granted full degree awarding powers by the Privy Council. From 1975 the College had been recognised by the Council for National Academic Awards as an appropriate institution to offer degrees validated by C.N.A.A. and, in the intervening period, a range of such degrees had been developed and operated successfully. Now, however, the next stage had been reached and it was time to assume full responsibility for the monitoring and validation of the College's degree programme.

At the time of this departure several of the larger Colleges of Higher Education (or polytechs) in Scotland and England were being granted the title, university. With a full-time student population of 2500 and a somewhat specialised range of courses, Queen Margaret College was just too small to contemplate such a leap. University status might have been obtained via absorption within one of the larger institutions in Edinburgh, but the College was simply in no mood to sacrifice its independence. On the contrary, Governors, Principal and staff were all confident enough in the high quality of the work of the College not to be unduly concerned about institutional titles. In its own fields of expertise the levels of attainment of students, the quality of degrees and of research, are rigorously maintained by the College and the educational environment is excellent. The future is, therefore, contemplated with confidence.

Whether or not a time will come when the continuing process of growth dictates a change in formal designation remains to be seen. What is clear, however, is that the university level education now provided by the College would have delighted the hearts of the pioneers who founded it in the 1870s. Moreover, the latter conclusion is no insignificant matter. As the story to be unfolded in the pages which follow attempts to establish, the remarkable women (and their male lieutenants) who were responsible for setting up the original college deserve no less than that their names should be for ever associated with an educational establishment of the first rank.

Education has always been important to the Scots, not least the cherished myth that Scottish education is different both in quality and approach from education in England. Such an attitude has, of course, its understandable roots in the acknowledged contribution which education has made to defining and establishing a Scottish national identity. The disadvantage of this position, however, is that it runs the risk not only of obscuring the non-Scottish roots of important developments in our education, but of significantly diminishing and undervaluing the contribution made by Scots to major advances on the wider British stage. As will be clear from the story of the founding of the college, the ladies who took the critical leading role were absolutely at the heart of the women's movement and the campaign for women's education in the second half of the nineteenth century. Full recognition of their seminal place in the history of education and in the progress and emancipation of women is long overdue.

CHAPTER ONE

The Context

*T*O understand why the original College was set up in 1875, why it took its initial form and what motivated the individuals who brought it into existence, it is necessary to understand the context. Any new institution is in a sense the product of its times and is the result of the experiences and attitudes of its creators. To understand Christian Guthrie Wright, Louisa Stevenson and the other central players it is, therefore, essential to know something of the environment in which they lived and to which they responded. Inevitably those interested in a full account of society in the mid-Victorian period must look elsewhere,[1] but a brief consideration is required of the social and economic setting, of the state of education and of the development of the women's movement.

Edinburgh is, of course, an ancient city, but its experience gave it no immunity from the ravages of rapid urbanisation in the 19th Century. Arguably, however, the problems were tackled with a style and ingenuity which was rarely matched elsewhere in the U.K. and it may also be true that the growth of the city, while often rapid, was never such as to entirely overwhelm the community and its leaders. Certainly the creation of the New Town in the period from the 1780s to the 1830s gave the city a formidable legacy of enlightened planning. On the other hand the Old Town, which was already in miserable condition by the 1830s, 'had by the mid century degenerated yet further, to become a fearful concentration of misery and vice'.[2]

The population of the city, broadly reflecting national trends, doubled between 1801 and 1831, when the total stood at 166,000. Over the next fifty years growth was only a little slower with the 1871 return showing 295,000 citizens. By 1901 the city's population had reached 413,000 inhabitants. In response to this pressure the city effectively became more and more divided so that 'there were two Edinburghs, not one'. Essentially the middle classes moved out to the New Town and beyond to the north and south, while the subdivision, overcrowding and squalor of the Old Town became steadily worse. This picture was illustrated in the vivid 1865 Report of the first Medical Officer of Health, Dr Henry Littlejohn.

The economic base of Edinburgh was, however, very different from many other Victorian cities. By contrast with Glasgow, for example, although Edinburgh and Leith had, by the 1860s, a population approximately half the size of that of Glasgow, it had less than one-third as many workers employed in manufacturing and virtually none in textiles. From the point of view of women in particular this meant that there were comparatively few opportunities for factory employment, and all through the century the dominant source of jobs for working class girls in the city was in domestic service.[3]

What Edinburgh did develop rapidly was a large and flourishing middle class. Proportionately, for example, it had five times as many lawyers as Glasgow, and its strong banking community was supported as the century progressed by the emergence of insurance and investment companies. The railway, with its host of managerial and commercial opportunities, had reached into the heart of the town at Waverley by 1846. In addition, the city remained the headquarters of the Church of Scotland and other presbyterian churches and was also a centre for publishing and journalism. To provide for this growing and prosperous community a multitude of small traders and service businesses developed, including cabinet makers, upholsterers, shoemakers, coachmakers, glass and leather workers and so on, adding constantly to the business interest within the city. Similarly, the retail sector became prominent early in Edinburgh, with almost the whole of Princes Street being commercialised by 1875.

None of the foregoing should be taken to mean that Edinburgh did not experience the horrors of slum housing, or the poverty, disease and chronic overcrowding associated with the working class areas of 19th Century British cities. However, what is suggested is that Scotland's capital was rarely overwhelmed by the extremes of industrialisation experienced elsewhere and if one were to look for a city in the U.K. of the 1860s and 70s where a confident, prosperous and growing middle class might be found, it would be hard to find a better example than Edinburgh. Indeed, if much of what we are about to consider has many of the elements of a genuine popular movement led by the middle class then the involvement of people from Edinburgh is not at all surprising in terms of time and place.

One of the factors which clearly motivated the middle classes was their concern about the threat to the health of all sections of society posed by rapid urban growth. Physical debilitation, frequent illness, incapacity through injury and premature death were the familiars of the urban working classes. In the teeming districts in which the latter lived the risks to life and limb took many forms and included chronic pollution of land, water and air, grossly inadequate provision for disposal of human sewage and often a desperate shortage of safe water. Similarly, their housing - typically in Scottish cities in towering tenements - was not only overcrowded and lacking in reasonable sanitation, but was also usually badly ventilated. Their diets were hopelessly unsuitable both in terms of quantity and quality - adulteration of food was widespread in urban communities and methods of storage and preservation were frequently primitive. And, of course, their incomes were often too low to permit either improvement or escape to a safer area. Small wonder that disease was a characteristic feature of life in such districts, but the epidemic outbreaks of typhus, typhoid and cholera which occurred from time to time at least had the effect of prodding middle class reformers into action. Although the latter could move their homes to more salubrious locations the dangers of infection were inescapable in the ordinary course of daily commerce, hence effective reforms had to address problems across the frontiers of class and neighbourhood.

The fundamental attack which was required to address the nightmare of mid-nineteenth century urban health had three basic elements. First, there was the essential requirement to undertake the major infrastructural capital works needed to make water and sanitation available on the appropriate scale. Undoubtedly, both in terms of capital cost and life-saving potential this was the most important programme and through the 1850s, 60s and 70s many cities made significant progress in this direction. In the 1850s a series of investigations in Paisley, Glasgow and Stirling showed water consumption levels ranging from 0.82 to 2 gallons per head per day in working class districts compared to as much as 12 gallons per day in middle class areas.[4] A series of water supply schemes thereafter began to transform the situation, notably in Glasgow, where, from 1859, the pure water of Loch Katrine was piped to the city over a distance of fifty miles, but also in Edinburgh where sustained pressure throughout the 1860s and 70s resulted in a great improvement. Bylaws of 1862 and 1864 compelled the introduction of water supplies and closets into rented housing; in 1869 the Edinburgh and District Water Trust was founded and a year later the major Moorfoot scheme associated with the Gladhouse reservoir was commenced. By 1878 average water consumption levels in the city had reached 34 gallons per head per day.[5] (Such a revolution obviously had major implications for standards of health, but, as we shall see, it also transformed the possibilities for housework and for the operation of households.)

The second element concerned the need to provide effective medical facilities, notably in the forms of infirmaries, dispensaries and clinics. As the knowledge, skills and reputation of doctors improved - particularly following the successful demonstration of more effective anaesthetics (1847) and disinfectants (1867) - so the influence of the medical profession became increasingly important. In 1862 Edinburgh appointed Henry Littlejohn as its first Medical Officer of Health and five years later the Scottish Board of Health was established with the enlightened Littlejohn as its principal Medical Officer. From then on the campaign to restrict population densities and to enforce tolerable standards of cleanliness carried an increasing authority.

The third major factor was obviously concerned with the way in which the mass of the working population lived. Reformers such as the Free Churchman, the Rev James Begg of Newington, in aid of his campaign for better housing, urged that 'the most important physical remedy for the woes of man is a comfortable and wholesome dwelling'.[6] But for most of the later 19th Century public policy was far more inclined to attempt to restrict and control slum nuisances rather than intervene in terms of the provision of housing. In these circumstances it is not surprising that the attention of voluntary activists should turn to life-styles and to education in the widest sense of the word.

Before considering the progress of change in the field of 19th Century education it is necessary to reflect on the impact of the industrial revolution on the home and, in particular, on women. As far as the middle classes are concerned the key point is that as factory based manufacturing developed their homes ceased to be units of production. Moreover, typically the home was also replaced by the office, shop or factory as the base from which economic activity was conducted. The result of this was that increasingly middle class women were detached from the day to day business of wealth creation and became more definitely associated with operating the house as a place of residence and relaxation. In addition, the gender division in the nature of middle class work became more sharply delineated.

From a working class point of view the pressing need to wage the ceaseless battle against poverty in an increasingly cash based society meant that unmarried women sought employment where they could find it. That could be in a factory or workshop, of course, but in a large proportion of cases it meant domestic service within a middle class household, with the result that the wives and daughters of the house were no longer required to carry out many domestic chores. Often such women came to be seen as dependent and, indeed, one public measure of a man's wealth and standing came to be the number of dependent women whom he was seen to support. Margaret Bryant is undoubtedly correct when she argues that the notion of the idle middle class woman was something of a myth[7], but it is also true that the well documented reality for many women in the households of the wealthy in the mid nineteenth century was that they had no real economic function and had few domestic tasks, perhaps beyond supervising household staff. As a momentary reflection on the garments of upper class women of the period will confirm, the clothing was almost entirely unsuitable for energetic labour and had a great deal more to do with conspicuous display. The thirty-one year old Florence Nightingale, therefore, was probably expressing a not untypical sentiment when she wrote in her diary in 1851 -

> The thoughts and feelings that I have now, I can remember since I was six years old. A profession, a trade, a necessary occupation, something to fill and employ all my faculties, I have always longed for ... Everything has been tried, foreign travel, kind friends, everything. My God! What is to become of me![8]

Josephine Butler echoed a similar sentiment in her brilliant 1868 essay on 'The Education and Employment of Women' when she wrote of the 'criminally thoughtless' men who refused to address the problem.

> I wish some of those men who talk as if they imagined our life a delightful one, could but be women for one little year, and could feel the dreariness I speak of, feel too the intense longing to be up and doing, helping in the world's work which is God's work, and know the depressing effect of that ineptitude, which is the want, not of capacity or of faculty, but of training. The serious work of life needs all the help that women as well as men can bring to it, and for helpfulness something more than goodwill is needed. Always have my own ignorance and helplessness been the hindrances to that for which I would have freely given my life; and I know that other women feel in just the same way: I have heard and known too much of thoughtful women not to be sure of this.[9]

The truth is that since they were likely to be dependent on men such women were all too often educated or trained for nothing other than marriage. Very often the emphasis of their education, such as it was, was on 'accomplishments', - music, drawing and so on - which might enhance their attractions. Moreover, since they were not expected to have an economic role it is probably the case that many parents were reluctant to lay out much money on a more formal education for their daughters, particularly if sons were also competing for available resources. Consequently many middle class girls of the period were educated very poorly, either at home, with the assistance of a governess of questionable abilities, or at a small 'ladies' boarding school, again of doubtful merit. Fortunately, this was not invariably the case for if she happened to be educated alongside a brother, or if her father had the time and inclination to involve himself, an excellent education might just be provided. There are important examples of this and it is clear that many of the women with whom we are here concerned fell into this category. But they were undoubtedly the fortunate few.

The real tragedy of this situation, however, was that it was disastrous for the large and growing numbers of women who were obliged to earn their own living. For an increasing proportion of women economic protection within marriage was not an option, and even where they did get married, there was no certainty that they would not at some point be thrown back on their own resources for survival as a result of the death or incapacity of their husband.

To some extent the problem lay in the increasing tendency of middle-class families to limit family size through delayed marriage; but even more significant were the major demographic changes which were altering the balance of the population. In the context of high levels of infant mortality girl babies were more likely to survive and this, of course, altered the balance between the sexes. Between 1851 and 1871 the numbers of single women over the age of fifteen increased from 2,765,000 to 3,228,700 and this represented a growth of 72.7 per cent in the surplus single women over a twenty year period.[10]

This was a problem which was addressed by Josephine Butler in her pamphlet wherein she analysed the 1861 census. She pointed out that of the just over 5.75 million adult women in England, less than 3.5 million were married, 756,000 were widows and 1.5 millions were spinsters over the age of twenty. Moreover, according to the census more than 800,000 wives and almost 500,000 widows had to work for their own subsistence, as well as 2,100,000 single women (including those under the age of twenty). Butler reasoned that the proportion of wives to widows and spinsters in 1861 was 3 to 2 and that nearly one quarter of wives were in some form of paid employment. From 1851 to 1861 the numbers of widows and spinsters having to support themselves economically had increased by half a million. To Butler this was 'the new order of things', with 'painfully significant' consequences in terms of female poverty and destitution.

About 3.5 million women had paid occupations outwith their own homes, but Butler thought that scarcely one thousand earned as much as £100 per year. The best paid were 'housekeepers in large establishments, a few finishing governesses, and professional cooks'. Because of the sheer numbers of unskilled, uneducated, untrained women seeking jobs, inevitably they tended to be concentrated into areas of employment characterised by low pay. People might scoff 'at the desire of women to be self-supporting: but starvation is a sufficient answer to sneers.'[11]

Butler pointed out that the principal employments open to women were in teaching, domestic service and sewing, but, as the Taunton Commission on Endowed Schools in England had just established, many of the female teachers were hopelessly unsuitable. The problem, in Butler's view, was a vicious circle.

> These women cannot teach, because they are so ill-educated, and again, they are so ill-educated that they can do nothing but teach. Many a woman rejected from the shop-till or housekeeper's room for ignorance and inefficiency, is compelled to offer herself among the lowest class of nursery governesses, or, failing all, (prostitution).
>
> The fault of this defective training lies mainly with the middle-class parents who, as the Endowed Schools Commissioners say plainly enough, educate their daughters to get husbands, and for nothing else.[12]

From the foregoing discussion it is perfectly clear that powerful economic and demographic forces were at work in stimulating the cause of the women's movement and the campaign for better female education and it is now necessary to set out some of the main elements of the latter development. Generally the focus of accounts of this phenomenon tend to be concentrated largely on events in England and on the gaining of female access to university education, particularly at Cambridge and Oxford.[13] This is not particularly surprising given the importance to women of scaling the heights both in terms of education and status. However, it may be argued that such an approach by historians has involved a tendency to ignore other facets of what happened as well as, perhaps, a degree of misunderstanding.

As has been explained, the key factor in stimulating change was economic. It was with 'the need for employment ... for a livelihood ... (for) middle-class daughters and the miserably qualified, miserably paid governesses ... that the revolution began. Here in the first half of the nineteenth century there is a deteriorating situation, a point at which pressure is building up.'[14]

A starting point in the campaign is sometimes suggested as being the foundation of the Queen's College in Harley Street in London in 1848. This college was originally created to provide some training for girls over the age of twelve who intended to become governesses, but it was quickly identified by some young women as a place wherein they might find an education. Women such as Sophia Jex-Blake, Dorothea Beale and Francis Mary Buss, who were subsequently each to exert significant influences, all enrolled at Queen's College.

The *English Woman's Journal* was an important 'rallying point and recruiting ground' for like-minded women on this subject and another key outlet was created when the Social Science Association (founded in 1857) admitted women to membership. Initially papers submitted by women had to be read by male colleagues - such was the contemporary abhorrence of women on the public platform - but it enabled the issues to be addressed in a rational and influential context. Since the Association's annual Congress was held in different cities, including Edinburgh, it attracted the involvement of regional interests and spread the ideas of reform.

A Society for Promoting the Employment of Women was set up in London with the object of advancing women's opportunities for education and employment and two of its members were Emily Davies and her friend, Elizabeth Garrett, who had already announced her intention of becoming a medical doctor. As early as 1862 the latter had unsuccessfully sought admission to the University of Edinburgh.

As far as Scotland was concerned the initiative was taken by a small group of women led by Sarah Siddons Mair who founded the Edinburgh Essay Society in 1865. The activities of this group will be considered more carefully in Chapter 2, but in 1868 some of its leaders were active in the formation of the Edinburgh Ladies Education Association.[15] According to its founders the purpose of the Association was not to encourage women to enter the professions, but to give women 'the advantages of a system (of education) acknowledged to be well suited for the mental training of the other sex'.[16] The interesting emphasis indicates a clear desire to avoid stimulating the opposition of male vested interests and this was typical of an approach dedicated to making steady progress while avoiding controversy. By contrast, a little later Edinburgh University was at the centre of the brief storm associated with Sophia Jex-Blake's first effort to secure medical training. She was in fact permitted to matriculate in 1869 and to attend classes, separately at first and thereafter in the Extra-Mural School. However, the famous Surgeon's Hall riot, when the male students prevented women from attending an anatomy lecture effectively brought this phase to a halt. Without admission to the Faculty the women could not take their studies further and subsequent attempts to obtain legal redress had failed by 1873 when the Inner House of the Court of Session declared the original admission of women as matriculated students to be illegal.[17]

According to Lady Frances Balfour, 'In the Women's Movement there were always three great fights going on. First Education, then Medicine, then the Suffrage for Women'.[18] As the above episode illustrates, the three facets of the struggle often overlapped, and it is interesting to note that 1867 saw the Scottish Women's Suffrage Society formed in Edinburgh.

In England the Taunton Commission on Endowed Schools marked a key turning point. This investigation took place from 1864 to 1867 and Emily Davies and her friends determined that the Commissioners should give attention to girls' schools as well as those exclusive to boys. She pointed out that available endowed resources were far too often cornered by schools which excluded girls. The Commission acceded to the request and eventually produced a devastating indictment of the quality of the education provided for many English girls. The education in girls' schools was characterised as unsystematic, slovenly, superficial, ignorant of basic skills, and disorganised. Undue time was 'given to accomplishments and these (were) not taught intelligently or in a scientific manner'. The Taunton Report was of 'vital importance to the cause of girls' education. Defying all the old prejudices ... it was the turning point, leading to the acceptance of a girl's right to the same education as her brother.'[19]

A vital influence on the Commissioners was Dorothea Beale's girls' school at

Cheltenham. The performance of her pupils made it perfectly clear that 'the essential capacity for learning is the same, or nearly the same in the two sexes', hence there could be no educational reason for neglecting the abilities and requirements of girls. The immediate results of the Report were the passing of the Endowed Schools Act of 1869 and the Elementary Education Act of 1870, which respectively ensured a better distribution of endowment funds and encouraged the setting up in England of elementary schools.

Meanwhile, a second and simultaneous investigation was considering Scottish elementary education. This was the Argyll Commission (1864-67). There were two basic problems in school education in Scotland. First, the growth of urban communities had progressively overwhelmed the ancient parochial school system; and second, the provision of elementary education had become hopelessly fragmented.

The slowness of the Church of Scotland to respond to the social and educational needs of city communities was one of the principal causes of the Disruption in the Kirk in 1843. The evangelicals were frustrated by the Church's inability to redraw parish boundaries and to respond to the needs of a burgeoning population. After the Disruption the seceders who formed the new Free Church set about a truly remarkable programme of church and school building. By 1850, for example, the Free Church claimed to be subsidising 657 schools providing an education for about 60,000 children, and a further 14,000 children, for whom no subsidy was being given, were also being educated in Free Church schools. Yet there was great awareness that even this huge effort was inadequate and there was a constant call for a re-energizing of the parochial school system. Dr James Begg complained to the 1850 Free Church Assembly of the unsatisfactory state of Scottish education both in terms of quantity and quality and for which he blamed the Established Church's exclusive control over parish schools. He argued that the Disruption did not settle the question of the national system of education: 'when we left the parish churches we should not have held ourselves to have left the parish schools.' He pointed out that the Church of Scotland now represented only a minority of the population 'and that unless immediate means are adopted for securing a comprehensive and effective system, the evil, instead of abating, will increase as the population advances'.[20] Moreover, it should be remembered while considering this situation that if the various denominational schools produced a patchy and fragmented system of voluntary education, the picture was further complicated by a range of independent philanthropic and industrial schools which also attempted to provide elementary education in certain localities.

When the various reports of the Argyll Commission were published the conclusion was offered that of the 500,000 Scottish children requiring basic education, 200,000 received it under reasonable and effective conditions, 200,000 were in uninspected schools of questionable merit, and 90,000 or so children were attending no school at all. The reporters concluded that of the 98,767 children of school age in Glasgow, only 48,391 were listed on school rolls. What attendance levels were like is another matter, and when considering these figures it should be borne in mind that at the time attendance by girls was likely to be more erratic since they were often required to look after younger children or to otherwise 'help their mothers'.

From the evidence collected for the Argyll Commission it can be seen that Scottish education was indeed inadequate, but it also has to be noted that there appear to have been significantly more Scottish than English children receiving elementary education and that, for the time, Scotland had a comparatively low rate of adult illiteracy.[21]

Following the Report Bills failed in Parliament in 1869 and again in 1871, but a year later the Education (Scotland) Act was passed. It was to prove to be a major point of departure and a considerably more powerful measure than the English Act of 1870. Under its terms a national and unified system of elementary education was established as the schools of the presbyterian churches were taken over by secular authority in the form of a network of locally elected School Boards. Compulsory attendance for all children between 5 and 13 years became possible almost at once and over the next three decades Scotland was provided with an excellent system of primary education as many fine schools were created. Only the Episcopal and Catholic schools stood out of the system and continued to be funded by voluntary means.

The Scotch Education Department was also created in 1872, but its location in London continued to foster allegations of the 'Anglicizing' of Scottish education and there is no doubt that the education system became somewhat centralised. However, the almost a thousand school boards which were created in cities, towns and parishes across Scotland ensured an important degree of local influence. The churches and other vested interests tended to dominate the boards, but they were particularly important to middle class women. In 1869 property-owning women had been given the right to vote in municipal elections, but the school boards offered one of the first methods by which women could not only vote, but also compete for public office and participate effectively in local politics. Flora Stevenson, a younger sister of Louisa Stevenson, was immediately elected to the Edinburgh School Board and was to become its first female chairman after the election of 1900.

What the Argyll Commission and the subsequent legislation did not tackle was, of course, secondary education. Indeed, the assumption seems to have been that such a thing was unnecessary for the mass of the population and, where the middle classes were concerned, post elementary education could be provided without state finance and via the ongoing development of endowed grammar schools. In the case of sons of the Edinburgh professional and merchant classes something of the kind was not unrealistic, but elsewhere few Scottish schools had the wealth or spread of endowments to be found in England.

Progress with children's education was obviously critically important, but something was also required at a wider and adult level and this was particularly true in respect of women. In the 1860s popular education in various forms became extremely fashionable. It was at this time for instance that W. and R. Chambers published their ten volume Encyclopaedia of useful knowledge and, similarly, the publisher, Sam Beeton, produced a variety of 'handbooks of popular knowledge'. The most famous of all such works was probably his wife Isabella's '*Book of Household Management*', which originally appeared in monthly instalments, but was thereafter published as a single volume in 1861.

Popular education, however, took various forms and one of the most significant methods was via public lectures. In 1866 Josephine Butler and Anne Clough founded the Liverpool Ladies' Educational Society which arranged lectures, typically given by sympathetic academics, and which dealt with challenging topics which required serious study. These proved to be so popular that other towns joined in and this led directly to the formation of the North of England Council for the Higher Education of Women with Mrs Butler as President and Miss Clough as Secretary.

As was mentioned earlier, the Edinburgh Ladies Education Association was set up in 1868 and its initial activities followed the same pattern. It was at first led by Mrs Mary Crudelius, the tragically short-lived wife of a Leith merchant and one of her allies was the important campaigner for women in Edinburgh, Sarah Siddons Mair. They received initial support from Professor David Masson, Professor of Rhetoric and English Literature at Edinburgh University. In 1867 he had called for women to be educated 'up to the very highest' level and in the same institutions, with the same teachers and by the same methods as were available to men. 'Till this is done our nation is unjust to half its members and exists spiritually, intellectually and in every other respect at but half its possible strength'.[22]

The lectures given by Masson in the first year were attended by 265 women and by 1873, 335 women were attending classes in such subjects as Mathematics, Moral Philosophy, Chemistry, Physiology, Botany and Biblical Criticism, taught by university staff and organised by the Association. Among the first students was Christian Guthrie Wright who was one of the early prize winners in both Literature and Philosophy. Miss Guthrie Wright went on to become Honorary Treasurer of the Association, raising funds for its activities by persuading people to support it through bequests and legacies. In 1877 the Association changed its name to become the Edinburgh Association for the University Education of Women. Louisa Stevenson, as Honorary Secretary, Miss Houldsworth and Professor Masson were other key leaders of the organisation and they saw its objectives substantially fulfilled in 1892 when, under the Universities (Scotland) Act 1889, Ordinance No 18 set out the regulations for the instruction and graduation of women.

In April 1893 the first eight ladies were capped at Edinburgh University. All of them had completed their studies earlier, but had only just become eligible for formal graduation through the new regulation. In the circumstances, the achievement of the women was remarkable and one, Miss Maitland, a Philosophy graduate, became the first female to emerge from a Scottish University with First Class Honours. On the following day *The Scotsman* drew attention to the fact that the ladies had been sponsored by the Edinburgh Association and that this was the culmination of 'a long, arduous and often discouraging struggle'. The paper particularly saluted Louisa Stevenson and Professor Masson as the 'moving spirits' behind the success of the Association and warmly congratulated them for their resolute insistence that the education offered to the women had to be identical to that undertaken by male students.

A little earlier Guthrie Wright had been forced by the sheer pressure of some of her other work to reluctantly withdraw from office in the Association, but no doubt she too richly enjoyed its 'triumphant close'.[23]

(An interesting footnote to the above subject is that Miss Stevenson and some of the others decided that the female students at Edinburgh University should have their own hall of residence, for which purpose funds were raised between 1894 and 1897. Louisa Stevenson herself donated no less than £1,000 and other notable figures including Elizabeth Garrett Anderson, Louisa Lumsden and Emily Davies also sent contributions. Through their efforts Masson Hall was opened in November 1897 with Louisa Stevenson as its first Honorary Secretary and Sarah Mair as Treasurer.)

If Emily Davies applauded the outcome of the efforts of the Edinburgh ladies to obtain University education for women, she had not always approved of the use of public lectures nor of the activities of the Education Associations. She had established a college at Hitchin in 1869 which three years later became Girton College, Cambridge. There she adopted an uncompromising 'cardinal principle' that the courses studied by women and the examinations undertaken, should be identical to those followed by male students. Her inflexibility on this position was part of her long battle not just to secure entrance for women to Cambridge University, but to obtain equality of educational opportunity and status for women. Miss Davies wrote, 'It makes me very unhappy to see the Ladies' Lectures, Ladies Educational Association, etc., spreading. It is an evil principle becoming organized.'[24] Her fear was that any form of dilution of the education offered to women would damage the pursuit of equality. As she told the Birmingham Higher Education Association in 1878,

> I confess that, for my own part, I would rather, in the interests of sound education, hear of small classes of real students, who genuinely respond to thorough teaching, than of large audiences flocking to popular lectures, listening with interest for the moment, and going away with some 'general ideas', perhaps, but without having really mastered any part of what has been put before them.[25]

Others, however, took a different view. Her friend, Anne Clough, for example, influenced by the huge reaction and response of women to the extra mural lectures offered in cities like Leeds, Manchester and Edinburgh, was perhaps more willing to respond to the needs of the current generation of women, few of whom had the educational foundation on which to construct a traditional university style course of study. She was also more willing to consider educational programmes which might be specifically geared to the perceived needs of women and, in particular, to provide credentials which would enable them to obtain employment as qualified teachers. It was in keeping with this approach that Newnham College, Cambridge was opened in 1875 with Miss Clough as its first Principal.

This fairly fundamental dispute between 'the separatists and the uncompromising' about the form which education for women should take oc-curred not just in this country, but apparently also in the United States at about the same time. In Britain it became associated with the emergence of Girton and Newnham at Cambridge and with their counterparts, Somerville College and Lady Margaret Hall, at Oxford.[26] But the issues involved had very much wider im-plications and also concerned the question of whether or not women's education should have a vocational dimension which clearly distinguished it from the education available to males. Moreover there was also the matter of how far the female reformers should strive for autonomy over female education, the implica-tion being that a degree of control might only be possible within a framework which was different.

Josephine Butler, writing in 1868, was well aware of the debate and attempted in some ways to steer a middle course.

> There are two classes of advocate of the improvement of the education and condition of women. The one class urge everything from the domestic point of view. They argue in favour of all which is likely to make women better mothers, or better companions for men, but they seem incapable of judging of a woman as a human being by herself.... ... The second kind of advocacy ... is to push into the ranks of men, to demand the same education, the same opportunities, in order that they may compete with them on their own ground. ... they have lost sight of the truth .. that men and women were made equal indeed, but not alike, and were meant to supplement one another ... each supplying force which the other lacks...[27]

Butler was a strong advocate of co-education so that males and females would be educated together wherever possible, but she was profoundly aware of the need for women to use education as a method of preparation for employment and as a means of learning to cope with every-day life. She realised that a purely elitist view was inadequate, 'for this question of women's education is far from being one of intellectual progress merely; it is a question of deep moral import, and enters far into the heart of society..' Above all, her position was that of a Christian evangelical who wanted women to be educated so that they could participate fully in the physical and spiritual regeneration of their families and of the community at large.

Butler's views were to some extent shared and taken forward by others such as Elizabeth Wolstenholme (later, Elmy) and the sisters Maria Grey and Emily Shirreff. The former was profoundly influenced by her concerns for the large and increasing numbers of women who were having to support themselves. While she applauded the setting up of Girton and called for many more such colleges she pointed out forcefully that more was needed 'for the multitude of women who cannot avail themselves of such an institution'. For these women, among whom she included 'young mothers seeking instruction ... teachers wishing to supple-ment their own fragmented education' and the thousands who only had the time and opportunity for a little instruction if it was brought virtually to their doorsteps, the best hope was the continuing development of the public lecture system.

Whether ultimately these lectures will develop themselves into genuine local colleges, offering the highest instruction attainable to women, whether they will form an important part of those educational agencies of the future which are to affect not only our women but our men, it is premature to say ... But we do see in these beginnings the germs of something far greater, of something indeed capable of almost indefinite expansion and development.[28]

Maria Grey agreed with this view, arguing that many different methods and channels were required to address the various educational needs of women and that it was not simply a case of meeting 'the wants of a picked few'.[29] It was the desire 'to bring into communication and co-operation all individuals and associations engaged in promoting the education of women and girls' that led Mrs Grey to take up much of the initiative in the setting up of the National Union for Improving Women's Education in 1871. The National Union attempted to stimulate local groups by disseminating the best available information and through mutual encouragement, but it also brought together established sympathetic national organisations such as the National Association for the Promotion of Social Science, the Society of Arts and the British Association for the Advancement of Science. In setting out the aims and objectives of the Union Emily Shirreff pointed to the urgent need to enhance the quality of female teachers, called for young, able women to dedicate themselves to the task and urged other women to uphold socially those who did so.

No law can alter social conventionality, but cultivated women can everywhere in their own home and by their own example discountenance a conventional vulgarism, and help to improve the education of the nation by receiving educators with honour.[30]

As Shirreff explained, much of the intention was to foster the development of female school education above the elementary level, but it was also the purpose of the Union to 'aid all measures for extending to women the means of a higher education beyond the school period'. Specifically, as Object Number 9 makes clear, the members wished to

assist the establishment of Evening Classes for young women already earning their own livelihood, and to obtain for women, where possible, admission to classes for technical instruction; thus helping them to fit themselves for better and more remunerative employments than are now available to them.

Members realised that it was essential to use every means possible to extend the educational provision available to women and this was why they applauded and urged an extension of public lectures on 'health and on domestic economy'. Moreover, they were well aware of the need to 'create a sounder public opinion with regard to education itself, and (to) the national importance of the education of women, by means of meetings, of lectures and of the press'. Influencing public opinion by whatever means was critical, above all because of the enormous difficulty of raising money for the education and training of girls and young women. Such was the weight of prejudice and indifference, particularly on the part of males, that almost anything which helped to stimulate a more sympathetic climate required to be encouraged.[31]

Mention of the National Union draws attention to a further point, and this concerns the question of the role of HRH Princess Louise, Queen Victoria's fourth daughter. As will be explained later, Princess Louise was for many years patron of the Edinburgh College, and it may well be the case that her influence has been somewhat undervalued in accounts of the campaign for women's education. She was a friend and confidant of Maria Grey and greatly admired the work of the latter's cousin, Josephine Butler. She wrote to Mrs Butler, 'I do take great interest in the happiness and well-being of women, and long to do everything that I can to promote all efforts in that direction', and she offered her help wherever that might be appropriate.[32] As far as the National Union was concerned, initially there seems to have been some difficulty in obtaining funds to support its efforts until Princess Louise was appointed President. Thereafter 'a long list of important Vice Presidents was not difficult to achieve'.[33] The first meeting of the Union was in fact held in the Princess's dining room in Grosvenor Crescent in London. Subsequently the group went on to establish the The Girls' Public Day School Trust and the Teachers' Training and Registration Society, both of which were to accomplish significant work in England over the next two decades.

All of the above has been explained in various sources, yet the suspicion remains that the Princess's place in this story has yet to be fully recognised. What seems to have escaped attention is not her sympathetic support for Mrs Grey and her sister and cousin, but the Princess's own personal position. Her husband was the Liberal politician, Lord Lorne (himself a member of her committee) and his father, the

Princess Louise aged 43, from an etching by Josephine Swabodow, 1891.

Duke of Argyll, had, of course, headed the Argyll Commission on Scottish Education, while his uncle, Lord Taunton, had led the simultaneous English enquiry.
Admittedly the marriage did not take place until 1871, but arguably no woman in
the country was better placed to be fully informed of the state of female education
than Princess Louise. It is known that she attended the Parliamentary debate on
the 1869 Education of Children Bill, which attempted to extend compulsory
education to all children, that she was extremely displeased at its failure to succeed
and that from then on she took a close interest in the subject. Moreover, it is
striking that someone like Sir Wyndham Dunston, who was later also to serve on
the Committee, should, in 1939, write of her 'life-long interest in women's
education, and particularly in the higher education of girls, which entitles her to
a foremost place among those pioneers to whom the people of this country must
be for ever grateful'.[34] A little more than gentle patronage would be required to
earn such an epithet from a knowledgeable individual like Dunston, hence some
further research into the role of the Princess would seem to be well justified. Given
her mother's lack of sympathy for some aspects of the women's movement, there
is no doubt that the young princess had to conduct herself with circumspection,
but her role may well have been considerably more proactive than has been
commonly recognised.

Another interesting point concerns the alliances forged by the Union which, in
contemporary writings, is variously referred to as the National Union for Improving
the Education of Women, or the Women's Education Union, or simply the National
Union.[35] Often the Union pursued its activities by and through other sympathetic
and influential organisations. In 1868 the British Association for the Advancement
of Science established a powerful committee to examine the lamentable state of
British research and education in scientific fields of study and this led directly to the
setting up in 1872 of an important Royal Commission on scientific and technical
education. Identifying a common interest, the National Union appears to have
forged effective links with the British Association at this time and it is interesting to
note that the organisation in which the Edinburgh ladies directly participated was
referred to by them as the British Association and not the National Union.[36] It is
known that both Miss Guthrie Wright and Louisa Stevenson gave time and effort to
the British Association and this may have been the channel which brought the
Edinburgh women into contact with the London leaders, including Princess Louise.
Some of the precise connections are unclear and this is a subject which deserves
further study. However, it seems certain that in consequence of their involvement
with the British Association the Edinburgh group developed an efficient and
intimate link with the National Union. For example, no difficulty was experienced
in obtaining Louise as patron at the time of the establishment of the Edinburgh
School of Cookery in 1875, and it is known that thereafter Guthrie Wright reported
regularly and informally to the Princess during subsequent visits to London. Moreover, what is absolutely clear is that the activities in Edinburgh which are shortly to
be described conformed absolutely to the objectives, principles and methods of the
Union which have been indicated above.

In setting this context three further matters may briefly be considered. First, there are the questions of the attitudes of and towards women and the sources of personal motivation which inspired to action those individuals who took the initiative. In one sense, the need to enlarge the economic opportunities of women in general presented an obviously worthwhile channel for the energies of the leaders. However, as Margaret Bryant pointed out, it is almost impossible to understand the motives of the women concerned unless due attention is paid to their strong religious faith and sense of Christian stewardship.[37] Denomination does not seem to have been particularly significant since various church groups were involved, but in Edinburgh the principals seem often to have been either Free Church or Episcopalian.

It is perfectly clear that women such as Guthrie Wright, the Stevenson sisters, Sarah Mair and so on, were entirely committed to the progress of women, but it would be quite wrong to assume that their attitudes were feminist in the modern sense. Inevitably they were of their own time and generation and they shared contemporary middle-class views in respect of the role of women within the family. They were of the generation influenced by Samuel Smiles and broadly appear to have shared his opinion that 'whenever woman has been withdrawn from her home and family to enter upon other work, the result has been socially disastrous'. They would have had no difficulty in accepting his assertion that the home was 'the most influential school of civilisation' and that 'one good mother (was) worth a hundred schoolmasters'.[38]

Essentially their view was that the woman at the heart of the home and family was crucial to the prospects of raising standards of living and conduct and that nothing could be more important than preparing (particularly working-class) women and girls for their undoubted role in life. This outlook was to some extent identified with Sir James Kay-Shuttleworth, the Lancashire doctor, trained in Edinburgh, who served as Secretary to the Privy Council Committee on Education during the 1840s. Ill-health forced Shuttleworth's premature withdrawal from public office, but it is interesting to note that in later life he became Vice President of the National Union and advised on the setting up of the Girls' Public Day School Trust.

During the 1840s, when Kay-Shuttleworth was in office, key conditions required to facilitate a major campaign in the realm of domestic education were probably lacking. As was pointed out earlier, during the years around 1870 major public works were in hand to improve the infrastructure of cities, particularly in respect of water supplies. Even when copious amounts of water were brought by the new pipelines into the cities, inevitably it took some time to distribute supplies and particularly to bring the water directly into the houses. In working class districts many decades were to pass before this was fully achieved, however, in a city such as Edinburgh major progress had been made by the 1870s, at least in the more prosperous localities. The technologies which enabled this development included cast-iron pipes, steam engines and filtration systems.

Caroline Davidson has claimed that 'the spread of piped water supplies was undoubtedly the most far reaching change in housework in Britain' in the three centuries up to 1950 and there is no reason to dispute this verdict. Undoubtedly the arrival of water in the home dramatically changed the locus of much housework and the frequency with which tasks were accomplished. Laundry work obviously moved in-doors and the possibilities of cleaning in general were enormously enhanced. As far as food preparation was concerned the situation for many households was revolutionised. In the absence of plentiful supplies of water and an adequate source of heat, cooking had been either primitive or almost non-existent in many urban homes. But as soon as women had piped water available domestic consumption levels shot up as their household activities were transformed. 'Women no longer had to carry great weights of water over long distances, queue up for it, do without or plan ahead; and cooking, washing-up, cleaning, and laundry all became simpler operations'.[39] Moreover, since the water was now generally pure it could be used straight from the tap and there was much less need to rely on drinks such as beer which had been prepared with boiled water.

By the mid 1870s the spread of piped water was sufficient to transform the prospects for the serious reappraisal of domestic cooking. Moreover, as we shall see, there was a widespread public desire for some education and training in order to take full advantage of the developing situation. In other words, earlier in the century in many urban households the scope for any kind of sophisticated domestic cookery would have been somewhat limited. By 1875, however, in Edinburgh and elsewhere, the prospects for a successful educational initiative in this area had been enormously enhanced.

As with water, so too with gas and, to a lesser extent, oil fuel. Gas as a fuel for street and factory lighting had been used from early in the century, but it was not extensively used for domestic illumination until the 1870s and 80s. Davidson argues that gas was not really developed for cooking and domestic heating until the 1880s and 90s, by which point electricity was similarly being utilised.[40] However, as we shall see, although coal fires and ranges were the typical heat sources for cooking within households in the 1870s, portable gas and oil cookers were used for teaching and demonstration purposes from the very first lectures. It is doubtful if this could have been achieved earlier, hence many of the locations in which lectures were given could not realistically have been used prior to the 1870s.

Finally, the last quarter of the nineteenth century witnessed a decisive change in the availability of food supplies in the U.K. (and in other parts of Western Europe). Up to the 1860s it may be said that the race between the increase in the population and the growth of the food supply was often uncomfortably close and that at different times and for various sections of society the supply of reasonable quantities of food of an acceptable standard was frequently inadequate. It is not surprising, therefore, that the processes of improvement were often erratic. After the ending of the American Civil War in 1865, however, the subsequent development of the North American rail network and larger and more efficient steam-ships enabled the produce of the American prairies (and of other developing parts of the world) to enter European markets in quantity and the consequence was a significant and long-run improvement in living standards.

Between 1868 and 1878 Britain ceased to grow the bulk of the wheat consumed by her population and the share of meat consumption met by foreign imports rose from one-seventh to one half.[41] By the 1890s she was importing no less than 80 per cent of her wheat requirement[42] and, whereas in the two decades up to 1868 the price of wheat in this country averaged 52s a quarter, by the 1890s cheap imported supplies had forced prices down to a typical 27s a quarter.[43]

While an improvement in the quantity of food was obviously of enormous importance to human development in this and other European countries, of great significance must also have been the level of knowledge as to how to make best use of the improved supplies and the efficiency of dissemination of that information within the community. By the 1870s the need to bring about an enhancement in these areas was clearly urgent.

Cometh the hour, cometh the women, in this case, and it is now appropriate to concentrate attention on the development of the College.

CHAPTER TWO

The Edinburgh School of Cookery 1875 - 1891

*I*N considering the origins of the Edinburgh School one final strand remains to
be mentioned. As was noted previously, the Victorian era was a period of great
demand for popular education and perhaps the most famous example of this
occurred when the Great Exhibition of 1851 attracted no less than six million
visitors to view the wonders of the Palace of Industry at the Crystal Palace in
London. The exhibition had been organised by a Royal Commission set up by the
Society of Arts and its enormous success encouraged the Society, over the next few
decades, to sponsor a whole series of smaller international exhibitions on a site at
South Kensington.

In 1873 a leading member of the Commission, Henry Cole, was invited to
supervise the exhibition for the year and he took the decision to include food as
a theme. The sub-committee appointed to organise the development of this theme
arranged to support the various exhibits by a series of public lectures to be given
by the accomplished lecturer on scientific and technical subjects, Mr J.C. Buckmaster. Buckmaster lectured while the various foods under consideration were
prepared by a French chef and several assistants.

Henry Cole was an energetic and exceedingly innovative individual. For
example, he originated the scheme for the erection of the Royal Albert Hall as
well as the training school which was eventually to become the Royal College
of Music. On this occasion he was extremely impressed by the popular response
to Buckmaster's lectures and realised that this was a consequence of a widespread need and desire for knowledge in this area. As a result, he persuaded
the committee which had organised the event to stay in existence and to
establish a training school of cookery which would work in alliance with school
boards and training schools throughout the country. The new school was not
intended simply to fill a local need. It 'was not to be a 'South Kensington', nor
even a 'London' school. It was to be a 'National' school in the sense that it was
designed to pioneer a national effort for the recognition of cookery (and
incidentally hygiene) as being vital to the interests and well being of the whole
country'.[1]

The executive committee set up to organise a National Training School of
Cookery had its first meeting in November 1873 and the following May an appeal

was launched to raise £8000 to fund the School. Despite the apparently favourable conditions - the clear interest in food and its preparation, the evident national scope for activity, the obvious demand for appropriately qualified teachers - money proved to be a major problem and in fact only £600 was raised. This prevented the more ambitious of the objectives from being attained and although the School was established successfully, it never made the hoped-for direct national impact. As Dorothy Stone concluded in her book on The National, 'nothing happened ...unaccountably the advantage was not pursued. .. The National was henceforth to be for ever haunted .. by the spectre of insolvency.'[2]

Nevertheless, at a more limited level, the National School did develop a distinguished history. In January 1874 a Lady Superintendent was appointed and a staff of cook-instructors was recruited. The first class of fourteen students was admitted on 23 March of that year and each student paid three guineas for a course initially lasting just two weeks. Thereafter courses developed quickly and by the end of the first twelve months 176 students had successfully completed training and obtained qualifications. Interestingly 27 of the latter were cooks accompanying their mistresses and their status was indicated on published lists by the omission of any prefix to their names.[3]

On July 7th, 1875, *The Times* carried an article commenting on the Second Report of the Executive Committee of the National Training School and noted that the School claimed to have clearly defined objects, established principles, agreed methods of operation and results tested by examination. Yet it grumbled that, 'last year everyone, except the people for whom the School was intended, was busy cooking'. The intention was 'not so much to teach good cooks how to cook better, as to show the great mass of the working people how to make the most of the food material which is nowhere so good, so abundant, and so vilely cooked as in England.' So far, most of the pupils had been 'fine young ladies' of the middle class and it was acknowledged that their small fees had helped to provide essential funds, but the most important objective was to make training much more widely available. 'With this aim instructors are being carefully and slowly trained to go forth to those towns which are following, one after the other, the example of South Kensington and setting up Schools of their own'. The article concluded by drawing readers' attention to the lack of financial resources which was thwarting 'so wise and practical a purpose'.[4]

(In passing, the National School never developed into a higher education institution and throughout its eighty-eight year history it was constantly dogged by financial problems. In 1962 lack of money finally forced its closure, but when its properties and other assets were realised the Executive committee was able to hand on £100,000 to endow the Nutrition Department of Queen Elizabeth College in London, hence its influence may be said to continue in the latter College.[5])

Watching these events with great interest from Edinburgh were a number of people and, in particular, Christian Edington Guthrie Wright. Either in late 1873 or in 1874 she told her friend Sarah Mair of her plans.

Christian joined me as we left St.Paul's Church, York Place, and confided in me her intention to proceed to London in order to visit the then recently opened classes for the teaching of cooking at South Kensington and of herself undergoing the training that she might on her return initiate similar work in Edinburgh.[6]

Sarah Mair dates this conversation in 1873, in which case Christian would have known of the plans in respect of the National when its Executive Committee had been established, but before a single course had commenced. However, Sarah was writing half a century after the event, hence it may just have been a slip of the memory since the comment refers to 'recently opened classes'. In any case it is clear that Miss Guthrie Wright was well informed of developments in London from a very early stage. At that time she was approximately thirty years old and looking for an appropriate outlet for her considerable energies.

Christian Guthrie Wright had been born in Glasgow on 19th April, 1844, and, as happened with so many women at that time, her mother had died of puerperal fever within days of the birth. Consequently Christian's apparently somewhat lonely upbringing was largely at the hands of her father, Mr Harry Guthrie Wright, Manager of the Glasgow and South-Western Railway Company. She was sent to a boarding school, but where it was located is not known, and she spent many of her school holidays with a variety of elderly relatives. However, her father was a man of 'wide knowledge and of elegant tastes, a singer and a writer, if not exactly of poetry, of neat and witty *vers de Societe*'.[7] He appears to have taken the time to cultivate in his daughter a genuine curiosity and interest in the world and its ways.

At some stage in the early 1860s Christian came to Edinburgh where she became companion and guardian to her father's venerable aunt, Mrs Stewart, who was in her late 90s. For an energetic young woman the restraint involved in caring for the old lady must have been considerable and Sarah Mair comments on the 'sweet temper and self-control exercised by the youthful partner throughout the restrictions and loneliness inseparable from the position. Country walks in which my sister and I shared occasionally and a few concerts were the chief contributions made to the gaiety of her life'. Eventually, after reaching her century, Mrs Stewart died, and Christian and her father ultimately settled down at No 2 Lansdowne Crescent where they were both to live out their lives.

Christian had been introduced to the Mairs by the well known Edinburgh doctor, Alexander Wood, and her circle of friends grew rapidly as father and daughter extended the hospitality of their new home and as she plunged into a variety of social and charitable activities which earned for her a reputation as a capable organiser.

As was mentioned in the first chapter, in 1865 the Edinburgh Essay Society was established and it is worth pausing for a moment to reflect on this association, which was later to be known as 'The Ladies' Edinburgh Debating Society'. It was originated by Sarah Mair with the support of her father and functioned throughout most of its seventy year history in the Mair's dining room, first at 29 Abercromby Place and, from 1875, at 5 Chester Street. Throughout its history this Association made an important contribution to the development of a galaxy of able Edinburgh women, but the original Society was particularly important in terms of the role which it played in bringing together and stimulating the young pioneers of the women's movement in the city. Its journal, *The Attempt* (later *The Ladies' Edinburgh Magazine*), published monthly, allowed their ideas to be circulated in print, first for private distribution and subsequently for public sale. Much of the Society's attention was taken up by matters of literary interest or by topics of a more lightweight nature. However, from the earliest days it 'reflected the growth of what might be called the Renaissance of Woman' - as early as 1866 the group debated the case for women having a Parliamentary vote, which they rejected by 20 votes to five - and a similar continuing interest was in women's education.[8]

Christian Guthrie Wright was one of the first members and among the other founders were such brilliant women as Charlotte Carmichael (later Mrs Carmichael Stopes, mother of Dr Marie Stopes, the early protagonist for birth control), Elsie Stirling of Kippendavie, Mary Lees (sister of Sheriff Lees) and Bessie Scott Moncrieff. In subsequent years other interesting recruits, listed as 'valuables' by Sarah Mair, included Flora and Louisa Stevenson, Margaret Houldsworth, Elizabeth Oswald, Margaret J Urquhart, Anne Dundas, Flora and Rosaline Masson (daughters of Professor Masson), and Louisa Lumsden (one of the original five students at Hitchin/Girton College, Cambridge).

Beyond doubt this society exercised an important influence by allowing a group of gifted young women to develop their interests and self confidence to the point where they, individually and collectively, could make a significant impact on the community of their day. 'The movement for the Higher Education of Women was colouring the horizon during all the earlier years of the Society's life, and the furtherance of the Cause frequently occupied its attention.'[9] Not surprisingly, therefore, the members were, and regarded themselves as being, pioneers. 'The leading figure throughout' was Sarah Mair, (known to her friends as Sally), and much later her many activities were rewarded when she was appointed D.B.E.. In 1920 she was also honoured by the award of an LL.D. by the University of Edinburgh.

In Sarah Mair's scrap-book Christian Guthrie Wright's name is recorded 'with affectionate pride' and the two remained firm friends and collaborators. As was noted earlier, Christian attended Professor Masson's extra-mural classes at the University, distinguishing herself as a prize-winner and subsequently becoming a leading campaigner for entrance for women to university by accepting office as Honorary Treasurer of the Association for the University Education of Women.

How Christian first became aware of the activities concerning the National Training School in London is not known and it is possible that either Dr Wood or, indeed, Professor Archer of the Industrial (Science and Art) Museum might have approached her on the subject. The latter, for example, might well have had direct contact with Henry Cole's activities via the Society of Arts. However, it is even more probable that she discovered the matter herself through the British Association

(National Union), which was committed to disseminating appropriate information, and that thereafter she personally took the initiative. Writing in 1925, Miss Ethel de la Cour, then College Principal, wrote that Christian

> had herself felt the want of definite training in Cookery and the other household arts, and she believed that the same desire for instruction was shared by other women, and that she would have their sympathy and co-operation in her endeavour to supply such classes. With her usual thoroughness Miss Guthrie Wright waited to give her ideas to the public until she felt she could do so with full success...[10]

On 21 April 1875 *The Scotsman* carried an advertisement for a public meeting to be held at four o'clock that day in the lecture theatre of the Industrial Museum 'to consider the expediency of establishing a Course of Lectures on Cookery with Demonstrations and relative arrangements'. The report on the meeting which appeared in the following day's *Daily Review* commented that 'Miss Guthrie Wright .. had been foremost in the movement' leading up to the meeting, hence her personal initiative may well have been crucial. However, the other leading participants on that day are also of interest.

The meeting was well reported in *The Scotsman*, the *Edinburgh Courant* and the *Daily Review,* the latter describing the 'large' attendance as being 'principally composed of ladies'. Lord Provost Falshaw chaired the meeting and the other principals were listed as the Rev Dr Robertson, the Rev Dr Begg, Dr Wood, Professor Archer and Miss Blyth. The two clergymen mentioned were both well known for their interest in educational matters. Rev Dr James Robertson was Church of Scotland Minister for Newington and Dr Begg's Free Church parish was in the same part of the city and their joint participation illustrates the interest of both denominations in being involved in any such venture. However, it is interesting to speculate that the resourceful Christian may well have gone to some lengths to secure the attendance of two such heavy-weight churchmen.

Begg's presence is particularly noteworthy. Not only had he been Moderator of the Free Church in 1865, but he was famous for his forthright views and had taken an active public stance on behalf of women. When the Disruption occurred in 1843 a key issue at the first Assembly of the new Free Church was whether or not women members of congregations should have an equal right to vote in the election of ministers and other office bearers. 'Dr James Begg came forward as the champion of Woman's Rights (and asserted) that the females of their congregations had an equal right with the males to give their voices in the elections..' This was bitterly contested at the Assembly, but after the matter had been sent to presbyteries for consideration the claims of the women were conceded 'without any very serious disturbance'.[11] This was one of the very earliest examples of women breaking through into something approaching a public democratic context, and it is very likely that Begg's presence on the platform was at Christian's deliberate invitation.

The main resolution, which was passed unanimously, was

> That in view of the great success which has attended the establishment of Schools of Cookery in London and elsewhere, and of the fact that School Boards are introducing

instruction in Cookery into Girls' Schools, it is desirable that some means should be provided in Edinburgh for acquiring a systematic knowledge of the general principles of this Art.

In fact, the motion is somewhat misleading in its suggestion that school boards were actively introducing cookery in Scotland since, as will be indicated later, it took no little time and effort to establish the subject in Scottish schools. However, the main intention of the motion is quite evident and it was proposed by Dr Wood. In his speech Wood made it clear that the movement to secure the proposed lectures 'had been set on foot principally with a view to benefit the working classes'. The object was to provide the skills of cooking to enable working class wives to 'secure the comfort of their husbands and families', and he had no doubt that the matter was also particularly important in terms of health. The selection of the right type of food and its proper preparation were of great importance. 'In the course of an extensive practice he had found more evil arising from indigestion than from almost any other cause'. Moreover, he earnestly hoped that an improvement in domestic cooking would contribute to a reduction in drunkenness by encouraging men to go home rather than to the public house.

The second motion, also passed unanimously, was to establish a provisional committee, under the chairmanship of Lord Provost Falshaw, to arrange the lectures and other means of giving effect to the first resolution. Begg was the proposer on this occasion and he urged the importance of a knowledge of cooking in women of every class, 'and in expressing a hope that in the new school the good old-fashioned Scotch dishes would not be neglected, (he) mentioned that he stood there as a living proof of the nutritious properties of Scotch porridge. (Laughter)'.

It was then also agreed to set in hand means of raising funds via a subscription list. Finally, Professor Archer told the meeting that he would make the lecture theatre of the museum and kitchen facilities available for the public lecture programme. The intention was that the first series of lectures would commence in the following winter, that they would be delivered by a professional lecturer recruited from London and that the necessary arrangements would be made by Miss Guthrie Wright.[12]

At the meeting Christian was appointed Honorary Secretary of the Provisional Committee and Mrs MacDougall of Gogar became Honorary Treasurer. Two days later Christian's minute of the meeting was published for display at the museum and in it the matters mentioned above are all noted. But in addition the minute also declares the intention of encouraging the leading citizens of the city to associate themselves with the venture by persuading them to allow their names to be included on a General Committee list. To promote this end it was agreed to invite 'Her Imperial and Royal Highness the Duchess of Edinburgh, Her Royal Highness the Princess Louise, and Her Grace the Duchess of Buccleuch, to do the Committee the honour to become Patronesses of the proposed School in Edinburgh'.[13] It was suggested that this procedure was following the example set by the National in London, but it is interesting that the method of attempting to give social status to female educational initiatives was as suggested by the National Union. All of the patronesses accepted the invitation and when the Dowager Lady Ruthven sent a donation of money, she too was promptly recruited as a fourth patroness. (As a matter of interest, the Duchess of Edinburgh was Marie Androvina, only daughter of Tsar Alexander II of Russia, who had, in 1874, married Queen Victoria's second son Alfred, Duke of Edinburgh. Her connection with the College seems to have been purely nominal.)

In its report of the meeting the *Edinburgh Courant* quoted Professor Archer as stating that Miss Guthrie Wright would, during the summer, go to London to make herself fully familiar with the arrangements of the National at South Kensington in order to ensure that the best practices would be adopted by the courses to be offered in Edinburgh the following winter.

The Courant was so impressed by the meeting that it felt moved to accompany its report with a leading article on the subject.

> ... The presence of some hundreds of ladies at the meeting in the Museum of Science and Art proved how warmly the movement is likely to be welcomed in the city, and we are disposed to augur the greatest results from the institution of the proposed school of cookery, if it be carried on with the necessary zeal and judgement. In point of fact, there is no question on which all classes of society can so well unite ... The upper classes, the middle classes, and the poorer classes are equally interested....
>
> ... Cookery is amongst the middle classes practically a lost art.... As far as women in still more humble circumstances, the question is one of really vital importance ... The gain, physically, morally, and pecuniarily, from an improvement in the dinners of hardworking people is simply incalculable.... The greatest care, then, should be taken to avoid any appearance of exclusiveness in the course of instruction offered.

The article then went on to call for very low charges for instruction to be set in order to ensure 'a lecture-hall filled to overflowing with the wives and sisters of all classes of the community'.[14]

By the early summer arrangements were sufficiently far advanced for an Executive Committee to be able to take over from the provisional committee and to announce that the programme of lectures, demonstrations and practical classes would commence the following winter in the Museum and under the superintendence of an 'Instructress trained and certificated in the National Training School of Cookery, South Kensington.'[15] The members of the new Executive Committee included Professor Archer, Dr Tuke, a Mr Clifton and Miss Guthrie Wright's father, but otherwise was composed of ten women. These included Mrs and Miss Robinow, Miss Anne Dundas of Polton and Miss Louisa Stevenson and, in November of the year, the latter succeeded Mrs MacDougall as Honorary Treasurer.

The attempt to find a suitable teacher to conduct lectures resulted in the appointment of Miss Isobel D Middleton, the daughter of an Edinburgh doctor, and she was selected from some forty applicants. Miss Middleton was sent to South Kensington to undertake training with an allowance of £40 to cover all her expenses and Christian accompanied her (at her own expense) and completed the same course of instruction as well as investigating the operation of the College. The two women appear to have been in London for three months, from July until the end of September.[16]

Interestingly, copies of the published exam results and of Christian's certificates in Artisan Cookery and Cleaning have been preserved and these are reproduced at Appendix A. It will be seen that she scored very high marks in her subjects and finished top of the first grade students in her written examination, scoring 965 marks out of 1000. Miss Middleton, with 750 marks finished top of the second grade. Despite these results there never appears to have been any question of Christian herself taking lectures or giving demonstrations and it is evident that some sort of social or professional distinction operated. Her designation as Honorary Secretary indicates that she drew no salary for her work and she certainly took care to explain to Lady Ruthven in the letter quoted above that she had gone to London at her own expense. She was, therefore, determined not to be seen as an employee or a member of staff, but rather as a lady giving voluntary leadership. Probably this was partly a matter of personal preference, but clearly it was an essential requirement if her social position was to be protected, and that had implications not just for herself, but also for her ability to mix with and enlist the support of leading men and women in society.

On October 19th advertisements in *The Scotsman,* the *Courant* and the *Review* announced that the public opening of the Edinburgh School of Cookery would take place on Tuesday 9th November in temporary classrooms in the Museum and that the programme of classes would commence from the following day. The prospectus indicated lessons in Superior Cookery, Plain Cookery and Artisan Cookery. Superior Cookery classes were to be held on Wednesday and Friday afternoons and would cost 3s for a single lesson or £1.10s for the course of twelve lessons. Plain Cookery classes were scheduled for Wednesday and Friday mornings from 11am to 1pm with the course of twelve lessons costing £1.1s and an individual class 2s. Artisan Cookery classes were to be available on Saturday mornings from 10am to 12am and again, on Saturday evenings from 7 o'clock. In this case the morning classes were specifically declared to be intended for teachers and pupil teachers in elementary schools and pupils in secondary schools, but members of the public were also to be admitted. The charge for the morning was 4d per class. The evening class was available for half that price and was declared to be 'for women only'. Clearly, the effort was going to be made to meet the needs of all sections of the community.

The advertisement then went on to illustrate another facet of the thinking of the Executive Committee for it indicated that following the end of the Edinburgh session, the Committee would be prepared to arrange similar public lectures in various venues in other towns and cities. Interested parties were invited to contact Miss Guthrie Wright.

On the same day as this notice was given a long article was published in *The Scotsman* under the heading 'The National Training School of Cookery, South Kensington' and it was written by Christian, although in the guise of 'a student of the School'. She set out the objects of the National as being to train and qualify teachers of cookery, to provide training in cookery for those willing and able to pay the fees, and to recruit, equip and prepare teachers and lecturers to go out to offer instruction in provincial towns and cities. The facilities of the National were described, as were its scale of charges and the attributes which were to be sought in a potential teacher. The latter should be well educated already and 'may well be the daughter of a clergymen, doctor, lawyer or half-pay army or navy man ..' In Christian's personal view, the candidate also required to have shown some interest in and aptitude for, culinary matters, since she had already seen more than enough to convince her that a talent for teaching cookery was 'by no means universal'.

The period of training for a teacher was twelve weeks, for which the fee was ten guineas. This could be paid personally by the student, but the preferred way was, as had happened with Miss Middleton, by a local committee sending her to London to equip herself to return to teach in the community. This was preferred because it was the method most calculated to result in the knowledge gained being disseminated to the common advantage.

The article also describes the content of the various courses in scullery work, artisan cooking and higher cookery. In the scullery the mysteries of cleaning various types of range and cooker were explained and it is interesting to note that these included gas cookers. Indeed, in her description of cookery lessons she makes it clear that gas cooking was best for the purposes of teaching and demonstration.

> The teachers cook chiefly upon gas stoves fitted into a kind of counter, as a large audience would not see the cooking on an ordinary kitchen range, and the latter mode would besides oblige the teachers to turn their backs upon the audience.

(It is noteworthy that this was taking place at a time when very few people had gas cooking facilities in their homes and a decade or so before the gas companies began seriously to compete in this area.)

Students were expected to complement lectures and demonstrations by reading the recommended texts and the fee for each examination was 2s6d. Intending teachers devoted the second half of their studies to supervised preparation of food, with the resulting products being either consumed by students and staff or sold to visitors.

Christian also pointed out that thus far only a limited number of intending public instructresses had come or been sent to the college. While she was there the only ones preparing to fulfil such a role were a lady from the proposed Liverpool School of Cookery (where Miss Fanny Calder had taken the initiative), two representatives of religious orders, and one or two ladies seeking to be qualified for the London staff. A few others were simply pursuing a personal interest. 'The school is still attended and supported chiefly by ladies and (their) cooks attending one or more of the classes'. She continued,

> The real difficulty lies in reaching working people. Classes that wives and mothers are expected to attend have, as a rule, proved to be failures. This difficulty is in England

met in the most practical of all ways, by active measures being taken to bestow instruction in cooking on the young.

She indicated the support being given by the London School Board and pleaded for the same back-up and consideration to be given in Edinburgh.[17]

Further adverts for the forthcoming launch of the Edinburgh School appeared in the local press on 27th and 30th October and on 8th November, and it is hard not to be impressed by the amount of effort which was made to excite public interest. Moreover, in private great attention was given to securing an impressive list of personages on the platform at the opening demonstration. The Lord Provost had agreed to chair the proceedings and letters of invitation were fired off to various dignitaries including Professor Sir Robert Christison, the Dowager Lady Ruthven, James Cowan, MP, Baroness Burdett Coutts, a host of distinguished academics from the university, Edith Nicolls from the National, Fanny Calder from Liverpool and, not least, the Earl of Rosebery. Names were delicately dropped in the correspondence, particularly of those whose presence had been secured, and the result was an impressive line-up on the great day, even although Rosebery was among those whose formal apologies were read out.[18]

The turn out at the opening of the School was nothing short of phenomenal. It was estimated that an audience of about one thousand, mainly ladies, crammed into the lecture theatre of the museum, blocking all the passages and doorways, and that at least a similar number were unable to gain admittance. 'All classes of the community were here represented - ladies of fashion, young and old, being quite as numerous as plump cooks and girls apparently of the domestic servant class', reported *The Scotsman*. Generally the press seem not quite to have known what to make of the excitement, but all fully reported the event and a few days later the *Dunfermline Saturday Press* produced an editorial on the subject. The occasion was likened to a religious revival and the editor described the

crowd of eager, interested persons .. seen hurrying to the rendezvous - pushing and jostling each other with that exquisite disregard of the ordinary civilities which has now apparently become the exclusive prerogative of a well-bred Edinburgh mob. Chambers Street seemed for the nonce turned into a cab-stand. University dons, influential citizens, blooming maidens, spectacled blue-stockings, grave matrons, with an occasional 'lewd fellow of the baser sort' were to be found converging .... And what do our readers suppose was the cause of this remarkable excitement? .... The new thing that in this instance brought the whole city together was - the cooking of an omelette![19]

Miss Middleton did indeed demonstrate the preparation of an omelette and a souffle, but before then various speakers had told the audience of the importance of what was being attempted. Dr Wood, for example, claimed that all sections of the community required to have a much greater knowledge of the digestive system and of the need for proper cooking and that such a reform could only be brought about 'through women and women alone'. He indicated his awareness of 'a great difference of opinion as to the proper sphere of women in educational matters', but there could be no doubt of their importance in this area. Professor Hodgson agreed with the need for attention to be given to cooking, but he had also always 'been an advocate for higher education for women'. Rev Professor Calderwood declared 'that it was no simple question of cookery that they were occupied with. It was something much wider and much more important..' The educational requirements of the community could not simply be met by the elementary schools of the school boards, hence the present initiative was greatly to be welcomed. It was noted that the School intended to be self-sufficient and that it was hoped to raise £500 in order to secure a permanent building. To warm applause Sir Robert Christison thereafter formally declared the School open, and finally, the one lady to speak, Miss Louisa Stevenson, proposed the vote of thanks.[20]

(In passing, it has to be noted that Professor Sir Robert Christison's involvement was a quite remarkable tribute to Christian's diplomacy. A year or two earlier Christison, the Queen's physician, had been the most implacable of opponents barring the progress of Sophia Jex-Blake and her friends in their attempt to secure medical education at Edinburgh University. His participation on this occasion, therefore, is the clearest possible evidence that Christian and her colleagues were deliberately following a method of operation which was designed to avoid conflict with powerful vested interests.)

The first session of classes commenced on the following day, but a week later the new School presented a second large public lecture. On hearing of the intention to open the Edinburgh School, J C Buckmaster, the famous lecturer who had occupied the stage at the Great Exhibition lectures at South Kensington in 1873, had written to Christian indicating his disappointment at not being invited to make the initial presentation in Edinburgh. By the time his letter reached Miss Guthrie Wright on 29th October the arrangements for the first lecture were too far advanced to alter, but it was swiftly decided that he should be given the platform on the afternoon of Monday 15th November.[21] Once again Christian applied herself to the tasks of securing maximum publicity and the support of leaders in the community.

On this occasion the local MP, James Cowan, was in the chair and he informed the 800 strong audience that the present law governing Scottish school boards prevented them from using ratepayers' money to provide examinable instruction on cooking in board schools. He urged his audience to petition Parliament for a change in the law since he believed that if a board could provide five shillings for each child 'who passed the test examination, and if 5s additional were given for each one who could cook a dinner for six persons at the cost of a shilling, that would pay for the support of the School of Cookery. That would surely be a small matter to take out of the ratepayers' pockets. (Hear, hear!)'.

The content of Buckmaster's lecture is extremely interesting, even from a modern perspective. He argued from the assumption that the art of cooking must logically be as important as the science of agriculture and that people had to learn what good cooking really meant. It should not be confused with expensive cooking because part of the concern was with good budgeting. 'The true object of cooking was to make food, not only more palatable, but more digestible; and properly prepared food would sometimes do more good during sickness than the doctor'. It was vital that the instruction was not confined to the middle classes, but that the message was passed on to poorer women. 'That seemed to him the true religion of common life'. As far as specific foods were concerned, he advised the School of Cookery to give close attention to the preparation of bread. From observations made on his visits to Scotland it seemed to him that Scottish bread was not properly baked and was often subject to adulteration. He also urged the use of macaroni,

> because it was made of the whole meal, and contained all the phosphates that were lost in the preparation of flour for white bread. It would be just as reasonable for persons to insist on blue carrots and green beef as to insist on white macaroni and white wholesome bread. In both cases they were the result of dishonest manufacture.

He advocated less dependence on meat and urged people to take their 'nourishment instead from the nitrogenous matter of vegetables, eggs, milk and cheese'. He claimed that most of the 'misery of bad food was not produced from poverty, but from ignorance'. He was enthusiastic for onions and potatoes and particularly approved both porridge and haggis which he considered to be healthy and nutritious. He hoped that haggis 'would never, for the sake of Scotland, cease to be a national dish. (Applause and laughter). In some parts of London it had been sneered at as 'boiled bagpipes' (Laughter), but it was an eminently wholesome article of diet ...(which)... was originally a French dish.' He commended the new School to 'thoughtful, intelligent ladies', and urged the school boards of Scotland to ensure that the instruction was made available to the children of the working classes.

Buckmaster's lecture was received with loud applause and as he spoke Miss Middleton demonstrated the preparation of vegetable soup, sole au gratin, and an omelette and showed how 'to boil potatoes properly'. Much later College mythology held that 'Buckmaster's cooking fat caught fire during his lecture', but the contemporary reports make no mention of such an occurrence and are quite clear that Miss Middleton did the actual cooking.[22]

Following this very high profile launch, the School's first winter programme of classes quickly settled down, but the local press sustained its interest. A few days after Buckmaster's performance *The Scotsman* carried an editorial on the subject, commenting that the Edinburgh School of Cookery was a 'useful institution (which) since its opening last week seems to have gained ground largely in the estimation of the female community'.

> All the classes have now been fairly set agoing, not the least important being one for artisan cookery, in which instruction is given in the preparation of the plainer kinds of food. To many careful housewives the 'superior cookery' class will no doubt prove of advantage; and that this is felt to be the case was evidenced by the large attendance at yesterday's class, when the lady teacher gave a 'demonstration' on the cooking of fish.[23]

As will be explained shortly, the earliest hopes of easily obtaining the co-operation of the Edinburgh School Board proved to be somewhat premature, but other sympathetic individuals and institutions soon took notice of what was being attempted. At the beginning of December the Governors of the Merchant Company School for Young Ladies in Queen Street resolved that its senior pupils should be given instruction on cooking and that the School of Cookery be invited to provide this facility. This, of course, was not quite the group of children that Christian hoped to target via school board schools, but it was a beginning.

Similarly, groups in other Scottish towns and cities began to respond to the lead being given in Edinburgh. On 1st December a delegation from Glasgow led by Sir James Watson and Lord Dean of Guild King visited the Edinburgh School. In fact when the request to entertain the delegation arrived Christian immediately arranged for her father to host a private lunch for the visitors followed by attendance at a class.[24] *The Scotsman* reported that the object of the visit was to discover what was being done with a view to establishing a similar institution in Glasgow. The visit appears to have been lengthy and thorough and the guests were particularly interested to watch Miss Middleton conducting a practical class. 'We understand that the directors of the School conveyed every information desired by the Glasgow deputation, who were well pleased with the scheme and its practical operation'.[25] From this account it is clear that Christian's instinct for every available scrap of publicity was being fully deployed. This visit was quickly followed by the establishment in Bath Street of a Glasgow School of Cookery and lectures commenced there from the spring of 1876. Most of the students apparently came from the prosperous west end of the city. At the end of its first session the Glasgow School Board declared its intention of introducing cookery in three of its evening schools in the autumn of 1876 and of using the School of Cookery, where Miss Price would be assisted by Mrs Black, to train teachers.[26] (This development provided one of the roots of what was eventually to become Glasgow's Queen's College.)

In these very early days the Edinburgh School remained at its temporary base in the Museum of Science and Art, an arrangement which obviously could not long continue. However, until such time as sufficient funds had been raised there was no possibility of purchasing a more suitable location, and Christian and the Executive Committee had to search frantically for premises which might be rented at a modest charge. Various alternatives were considered, but eventually a better temporary base was found almost directly across Chambers Street from the museum. Towards the end of December a short lease, lasting until the end of April 1876, was obtained for a large lecture hall with adjoining room and a small lecture hall, both located at the Watt Institution and School of Arts. The rent for the period was £50 and the large hall was to be available on Thursdays and Saturdays while the smaller theatre was required on Wednesdays and Fridays. Utensils and equipment were located in the ante-room and gas cookers and other appliances were positioned in a manner agreed with the Institution's insurers. The School agreed to pay for the installation of gas pipes and meters as well as the gas consumed, and to restore the premises to their original condition on termination of the lease.[27] In fact the School continued to function with the use of these short term facilities for another full year.

As far as equipment is concerned, Christian and her committee appear to have become adept at persuading local businesses to donate their products which would then, of course, be seen being used during demonstrations.

Since Isobel Middleton was as yet the only available demonstrator there was an obvious limit to the activities of the School, however, as soon as the Edinburgh winter series of classes was completed a start was made to providing some instruction in other centres, initially elsewhere in Scotland. As was mentioned earlier, interested parties had been invited to contact Miss Guthrie Wright and in the spring of 1876 the first of the provincial lectures commenced. At the beginning of May Miss Middleton demonstrated in Perth, where she was applauded for her 'clear and admirable address'. Later that month she conducted classes at the Corn Exchange in Alloa and the *Alloa Advertiser* was fulsome in its praise, claiming that her audience 'never had, and never will have, a better instructress, than Miss Middleton, in the particular sphere of domestic usefulness now under consideration'. The public lectures were in the form of two courses of twelve lessons and 'were worthy of the highest commendation', although the paper noted the relative absence of working class women. Nevertheless attendance was estimated at seventy for morning sessions and about a hundred in the evenings. As the word spread, however, so the numbers grew and no less than two hundred women packed into the hall for the last class. Early in June Miss Middleton's classes were being held in Auchtermuchty, where she demonstrated high class cookery during day sessions and artisan cookery in the evenings. Again, the reception was enthusiastic, with attendances increasing each night.[28]

If Miss Guthrie Wright was delighted with the progress being made, and carefully gathered and preserved all the relevant newspaper accounts, she was less than happy with some aspects of Isobel Middleton's conduct, particularly once the latter commenced her touring programme. She was not confident that the younger woman maintained her accounts accurately; nor was she certain that all the portable equipment was being properly looked after; and she disliked the idea of Miss Middleton accepting direct payments from the local committees which were organising the arrangements for the classes. Indeed, it seems that when challenged about the apparent disappearance of some utensils Miss Middleton had some difficulty in providing an explanation and accordingly she received a very curt one line note demanding an immediate reply by return of post.[29]

Despite these tensions it was obvious that Miss Middleton had made a vital contribution to the early months of the School's existence and, not surprisingly, before she commenced an eight week summer break, she was offered a new contract, albeit in somewhat qualified terms. On 1st June 1876 Miss Guthrie Wright wrote to her as follows:

> I am directed by the Executive Committee to offer you a re-engagement as instructress in the Edinburgh School of Cookery from the first of November next, at a salary at the rate of eighty pounds (£80) a year, the rise of ten pounds from your present salary being on account of your excellence as a demonstrator. I am instructed to state that the rise would have been much greater but for the grave causes of displeasure mentioned

verbally to you by Miss Stevenson and myself. On account of these causes, the committee have also decided that the re-engagement shall be terminable at any time at a month's warning on either side.

They undertake to pay your salary at the above rate, monthly, to give you travelling expenses first class, while teaching out of Edinburgh, and to give you at the rate of one pound (£1) a week extra while teaching and resident out of Edinburgh.

They require that your time be placed at their disposal for teaching in and out of Edinburgh; and that you do not engage in any other teaching of cookery than in connection with the Edinburgh School of Cookery.[30]

A fortnight later the Committee decided to make two further appointments to the teaching staff. Interviews had been going on for some time to find suitable individuals and now posts were offered to Miss Dodds and Mrs Macpherson. The conditions of their appointments were that they successfully completed courses of instruction at The National School in South Kensington, during which period they would receive £30 to cover fees, board and lodging, travelling and incidental expenses. Thereafter the salary would be £60 per annum and the engagement would be terminable on three months' warning on either side. If however, the notice was submitted by the teacher less than two years into the contract, then the £30 paid to cover training costs would require to be refunded. As with Miss Middleton, the teachers were required to work either in Edinburgh or elsewhere, had their first class travel expenses paid, received an extra £1 for each week spent working away from Edinburgh, and were expected to teach exclusively for the Edinburgh School.[31] When the two new recruits returned to Edinburgh to commence their duties the Committee was so delighted with their early demonstration work that it was decided to increase their salaries from 1st November to £70 per annum, the salary at which Miss Middleton had commenced, and to increase their additional payment when teaching away from the city to £1.10s per week.[32]

As the letter to Miss Middleton quoted above makes clear the School was not run entirely by one individual and the Executive Committee was now functioning effectively. Professor Archer had presumably played a useful role in securing the temporary base, but it seems that the leadership of the School was firmly in the hands of the female Committee members. In particular Miss Louisa Stevenson and Mrs Robinow were becoming Christian's increasingly important lieutenants. Mrs Robinow, an older woman whose daughter was also on the committee, seems to have had some book-keeping skills and she attempted to provide instruction to assist Miss Middleton to maintain better accounts. In addition she took up the task of maintaining a record of the materials used during lectures and presentations and of the sale of the resultant products. This duty she was to discharge voluntarily for many years and the initial financial control which helped the School to flourish and grow in these early years was undoubtedly due in no small measure to her care and attention.

Louisa Stevenson was, of course, a very important participant and it may be worth pausing here to consider her position with more care. Louisa was born in

Glasgow in 1835 and was a member of the large family of Mr James Stevenson who became senior partner of the Jarrow Chemical Company of South Shields. Her younger sister, Flora, as has been mentioned, was also to make an important contribution to the women's cause in Edinburgh, particularly through her membership of the Edinburgh School Board from 1873.

It is very interesting to note that many of the Stevenson girls' early years were spent in South Shields, only a matter of miles from Gateshead where, through the Crow sisters, Emily Davies was establishing her friendship with Elizabeth Garrett.[33] Margaret Bryant has pointed to the extraordinary element of chance in the bringing together of many of the key players in the women's movement in the 19th century - 'there is an almost disquieting, even ludicrous, element of chance in the story' - and that may indeed be true.[34] However, the personal connections may be even more remarkable than Bryant realised since friendships made by the Stevensons in the 1850s and early 60s in the north of England may well have created a key connection between the leaders of the women's movement in Scotland and England. (The present writer has not had the opportunity to research this matter, but the early backgrounds of the women in question would be an appropriate subject for further study.)

When James Stevenson retired he moved with his family to Edinburgh, where he became an elder in St George's Free Church. The family ultimately settled at 13 Randolph Crescent where, following their father's death in 1866, his four unmarried daughters lived out their lives. 'There they entertained most of the distinguished strangers who came to Edinburgh, on such occasions as meetings of the British Association and graduations at the University; and these Receptions were for many years a great feature of Edinburgh Society'.[35]

Over the years Louisa Stevenson committed herself to many aspects of the women's movement and, as noted earlier, she was a prime mover in the Edinburgh Association for the University Education of Women. Indeed, Louisa's involvement in this activity commenced early for, in 1871, she had been one of the Honorary Treasurers who had raised the money to cover Sophia Jex Blake's legal expenses as the latter and her four friends struggled to complete their medical training at the University and to defend themselves from various attacks. One of Louisa's relatives who sent support at that time was the writer, Robert Louis Stevenson, who wrote praising the putative female medical students as the 'first of a noble army, pioneers ...'.[36]

As with her sister Flora, Louisa was from an early stage a supporter of the cause of women's suffrage and was one of the first two women to obtain election to the Edinburgh Parochial Board 'where she devoted herself specially to the nursing arrangements in the Poor-house'.[37] When, at the Debating Society in January 1885, she criticised the operation of the Poor Law, her argument had a strangely modern note. Her particular concern was the dilemma of allowances to deserted wives. The provision of such allowances by the community would, she argued, encourage desertion, but the present system was, nevertheless, quite unacceptable since it left deserted wives without any support.[38] In these days, of course, there was sometimes intense opposition to the public activities of women and when Louisa was appointed to be convener of one of the Parochial Board committees, one of the male members protested. 'I object to Miss Stev'son because she's a wumman. Now you'll be telling me that Queen Victoria's a wumman, but the Queen is only a kind o' a figureheid. But Miss Stev'son's no a figureheid; she gangs into everything.'[39]

Another male sceptic served with Louisa when she was on the Board of Managers of Edinburgh Royal Infirmary, but although at first 'he had been strongly opposed to the idea of women on such Boards' he had been compelled by her to change his mind completely. Indeed, he had eventually concluded that 'Miss Stevenson was the most useful member the Board had had during all the twenty years he had been a manager'.

A lovely story told of Louisa Stevenson concerned her dealings with a rascally Governor of the Poor-house. Convinced that he was appropriating the contents of the wine-cellar, which were properly for the benefit of the poor residents, Louisa persuaded members of the Parochial Board to pass a resolution instructing that the key to the cellar be transferred to the safekeeping of the local doctor. Not content with this achievement, however, on the evening before the key was due to be handed over, together with another female colleague, she paid an unannounced visit to the house, arriving in time to catch the Governor and his cronies in the midst of a carousal during which they were attempting to dispose of all the available wine and beer. Her triumph was complete, and perhaps her real purpose achieved, when the Governor was summarily dismissed from office.[40]

Louisa Stevenson was a particularly able women and a sound business and financial manager, and she was ideally suited to the duties of Honorary Treasurer of the School, a position which she fulfilled for no less than fifteen years. Moreover, she was a gifted public speaker with a 'naturally beautiful voice' and she was precisely the kind of woman who could tackle the barriers of prejudice and ignorance while giving rise to the minimum of offence and opposition.

There is no doubt that Christian Guthrie Wright was the real leader and driving force behind the successful establishment of the Edinburgh School, but the others also had vital roles. From Christian's point of view Louisa Stevenson's steadily growing public reputation was an important asset, hence she was quite content that her close friend should assume a leading role in public.

In June of 1876 Christian once again tried to obtain the support of the Edinburgh School Board and wrote to its Chairman, Professor Calderwood intimating that the staff of the School was being extended to three and that it would therefore be willing to provide instruction in Board schools. Her letter was quoted at length in The Scotsman of July 15th in a report of the Board's meeting of the previous day. Interestingly, while the report indicates that Dr James Begg supported Miss Guthrie Wright's request, Miss Flora Stevenson took a more cautious line. She noted that after earlier discussions a committee had been established to consider the question of cooking in Board schools, but that it had been decided to do nothing further since 'more directly educational questions required more immediate action'. Obviously the recently established Board was finding it difficult to meet all the calls on its available resources.[41] Nevertheless, if Edinburgh proved slow to respond, encouragement came in the form of an invitation to provide classes in the schools of the Boards of Leith and Portobello.

In July Christian wrote to Isobel Middleton advising her of the appointment of the new members of staff and setting out the arrangements for her autumn programme of provincial lectures. These involved nine days in Cupar, and twelve days in each of the towns of Stirling, Aberdeen and St Andrews. This letter, however, illustrates that the stress between the two women was continuing to build. Having now had the chance to examine the contents of the crate of travelling equipment Christian was irritated to discover that utensils were indeed missing and that the vital portable 'Leoni' gas stove had been damaged. She understood, of course, the risks involved in moving equipment from place to place and proposed to retain the stove, once repaired, for use in Edinburgh, while providing a 'Gray's' stove for the peripatetic classes. The 'Gray's' had not functioned well in the past, but it was suggested that faulty piping in the gas supply was the problem. A new one was being made and she invited Miss Middleton to suggest any modifications.

Throughout August and part of September Christian spent a holiday with her father at Almote Cottage, Moffat, but there was no slackening in her correspondence on behalf of the School, with letters being dispatched to confirm the details of the autumn and winter programmes. Miss Middleton was bluntly told that her eight week holiday could not be extended and she was 'strongly advised' to report to Mrs Robinow for instruction in keeping her accounts.

When Christian returned from Moffat a fascinating public exchange took place between her and Flora Stevenson and this not only explains some of the problem being experienced with the Edinburgh School Board, but perfectly illustrates the central debate about the nature and shape of the education of girls.

Stung by public criticism of the comparative slowness of the Edinburgh Board to introduce cooking to Board schools, Flora Stevenson submitted a long letter to *The Scotsman* on 28th September. She admitted that the Board had done no more than agree in principle that cookery should be taught in its elementary schools, provided satisfactory arrangements could be made. She pointed out that suitable accommodation with the necessary space, ventilation and light was often lacking in the schools. However, the other important question was one of time, particularly in the schedules of girl pupils. She explained that in addition to the lessons which girls attended together with boys , the girls were also required to spend five hours per week on sewing.

> People seem to forget in speaking about training school girls in the art of cookery that there are other branches of instruction which are equally important, and which they can only acquire at school; and they forget, too, that very few girls attending elementary schools remain at school after eleven or twelve years of age.

She pointed out that girls had to be examined in their various subjects at the same age as boys, but with the handicap of five hours less teaching per week on mainstream topics for which grants were payable. She admitted that under the most recent changes to the regulations governing school boards money could now be spent on cookery classes, but since these changes had only just been introduced by the Code of 1876, it was not reasonable to charge the Edinburgh Board with tardiness in its response.

> I have no desire to undervalue the importance of this kind of training for girls, and I think we are greatly indebted to Miss Guthrie Wright and the other managers of the Edinburgh School of Cookery for all they are doing in providing instruction in cookery for all classes in the community. I do however, deprecate the tone which so many people assume in speaking of the importance of teaching women the art of cooking, as if by this means, and by this means alone, society is to be regenerated, and an end put to all intemperance and imprudence..... By all means let the girls of this generation be trained to be good 'house-mothers', but let it not be forgotten that the well-being of the family depends equally on the 'house-father'.

She then went on to plead that equal time and attention be given to instructing boys on saving and on the duties and responsibilities involved in maintaining a home and family.[42]

In the prevailing climate Flora Stevenson's letter was in many ways a brave effort at advocating the maintenance of a fair balance in the education of boys and girls. What is especially interesting, however, is that her letter was a very clear exposition of what might be described as the Emily Davies point of view that girls should be able to compete on equal educational terms with boys, should not have their school time unreasonably diverted into 'female' subjects, and that ideally boys and girls should complete a common syllabus. She could applaud cookery instruction for women, but was clearly reluctant to have the education of school girls skewed in such a way as to make it more difficult for them to compete on even terms with boys. One suspects that a stiff action was being fought to that end on the Edinburgh Board and that concessions were being made only slowly and with reluctance. Incidentally, these opinions also lend some circumstantial evidence to the view that Flora may indeed have been influenced by contact with Emily Davies.

Miss Stevenson's intervention, of course, provided an opportunity that was eagerly seized by Christian. On the same day she had published an article in the *Annandale Herald* and it now became the basis for an even longer response which was published in *The Scotsman* on September 30th. She noted that those who were uncertain about the provision of training in cookery in elementary schools could nevertheless admit that some such training was essential. Unfortunately the fact was that most mothers were themselves far too ignorant to provide this training to their daughters and, in the case of girls from working families, it was necessary to teach them how to get the most out of available household resources. She pointed out that good domestic practices would strengthen families and commented that 'whatever adds to home comfort and family health adds also to home happiness and family peace and prosperity'. She described the prevailing ignorance of the selection and preparation of food in most working class homes and emphasised the health issue. She pointed out that different foods achieved different tasks for the body - some to provide heat, some flesh and others to make strong bones - and that eating good food in the correct combinations was important.

> If we can get the learner to understand why animal and vegetable food should be combined, why it is good to eat bread with cheese, pork with beans, liver with bacon, rice with milk and eggs, the greater is the gain; but if, without insisting on the reason being in every case understood, we put the learner in the way of making the mixture, whether the scientific reason for it is known or not, a great good will necessarily result from our teaching.

She contrasted the ability of French women to produce excellent meals from odds and ends with the wastefulness and unimaginativeness of most Scottish and English housewives. 'If working-men's wives could be prevailed on to put in the stock-pot what they now put in the ash-pit, the year's outlay on food might be reduced by one -fourth'. Moreover the happiness of the homes would be promoted and temperance encouraged.

> Such are some of the lessons which it is thought desirable to teach working-class girls.....The great aim is to teach them method, cleanliness, tidiness, skill of hand and thrift. Some effort (should be) made .. to give them command of as great a number as possible of the simplest, cheapest and most wholesome every-day dishes..

She argued that girls should certainly be taught such matters as part of the 'ordinary school course'. The only other alternative was for the lessons to be given by a separate institution, but that would be inefficient and wasteful. It was 'as right and natural' that girls should be taught to cook as to sew and knit and the knowledge was likely to be a great deal more useful to most girls than many of the subjects currently studied. Moreover, well taught cookery could be a practical vehicle for the teaching of both physics and chemistry. She wrote

> where the experiment has been tried, no interference with the ordinary work of the school has resulted. Almost the invariable testimony is that, 'the girls who passed the best examination in cookery also passed the best examination in the Standards'.

She then described how school boards in England - London and Birmingham - were providing cooking classes in their schools, and in Scotland, Glasgow and Portobello School Boards had just started classes while the Dunfermline and Stirling Boards were sympathetically considering the matter. In Edinburgh itself nothing has yet been done ... on the ground, as stated by Miss Stevenson, that 'it was thought that some more directly educational questions required more immediate attention', but the School of Cookery was willing to provide the same service as was being given in Portobello school. She concluded by explaining that under the new Code, boards were perfectly able to make the funds available to have such instruction given in their schools.[43]

It was a truly remarkable exchange and the two contributions clearly illustrate the nature of the dilemma which confronted the female reformers. On the one hand, there was an obvious desire to enable girls to compete on equal educational terms with boys, and this meant that they should study the same subjects and sit for the same examinations with an equal chance of success. This is what Emily Davies had described as the 'cardinal principle', and in many ways, particularly in the longer term, it was an entirely valid position. On the other hand, however, deep seated ignorance in domestic kitchens was undoubtedly profoundly damaging to the health and happiness of the community and, in particular, to its poorest members. As Christian Guthrie Wright pointed out, girls had a right to this knowledge and how else was it to be provided if not in the schools? From a practical point of view training in cooking could make an invaluable contribution to the health and well being of the community and, in Dr Wood's words, this revolution could be achieved through 'women and women alone'. Equality of opportunity in schools would, therefore, have to make space for practical necessity.

(Helen Corr argues that Flora Stevenson subsequently became one of the 'staunch nucleus of female supporters of the 'Home Rule' campaign' on the Edinburgh School Board who sought to persuade their male colleagues to provide for domestic teaching in Board schools.[44] It may well be the case, therefore, that Flora subsequently adjusted her views, perhaps in deference to her sister and to Christian.)

On the 18th and 19th October Christian visited Liverpool[45] where she joined representatives of the Cookery Schools of Liverpool, Leeds and Glasgow. They met at the Royal Institution in order to set up The Northern Union of Training Schools of Cookery. The Union was 'for the purpose of training teachers and conferring diplomas and certificates' and the object was to try to provide courses and qualifications of an agreed uniform high standard. Miss Fanny Calder of the Liverpool School was appointed Honorary Secretary of the Union and the task was 'to provide some guarantee to the authorities that the teachers they needed to employ were efficiently trained'. Bearing in mind the subsequent divergence between English and Scottish education it is interesting that at this brief point in time the developing Cookery Schools of the North of England and Scotland were apparently willing to bind themselves 'to a common course, with one examination and one examiner for all, pledging themselves, moreover, to exchange the fruits of their experiences..' Interestingly, one of the first examiners appointed by the Union was Miss Agnes Maitland, who went on to become the second Principal of Somerville College, Oxford. The initial list of prescribed text books agreed by the Union included - *Elementary Physiology* by Dr Lankester; *Domestic Economy for Girls*, Nelson's Royal School Service; *Health in the Household* by Mrs Buckton; *A Scholar's Handbook of Household Management* and *Cookery* by Tegetmeier; *Food*, by A C Church; and *Elementary Physics* by an unnamed author.[46]

The first AGM of the School was held shortly after Christian's return from Liverpool, although she was ill on the night and the report had to be read to the Lord Provost and large audience by Louisa Stevenson. The Committee was able to declare a surplus of £256. Cannily this ignored the £433 which had been subscribed in Donations by School supporters and simply referred to the balance between receipts for classes and expenditures. It was also pointed out that for the first two months the School had paid no rent and that further funds were urgently needed to obtain and furnish suitable permanent premises. Moreover, they were concerned to be prudent.

> The experience of other similar institutions has taught the Committee the fact that a season of commercial depression is almost certain to overtake them sooner or later, and they are most anxious to lay aside a sufficient sum of money now, to tide over such a time, without interfering with the efficiency of their classes.[47]

The report indicated the large numbers which had attended for instruction, both in the city and elsewhere. It was noted in particular that the Edinburgh artisan classes had attracted many working women, no less than 525 on one evening occasion. In addition, it was also noted that lessons were being given to 100 pupils at George Watson's Institution, to 180 pupils of the Queen Street Merchant Company School, to 140 pupils of the Free Church Training School (Moray House) and to 60 pupils at Portobello Board School. Finally, public lecture courses had been successfully presented in ten centres outwith Edinburgh.[48]

The summary prospectus for session 1876-77 is reproduced at Appendix B and it indicates a programme divided into demonstration lessons and practice lessons, lists the range of fees and some of the subject matter. It also points to the beginning of a public lecture programme on medical and health matters, with the first lecturer being Dr Stevenson Macadam. This latter series became quite a feature of the College's activities and subsequent lecturers included the city's Medical Officer of Health, Dr Littlejohn.

The programme of classes in other centres was now also rapidly gaining momentum in what was becoming an authentic popular movement. Usually contact would be established with Christian by a letter from a local provost or other civic leader pleading for assistance. Whenever possible, the challenge was taken up, although lack of qualified staff continued to be the main restriction. Provost Nairn of Montrose was one of those to challenge the new financial arrangements and in her reply to him of 2nd November, Christian set out the position of the School at the time. At first the courses typically extended to two sets of twelve lessons provided over a fortnight and for which the fee was £1.11s 6d per day. The local organisers had been expected to pay £2.2s plus the cost of carriage for the use of stove and cooking utensils, as well as the teacher's first class travelling expenses. Finally, one half of the net profits had been required by the School, the other half typically being passed on to some appropriate local charity. These were the initial terms, but they had had to be reviewed in the light of experience.

> From what we have heard of the only two Schools of Cookery in England that have existed for any length of time - it has seemed to us to be absolutely essential - if we wish to be able to maintain a permanent staff of teachers for other towns as well as Edinburgh - that we must lay aside money during the early years while the novelty and need of the teaching brings large classes.

As a consequence the arrangements had been altered so that all of the risk and profits were henceforward to be taken by the School while large towns would be given priority over village communities. She denied that the school was being unreasonable and urged him to make an early decision on behalf of Montrose since other towns were waiting to have the service.[49]

What emerges from this letter and, indeed, from the decisions which were announced at the AGM, is that some very clear business heads were being applied to the affairs of the school. Either the female leaders were being extremely well advised, or they were themselves demonstrating shrewd business acumen. In any event, they were calmly playing to a long-term agenda.

Whatever may have been her shortcomings in other respects Isobel Middleton seems to have been a very fine teacher and soon rapturous reviews of her autumn classes were being gathered from the various local newspapers. The Fifeshire Journal described the last of her series of lectures in Cupar which 'was given before even a larger audience, if possible, than any hitherto which has attended upon her instruction ...every available seat and standing place was crowded'. The chairman of the meeting expressed his delight that so many young women had attended and that, in particular, large numbers of working women had come to the evening sessions. He admired three aspects of Miss Middleton's work - the avoidance of waste; the orderliness of her technique - 'there is a method in her manner of cooking that at once indicates it is the cooking of a lady, to see whom perform is one of the great treats of these lectures' - and her emphasis on cleanliness. As a gesture of appreciation Miss Middleton was presented with 'a purse of sovereigns'. In her reply the young teacher explained that she had anticipated no such reward. She said that the teaching she had given at the evening classes were

> lessons of experience. I was one of a family that was not rich, and there was a great deal of economy required ... The first or second day I came here I was told it would not be a success, and I was very down-hearted ... I thought it deserved every effort on my part, and I did all in my power to make a success, and I am very happy indeed at the result. I have met with every kindness from the Ladies' Committee and others, and I again (here Miss Middleton broke down) thank you all. (Great cheering.)[50]

The new demonstrators also swiftly proved themselves to be capable and Mrs Macpherson's initial presentations for the School Board in the new school at Portobello were well reported. *The Daily Review* noted that she used a cast iron gas stove made by Messrs Gray & Son, 85 Princes Street, that it cost £8.10s and that it could readily be moved from place to place. The gas was 'mixed with atmospheric air at the burners' which was better for cooking and more economical. At her afternoon class Mrs Macpherson prepared baked haddock, veal cutlets a la Talleyrand, vanilla souffle, roly poly, and cauliflower au gratin. At the evening class for artisans' wives she demonstrated the preparation of such articles as 'Irish stew, clarified fat, fried fish, rice and cheese, onion soup etc. At all the classes tea and coffee is made, proper instruction in the making of which is, in the opinion of the School of Cookery, too much neglected'.[51]

In Aberdeen, at the Song School, Union Street, Miss Middleton's classes were again received with enormous enthusiasm with the evening demonstrations 'being attended by hundreds of females, and large numbers are every night turned away from the doors, there being no room to accommodate them'. The *Daily Free Press* reported that the hall was besieged long before the class was due to commence and that Miss Middleton was 'an excellent teacher, clear and distinct in utterance, and unambiguous in everything that she says. She has the faculty of interesting her audience in what she is doing, and altogether helps them to spend not only a profitable but a pleasant evening'.[52]

At about the same time the new Dundee Cookery School commenced operations in a converted building at the rear of the Town House. On the opening night the lecture was given by Buckmaster and it was reported that the School had received 'valuable aid from the energetic and devoted Secretary of the Edinburgh School of Cookery, Miss Guthrie Wright'. In his lecture Buckmaster spoke of the successful establishment of Cooking Schools in Edinburgh and Glasgow and 'remarked that he should not be surprised if he found the Edinburgh Committee taking possession of the Mansion House and teaching the Londoners'.[53]

In mid November Mrs Macpherson commenced a series of classes in Dunfermline and the *Dunfermline Press*, in commending the instruction to the townswomen produced an editorial on the subject under the title 'A Popular Movement', and which reviewed the progress of events over the past year. It concluded,

> it will thus be seen that no social movement of modern times, either in Scotland or England, bids fair to become more popular than that of instruction in the art of cookery.[54]

At the end of that month the first classes were held in an Edinburgh School Board school, at Fountainbridge, although this was stated to be still only 'an experiment'. The chairman on this occasion was Dr Begg, who was a member of the Board, and in his address he referred to the debate on syllabus content. He said that 'education to some extent ought to be common to boys and girls' - particularly in respect of reading, writing, arithmetic and religion. However, it was, in his view, equally essential to teach young girls how to run their future homes.[55] Clearly Christian's volley had struck home and the Board had been forced into a response, however grudging on the part of some of its members.

As 1877 opened so the flood of requests for classes increased to something of a torrent and came from both sides of the border. Given the limited number of instructresses not every invitation could be accepted, of course, and the matter was further complicated by a breakdown in relations with Isobel Middleton. The latter had been unwell for a few days following her Aberdeen classes and when there she had evidently expressed some critical comments about the extent to which she was being over-worked. Christian had found it necessary to reply to a letter from the Aberdeen organiser, Mrs Geddes, explaining that Miss Middleton's salary compared very well with the London pay scales and that she was given a good holiday allowance. Previously there had been a somewhat similar exchange with the organising committee in Stirling. Essentially, the main difficulty seems to have been that Miss Middleton had become aware that trained demonstrators were scarce and that there was real demand for her services. Local people were more than willing to pay (the instructresses often received a gift of money at the end of a series) and she may well have been under pressure to give private classes or classes for other agencies. Several times Christian responded angrily to suggestions that such events had taken place for she was adamantly determined to insist that staff worked exclusively for the School.[56]

In another letter to Mrs Geddes Christian acknowledged that the Aberdeen classes had been so profitable that it was reasonable for the local committee to retain £50 for local purposes. However, she pointed out that the occasional large earnings were necessary to the School to enable the establishment of a permanent base and in view of likely harder times ahead. She commented that the Schools in London, York and Leeds were all in considerable financial trouble.[57] Indeed, 1876 seems to have been a hard year for the English schools of cookery and in a letter to Mr Dick of Dunfermline in December, Christian commented on their difficulties and wrote that the National's predicament was so serious that it was seeking assistance from the Government.[58]

Nevertheless, the buoyant conditions in Scotland permitted another member to be added to the staff and this was a French lady, Madame Guillaume, who was awarded the larger salary of £100 per annum plus £1.10s when teaching away from Edinburgh, first class travel and dinner at the School.[59] Clearly Christian too was coming to terms with the market value of her staff.

Sadly, Miss Middleton's connection with the School was soon to end in some acrimony. Shortly before Christmas Christian received a letter from Miss Hall on behalf of a committee attempting to open a school in Manchester and asking if a reference could be supplied for Miss Middleton. In a curt letter Christian replied that in her year at the Edinburgh School she had 'given much satisfaction' so far as her teaching was concerned, but otherwise effectively damning her with faint praise. When pressed by a subsequent request from Miss Hall, Christian declined at first to express a further opinion and, presumably in the belief that she had secured employment in Manchester, Isobel resigned on 3rd January 1877. However, Miss Hall seems to have been determined to get to the bottom of the matter and pressed yet again for information. Christian responded that Miss Middleton 'is an excellent demonstrator, clear and distinct in her speaking and teaching, and also a good teacher of practice classes. We very much regret however that we must decline to enter into any further particulars regarding her'. The letter went on to outline some of the teacher's terms of employment and duties and concluded that at its December meeting the Edinburgh Committee had decided to give Miss Middleton notice in January that her employment would be terminated, but that this had been forestalled by her resignation. That letter appears to have ended any move to Manchester and Isobel Middleton now found herself in dire need of a testimonial. Christian agreed to lay her request for such before the Committee, but at a meeting on 16th February she was instructed to inform Miss Middleton that no testimonial could be supplied. Later that month a letter from Miss

Paterson, presumably Grace Paterson of the Glasgow School, indicated that she had employed Miss Middleton for a trial three month period, but her request for further information was abruptly rejected. It was a sad conclusion to Isobel Middleton's career with the School, but her contribution to the first year of its existence is indelible.[60]

This was not the last occasion in which there would be a problem with teaching staff and a year later a somewhat similar episode involved Miss Dodds, although in this instance a warm reference was immediately supplied and there seems to have been no long term animosity. Again, however, the root problem appears to have been a desire to independently exploit the commercial attractiveness of appropriate cookery qualifications.[61]

Despite such problems 1877 was a year of enormous and exciting growth for the Edinburgh School and by its end there were no fewer than five demonstrators in place, while strenuous efforts were being made to recruit others. Late in the year Madame Guillaume was promoted to become the 'resident' teacher and the other members of staff were Mrs MacPherson, Miss Kelman, Miss Drummond and Miss Smellie. With the exception of the last named, all of the teachers had been trained at the National in London. In the case of Miss Smellie, however, in order to support the aims of the Northern Union, it had been decided that she should be sent to the Leeds School of Cooking and from whence she was due to return at the end of December.

It seems in part to be the case that the financial problems being experienced by the English Schools presented an opportunity which was eagerly seized by Christian and her committee. The annual report of October 1877 indicates that the School supplied Demonstration and Practice lessons in High Class, Plain and Cheap Cookery in its temporary rooms at the School of Arts and gave public lessons on Cheap Cookery in various locations throughout Edinburgh, Leith and Portobello. Classes were also provided for students at Moray House Free Church Training College and to pupils at The Ladies' College, Queen Street, at George Watson's, and at the Board schools at Fountainbridge, New Street and Newington, at Leith Board schools at Leith Links and North Fort Street and at the Portobello Board school. In addition to these local activities, however, the School also supplied classes at no fewer than forty-one locations, twenty-five of the latter being in Scotland and sixteen in England. Classes in England were provided in such places as North and South Shields, Sunderland, Hexham, Kendal, Shotley Bridge, Huddersfield and, in particular, Newcastle. In most cases the courses included twelve day lessons and twelve evening lessons, but in Oswestry, Chester and Newcastle the day and evening lessons were supplemented by Practice lessons and by classes provided to Board schools. In Newcastle twenty day lessons, forty evening lessons and forty Board school lessons were supplied.[62]

At the time when the annual report was compiled there was some uncertainty as to exactly how many lessons had been provided in Birmingham over a ten week period and this was later the subject of a somewhat heated exchange. Apparently the Birmingham School was in disarray and, to help out, the Edinburgh School had agreed to take on some of its classes. Madame Guillaume had been sent down to assist and she had been required to undertake no fewer than 117 demonstrations not only in the city, but also in such places as Kidderminster, Coventry, West Bromwich and Handsworth. On her return to Edinburgh the young woman was exhausted and ill and the Edinburgh committee reacted angrily to what members considered to be an abuse by the Birmingham School.[63]

However, what is clear is that the entrepreneurial Edinburgh Committee had eagerly seized the chance to assume a leading role in the provision of cooking classes in many parts of the country. Perhaps not surprisingly, some of the other Schools were less than happy about what they considered to be encroachments into their territory, but in a reply to one such complaint Christian made her position clear. 'As a matter of courtesy' the Edinburgh School would not offer classes in the vicinity of another School of Cookery, but refusing requests for assistance from local groups was another matter. Such would be 'contrary to all principles of business or of free trade'. She maintained that the Edinburgh School was simply reaping the fruit of developing an effective 'system of working branch classes'.[64]

The fame of the School was obviously flourishing all over the country and the Committee found it necessary to gently, but firmly reprove the National in London for referring in an advertisement in *The Times* to the Edinburgh School as being connected to the National. While no doubt enjoying the compliment implied in the advert, Christian and her friends were not prepared to allow even the National a share of the School's growing prestige.[65] Similarly, the Directors of Moray House College were firmly informed that the demonstration lessons currently given to the College's students were far from being sufficient to enable them to properly teach the subject. The School's Executive Committee fully supported the idea that teachers trained at Moray House should be able to teach cookery in schools, but for such a purpose a minimum period of at least ten weeks of continuous and systematic training and practice was required and the School was as yet unable to provide training at that level. One suspects also that those guiding the affairs of the School were not exactly falling over themselves to develop a potential competitor within the city.[66]

The most encouraging feature of the courses being presented in various parts of the country was the huge attendances at the evening classes on Cheap Cookery. In session 1876-77 'in three towns, the evening attendance reached nearly one thousand, and in many towns it was not unusual to see a class of from five to seven hundred persons'. The charges were deliberately kept to 2d or 3d in order to enable working class women to attend, but even so the proceeds from twenty-four lessons on Cheap Cookery in one town amounted to no less than £130,12s,10d. 'As a result of these branch classes, Local Committees have reported, not only great general improvement in the cookery and economy of the district, but many individual instances of improved comfort in the homes of the working classes.' While a touch of triumphalism may be evident here, it should be remembered that in the prevailing climate of ignorance a little knowledge probably did go a very long way in bringing some obvious improvement to the lives of many families.[67]

As noted above, the system of branch classes typically involved Christian responding to a request for help by advising that a local Ladies Committee be set up. This committee would then make the local arrangements in accordance with a set of instructions and, once these had been agreed, the School would supply the teacher and equipment. Christian was always careful to advise on pre-publicity, normally supplying leaflets, posters and admission tickets, and she urged the local groups to ensure the involvement of doctors and clergymen and to obtain at least one local community leader to provide platform support. Usually she conducted the correspondence and then allowed the staff to get on with their job, but she was not averse to personally getting her jacket off if the need arose.

A flavour of these occasions is given in the report of the *Elgin Courant* of January 9th, 1877. It commented that the Edinburgh School was likely to remain Scotland's premier cookery school because of the time and trouble which was taken to provide the best possible instruction. It reported that when Miss Guthrie Wright arrived she found the venue, the Concert Hall, to be in a dirty condition, whereupon she

> put in operation a process of scrubbing and brushing that produced results, even in the short term at command, which were truly wonderful. The floors, the seats, the stage, the ante-room, the stairs, everything was scrubbed and washed till the wood appeared bare and clean. Cushions were beaten and brushed. Windows never opened before were made to admit the pure air of heaven. The table for cooking on, in front of the stage, was nicely covered with red and white cloth. (The stage was decorated in order to)...give it an air of home cleanliness and peaceful home comfort...

In addition the hall was decorated with flowers and altogether made to be more attractive than at any time since it had been built thirty years previously.

The *Banffshire Journal* reported that the teacher, Miss Kelman had taught 'in the presence of large crowds of attentive listeners, without embarrassment, and certainly without committing any error either in word or action'. She not only provided instruction on cookery, but gave guidance on the nutritive properties of the various foods. Moreover,

> Not the least valuable portion of her addresses consist in the many pointed hints she gives to all, if they would be good housewives, to study and practice economy in cooking so as not to allow the least scrap to be lost or cast away.[68]

As was noted previously, on the various provincial classes the demonstrators typically used a portable gas stove, but, of course, in many parts of the country the option to connect up to a gas supply did not exist. In these circumstances use was made of what was described as an 'American' stove, and this was oil fuelled. Later the standard appliance on such occasions was a 'Rippingdale' cooker. Apparently, however, in the early days, when teaching classes including the daughters of crofters and other working women, it was necessary to restrict demonstrations to one or perhaps two saucepans at a time since that was all that could be used on the open fire 'which was the solitary form of heat available' in many households.

As far as Newcastle and the north of England was concerned the lead, not surprisingly, was taken by Louisa Stevenson. In November of 1876 she visited Newcastle and persuaded local ladies to set up a branch school. A lecture room was hired and an extremely successful session of classes commenced early in the following January.[69]

Shortage of suitably qualified staff remained a problem over the next year or two and this was not helped by the fact that the training supplied to Miss Smellie in Leeds proved to be a sad disappointment. On her return to Edinburgh it was quickly evident that despite having obtained a first class diploma, her cooking and teaching skills were hopelessly inadequate. Christian wrote to Mrs Fenwick, the Leeds Principal, protesting that the guidelines set out by the Northern Union for the training of instructresses had been ignored and that the student had not been required to present anything like the necessary range of demonstrations. 'We have thought it wise to state these facts frankly to you, as it will bring discredit on our whole union if such teachers as Miss Smellie are sent out holding first class diplomas'.[70] For the immediate future only teachers qualified at the National in London would be considered and considerable pains were taken to obtain more from that source.

This exchange, in fact, was a prelude to the Edinburgh School withdrawing from the Northern Union. In the records of the Union held at Liverpool it is evidently maintained that the Edinburgh School had withdrawn on the grounds 'that it was a capital city and should stand alone',[71] but no such sentiment appears anywhere in the contemporary correspondence or records in Edinburgh. In a letter to Fanny Calder dated 5th March 1878, Christian makes it quite clear that the problem was a lack of confidence in the qualifications being issued by some of the member schools. The Edinburgh Committee was quite certain that its School was not yet in a position itself to train teachers, but Christian and her colleagues did not accept that the answer for it or for the other schools was to lower standards. 'We are of opinion that it was a mistake to form a training Union before the powers of the different Schools had been more fully known and tested'.[72] In other words, they were not prepared to permit the hard earned and growing reputation of the School to be dissipated by accepting the products of schools which were attempting to provide a level of instruction beyond their competence. The Edinburgh Committee members were perfectly well aware that the standing of their School rested first and foremost on the shoulders of the young women who represented it on an ever increasing number of public platforms up and down the country.

(As a matter of fact at about this time the School was doing some limited training of teachers, in that it was giving some specific instruction to its own members of staff. For example, when Miss Drummond was appointed in November 1877, a condition was that she should undergo training in high class French Cookery at the hands of Madame Guillaume. But, of course, Miss Drummond had received her basic qualifications in London. The interesting point here, however, is that the Committee shrewdly was taking the precaution of ensuring that no course should be dependent on a single member of staff.)

The teaching staff at this time was indeed very young and, writing many years later, Ethel de la Cour noted that none of those employed in the early period was older than twenty-six years of age. Inevitably, dispatching them all over the country was not without its worries and on one occasion Christian insisted on giving one of her black velvet bonnets to a pretty young teacher in order to make her appear slightly older.[73]

From the School's long term point of view, the main achievement of these early years was that the success of the various classes had resulted in the finance being obtained with which to secure a more permanent base in Edinburgh. The annual report for 1876-77 declared that the 'town and country' classes had raised no less than £3482 and, after the deduction of expenses, this left a balance of £1883. The Committee pointed out that such an income could only be considered quite exceptional and should not be regarded as typical of what might be raised in future. Despite this caution, however, more than enough had been secured to permit the leasing and fitting out of permanent School premises in the Albert Buildings, Shandwick Place. Included in the premises were a Lecture Hall of 25x30 feet and a slightly smaller Dining- Room, and, in addition to residential accommodation for one teacher (initially Madame Guillaume), space was also provided for a Ladies Club Room, principally for the use of ladies from outwith Edinburgh who were visiting the city.[74]

The move to Shandwick Place took place in December 1877 and in the early months Christian had to work very hard to persuade or bully the landlord's factor to make necessary alterations and adaptations to the building, but gradually unpleasant draughts were excluded, new doors and gas pipes were fitted and so on. Moreover she also proved herself to be particularly adept at securing equipment. For example, when the Eagle Foundry of Birmingham offered the School an 'Eagle Stove at a large discount', Christian responded that the School did not intend to purchase one;

> but if you think it worth your while as an advertisement to present an Eagle Stove to the Edinburgh School, it will be accepted and fitted into one of the rooms in the new premises, Albert Buildings, Shandwick Place.
> Messrs James Gray & Sons have presented a Close range, value about £35.[75]

Very interestingly, in January 1878, Christian wrote to Messrs Woolf & Co (no address noted) thanking the firm 'for the present of a freezing machine'. One can only speculate as to what this might have been, since the building had no electricity and, for example, was lit by gas; but it seems clear that the various interested firms saw the School as a vehicle through which the latest technological advances might be introduced to the public.[76]

In the following year the progress of the School was maintained and the range of classes provided in the new accommodation expanded. Moreover, if the Edinburgh School Board was still not prepared to make cookery available in all its schools, classes were nevertheless extended to schools at Stockbridge, Leith Walk, Bristo Street and Dean. Outwith Edinburgh classes were offered in thirty-eight locations and these ranged as far south as Liskeard, Truro, and Falmouth in Cornwall and St Peter Port in Guernsey. £505 had been spent fitting up the new School building, but the clear profit for the year still amounted to more than £500.[77]

In its Report at the end of 1878 the Committee made clear its view that Cookery should be an essential part of the school education of every girl and to further that end Christian had compiled and edited a *School Cookery Book* (London, Macmillan & Co, 1879) which was suitable for use in elementary and other schools. It was said to contain 'in simple language all that is necessary to give a clear knowledge of the theory and practice of good economical cookery. The use of technical terms has been carefully avoided ...'

This little book was, in fact, a considerable publication. Published by Macmillan as one of a series entitled *Science Primers*, under the general editorship of the celebrated naturalist, Professor T.H.Huxley and including texts by such distinguished individuals as Sir H.E.Roscoe (Chemistry), Sir Archibald Geikie (Geography and Geology) and W. Stanley Jevons (Logic and Political Economy), Guthrie Wright's 158 page volume is more or less representative of the state of knowledge in respect of food in terms of the late 1870s. Indeed, the inclusion of her book in a limited series written by scholars of such eminence gives a very vivid indication of the regard in which she was now being held. Her book does set out to give in plain language (but with technical notation) an account of the human requirement for food, the chemical nature of different foods, the uses of foods, and the principles of cookery. The various authorities on which she has drawn (such as Professor Parkes - who studied the diets of British soldiers - Dr Lankester, Dr Pavy and so on) are indicated, hence it is possible to be fairly confident that the analysis does indeed reflect the level of knowledge at the time. A range of recipes and cooking techniques are set out and finally, an appendix gives guidance on how cookery classes and facilities might best be organised in an elementary school. It is an excellent, straightforward and scholarly little volume and a year later it was reported that the book had been favourably reviewed and that 5758 copies had been sold thus far.[78]

The Committee, of course, also had to comment on its decision to withdraw from the Northern Union of Training Schools of Cookery, and did so by explaining its concerns about the abilities of some member schools to train teachers appropriately. The Committee had not felt 'warranted in sharing the responsibility of granting Diplomas to Teachers trained in schools holding varying standards of efficiency'. If, however, there was a genuine increase in the demand for trained staff, for example, through Cookery being fully accepted as an essential part of a school-girl's education, then the Edinburgh School would certainly open teacher training classes. Obviously, the subject was not only an educational question, but a matter of business and of matching the supply of teachers to the level of demand. Again, the evidence of outstanding business awareness is impressive.[79]

When this commercial acumen was noted earlier it was in the context of an indication that the Committee was planning to survive what members saw as an inevitable period of economic downturn. This duly arrived in 1879 and was associated in the minds of Committee members with the aftermath of the collapse of the City of Glasgow Bank in 1878. 'Public attention was absorbed with the national calamity' and this 'seriously affected the Classes at the Central School, and also branch classes in other towns'. Many classes had to be abandoned or deferred, but by the end of the year classes in Edinburgh at least had returned to the average. Classes outwith Edinburgh were only provided in five locations in that year, one of these being in Jarrow, and income from fees fell to a mere £753. Indeed, it can be said that the provincial classes never returned to the levels obtaining prior to the bank failure and it may well be that some of the original novelty of cookery demonstrations had simply begun to wear off. Nevertheless, the prudent preparation for such an eventuality paid off handsomely and the development of the School soon picked up its former momentum, particularly in Edinburgh. Even at the height of the depression the decision was made to broaden the teaching base of the school by including classes on related subjects. Accordingly, the School name underwent its first change when it was retitled 'The Edinburgh School of Cookery and Domestic Economy', and new courses were offered in dressmaking, sewing and etc, lace-making, the 'Theory of Food', on domestic economy and on 'Sick Nursing'.[80]

A lecturer recruited at this time was Miss Barnett of the National Health Society (London) and her task was to provide classes on Health and related topics. She offered a programme of lectures on such subjects as the requirement for ventilation, on water, on the care of the sick, on baby care, on accidents and emergencies and on housing, and interested organisations, such as churches and young mothers' groups, were invited to contact the School for her services.[81] This development indicated an interest which was to become very important to both Christian and Louisa Stevenson in the later 1880s.

In November 1879 Christian again attempted to persuade the Edinburgh School Board to be more helpful. Pointing out that Demonstration Classes had been provided successfully in Board schools for three years, and that no fewer than sixteen Board school children had found employment in the School of Cookery, where they had proved 'apt and intelligent'- presumably they were employed initially as assistants and maids - it seemed to the Committee to be time for the Board to extend the teaching of Cookery in its schools. In the Committee's view Practice lessons were also required in order to ensure that the children obtained some realistic 'hands on' experience of cooking under instruction. Secondly, demonstration classes were currently conducted after normal school hours and although attendance levels were good, the children were often too tired to enjoy the full benefit of the instruction. In reality, the problem was probably a reluctance on the part of the Board (and many other Boards) to accept the costs involved in equipping schools with cooking facilities and similar concerns about who was to be responsible for providing the ingredients which the pupils would require to use during practice sessions. Again, therefore, the appeal appears to have fallen on deaf ears.[82] Nevertheless, an interesting side effect of many of the provincial classes was that local people often followed up a course of demonstrations by voluntarily installing some cooking equipment in the neighbourhood school and within a few years this made possible the introduction of cookery in schools in many parts of the country.[83]

The financial crisis of 1878/9 produced a remarkable extension of the Edinburgh School's activities. A Manchester School of Cookery had had an erratic and somewhat precarious existence until 1878, at which point it was forced into liquidation, even although it had reputedly been doing good work. By 1880 the lack of such facilities in the Manchester area was proving to be a significant deficiency and on 22nd October a large meeting gathered in the Manchester Town Hall to consider whether or not the school could be re-opened successfully. Christian's cousin, Miss Romily Wright, was a resident of Manchester and, perhaps through her, an invitation was sent to Christian inviting her to address the meeting. The opportunity was too good to miss, and she offered the assistance of the Edinburgh School. She pointed out that the objective of the Edinburgh School was to have cookery introduced into the ordinary curriculum of board schools, but Miss Becker of the Manchester Board indicated that this could not yet be done although her Board would make space for 'extra' classes in cookery. Thereupon Christian more or less offered to establish a Manchester branch of the Edinburgh School. This offer was not made 'without careful calculation and mature consideration'. Moreover it was emphasised that 'while the Edinburgh Committee will only continue to hold classes in the Manchester district so long as these are self-supporting, they are prepared at any time to withdraw if an efficient Local Association undertakes to provide the teaching desired'.

By this stage Christian was once more in touch with Miss Dodds, who, in addition to working for the School, had taught for a time in both England and America. She was now re-employed and dispatched to Manchester to work under the general guidance of Miss Romily Wright. Other staff were to be seconded to Manchester as required. Initially, the Edinburgh staff had to bring with them all the usual paraphernalia, including gas stoves and this appears to have caused some confusion. It was noted that 'Manchester plumbers at that date, having so small an acquaintance with gas stoves, .. one of these was duly fixed in a school-room, with its feet in the air, and the gas supply pipe wandering over the floor'. However, despite such obstacles, in its first session, 1880/81, the Manchester Branch supplied courses of Artisan Demonstrations, Demonstrations to Ladies and, in a few cases, Practice lessons in such locations as Collyhurst, Kersal, Salford, Ancoats, Stalybridge, Ordsal, Pendleton, Rusholme, Chorlton-on-Medlock, Radcliffe, Atherton, Middleton, and Lymm. In the following year classes were also given in Burnley, Sale, Hyde, Sheffield and elsewhere.

On November 9th 1880 the Manchester Guardian reported that the first public cookery classes held under the auspices of the Edinburgh School had taken place on the previous evening at St James' School, Collyhurst. About one hundred people attended and these were reported to be mainly 'women of the working class'. The standard fee for the course of twelve lessons was two shillings, but it was noted that blocks of fifty tickets could be purchased for half price to encourage charitable organisations and employers to assist poor women to attend. Miss Dodds conducted the class and 'at once plunged into the subject by demonstrating in a practical manner the preparation of a number of dishes'. The paper reported that the audience paid close attention during the one and a half hour demonstration, taking notes, and at the end, sampling the dishes.[84]

The Manchester branch did not initially establish a permanent base and for the next few years its classes continued to be held in a variety of schools and halls throughout the district. In Salford, for example, the Greengate Institute was used.[85]

One interesting stipulation passed on from Edinburgh was that for every course of instruction provided for working people at low fees another should be opened for better-off women. Clearly the practical good business sense was also to be applied in Manchester and it is noteworthy that in nine of the ten years that the Edinburgh School operated its Manchester branch a profit was returned. Indeed, in 1884, which was another awkward year financially, Manchester earned a profit of £42 as against the School's total surplus of just £56.

The direct connection with Manchester was severed in 1890. Significant losses had been incurred by the branch over the previous year and it was now felt to be an appropriate time for Manchester to take control of its own affairs. At the time of hand-over there were outstanding debts of £125, but the Edinburgh School declined to accept the liability and instead made over as a gift to the new Manchester School stoves, equipment and various other fittings.[86]

The 1880s were years of consolidation for the School in Shandwick Place and as it was steered through what were often tricky financial conditions. The base of courses was gradually broadened and from 1881 training was provided for intending teachers of Cookery. At first the numbers accepted for such training were very small and the focus was limited to the teaching of Artisan Cookery. However, in that area a competence was gradually built up and Christian reacted angrily to an apparent throw-away comment by an official at the Education Department to the effect that he 'knew of no Scotch (Cooking) School capable of presenting teachers' Certificates'. She pointed out that unlike some schools elsewhere the Edinburgh School had been unwilling to risk devaluing teachers' qualifications by granting a local certificate, but 'special attention has been given to the training of teachers of Artisan Cookery in our School, and it will stand comparison with that of any school in the United Kingdom'. She demanded that the official concerned should check her claim with the Scotch Department and thereafter retract and apologise for his comment.[87]

The cautious development of training teachers of Cookery was deliberate. The School's Committee was determined to ensure that the status of instructresses was maintained and that their training did not become so trivialised that it could be taken up on a large scale by non-specialised teacher training schools such as Moray House. Attendance at a few demonstration classes and some theoretical work would not, in the Committee's view, produce a properly competent specialist teacher. Moreover, when considering this matter it should be remembered that Christian and the others were also concerned about developing careers for women which were capable of commanding a good salary. At this time a typical domestic maid earned less than £20 a year with full board, and a nurse might have earned about £40. By contrast, although salaries fell back in the 1880s, a qualified School instructress had a salary of from £40 to £100 per year, and an outstanding lecturer could easily top the latter sum, particularly if she was also engaged in delivering peripatetic lectures for the School.

In 1887 the position in respect of teacher training was set out in correspondence to applicants. Mrs Wagstaffe of Macclesfield (applying on behalf of her daughter) and Miss Fleming of Carlisle were told that students had to be over 17 years of age and could expect to be in training for a continuous period of five or six months, the exact duration depending on their practical level of competence in both cooking and demonstration. The course comprised Artisan, Plain and High Class Cookery teaching, although the emphasis was on the first two elements. There were also classes in Elementary Chemistry of Food and on the Physiology of Digestion, and instruction in these areas was provided in the Heriot Watt College. It was open to students completing the latter courses to sit the South Kensington Science and Art Examinations. At the end of the five or six month period a student receiving a first class diploma would be enabled to hold 'any kind of cookery appointment' and, although the School could not undertake to secure a position for students, 'the ladies who have trained here have hitherto been very successful in finding work'. The fee for this full course was £15.15s. If, however, a student wished only to concentrate on Artisan Cookery, which would qualify her to give instruction in an elementary board school, the course would last for three to four months and would cost eight guineas.[88] However, as has been explained, the numbers undertaking this training were very small.

The letters referred to above were written by Dorothy Mary Scott. From the early days an administrative assistant had been employed to help with the day to day affairs of the school. Miss Scott was appointed to this post in 1884 and she was also given the title Lady Superintendent. Her job was described as 'the general management of the house and servants' as well as keeping 'part of the books and accounts of the School'. Interestingly, however, her salary of £50 was much less than could be earned by one of the main instructresses.[89]

Miss Scott was involved in an interesting exchange in the autumn of 1888 when she negotiated with Messrs R & A Mair of Glasgow for the purchase of a new improved gas stove which was referred to as stove number 8. She appears to have been able to secure this at a nominal price of £3.8s even although it seems to have been custom manufactured to her fairly specific instructions as to how cooking plates and grills should be arranged. When she received notification that the cooker was available she demanded its immediate delivery since the School intended to sell the old stove to a 'gentleman who is anxious to have it fixed in his house'.[90]

The main activity of the School in the 1880s remained firmly in the provision of classes in cookery, and these were held in the School buildings, in public lectures in various communities and in schools and other institutions. A few classes were also provided in sewing and other aspects of domestic work such as laundry-work.

1887 seems to have been a somewhat severe year and through that summer Christian worked very hard in attempting to organise a programme of lectures for Miss Musgrove. The latter had evidently been specially trained at the Manchester branch and specialised in the teaching of 'Sick Nursing'. Many of the contacts all over Scotland who had organised cooking classes within their communities were contacted and invited to similarly make the arrangements for Miss Musgrove. Writing to Mrs Paton of Alloa, Christian quite openly explained that because of the severe prevailing economic conditions the School had anticipated financial trouble and had 'hoped by trying sick nursing lectures in Scotland - as they are still novel - to make some money'. Miss Guthrie Wright was not usually quite so blatant, but she had to write many letters in order to complete the required list of engagements.

In the event, Miss Musgrove's classes were a resounding success. A typical set of her lectures, extending over a week, included six afternoon sessions for the benefit of ladies and four evening classes for working women. The subjects dealt with included changing sheets, making poultices and so on, and involved the display of a range of appliances. The fees charged were 7s6d for day classes and 2d for each of those held in the evening. At the end of her secondment in Scotland, Christian wrote on behalf of the Committee to congratulate her on the 'excellence and practical usefulness' of her lectures and on the warm response which they had received. 'Lady Lothian, patroness of the Jedburgh lectures, and the secretaries elsewhere, all speak in hearty terms of them'. She continued,

> I have also the pleasure of stating that you have personally made a favourable impression - I specially mention this because while it may doubtless in itself be pleasing to you to hear it - there is the further consideration that when the personal conduct and manner of a teacher or lecturer is unaffected and kindly, she not only does credit to herself, but she also paves the way for a favourable reception of other women engaged in public work.

In recognition of Miss Musgrove's success she was voted a bonus of three guineas by the Committee.[91]

Although quite explicit in her letter to Mrs Paton about the financial interest, the subject of sick nursing within the home was one which was very dear to both Miss Guthrie Wright and Louisa Stevenson and it may be appropriate here to digress a little on this matter, since it illustrates another important aspect of their activities.

Over the years in question Christian and Louisa had devoted themselves intensively to building up and developing the School. However, it would be a mistake to imagine that this was the extent of their voluntary service. The truth is that they were involved in many aspects of the women's movement and, if the School was first in importance to them, there were other major preoccupations. As was noted previously for example, over the years up to 1887 Christian was Honorary Treasurer of the Association for the University Education of Women. In addition, however, she was also active in the organisation set up in the 1860s as the 'Poor Association' and which eventually became 'The Council of Social Service'. Similarly, of course, Louisa was active on the Parochial Board and was on the Board of Edinburgh Royal Infirmary.

Through such activities both women were acutely aware of the appalling suffering associated with many illnesses, particularly among the poor. At the time most sick people were simply cared for at home. Hospital accommodation was limited and in any case 'many illnesses (were) inadmissible ... chronic phthises, paralysis, advanced cases of cancer, incurable ulcers, long standing rheumatism ..'[92]

1887 was, of course, the fiftieth anniversary of Queen Victoria's accession to the throne and it was decided to mark her jubilee by raising the funds to establish what became known by Royal Charter as Queen Victoria's Jubilee Institute for Nurses. The purposes of the Institute were

> the training, support and maintenance of women to act as nurses for the sick poor and the establishment (if thought proper) of a home or homes for nurses and generally the promotion and provision of improved means of nursing the sick poor.[93]

Effectively what was being attempted was to provide training of a high standard for district nurses and , indeed, where necessary, to encourage the introduction of such nurses who might specialise in assisting the care of sick people in their own homes.

Here was a cause which was bound to appeal strongly to Christian and her friends particularly when it is realised that one of the prime movers in the campaign was Florence Lees (later Craven), a lady who advocated the creation of a higher grade of nurse with 'a superior education'. She wished to create a 'profession in which a lady would not feel she was sacrificing herself, but on the contrary would feel that she was raising herself by entering a profession at once noble and honourable'.[94]

Subsequently Mrs Craven and three distinquished doctors examined the subjects which were not taught to nurses training in a hospital, but yet which ought to figure in the training of a district nurse. Their list included such matters as sanitary reform, the giving of instructions on health topics, ventilation, drainage, water supply, diets for the healthy and the sick, the feeding of infants, infectious diseases, monthly nursing of the lying-in women, and the care of new born infants. Monica Baly comments that 'the list is interesting because it encapsulates the main causes of mortality in the late nineteenth century when the infant mortality rate was 154 per 1000 live births.'[95]

This then was precisely the kind of activity and enterprise which interested Christian and it clearly offered a fresh opportunity for an initiative on her part. In

1887, therefore, she took up the Honorary Treasurership of the newly formed Scottish Branch of the Institute, and she continued in this office when the Branch was reconstituted as the Scottish Council under the Presidency of the Countess of Rosebery. In addition, she was appointed to the National Council of the Institute where one of her fellow members was H.R.H. Princess Louise, the Marchioness of Lorne, Patroness of the School of Cookery. Apparently, Christian persuaded Princess Louise to take a particularly close interest in the Scottish Council, with the result that the Princess agreed to become its president on the death of Lady Rosebery, and, under her protection, the Scots were able to achieve a high degree of autonomy.[96] Louisa Stevenson was also an active member of the Scottish Council.

By 1890 the Edinburgh group had established a 'Central Institution' in Charlotte Street as its training centre with Miss Peter as its Superintendent. The latter within a few years was to become the national Superintendent of the Institute and responsible for maintaining training standards all over the country. Right from the introduction of the first three students the attempt was made to ensure that they were 'highly trained and educated because, although they work under the direction of medical men, they rarely meet'. Remarkably, in their first year of existence the Edinburgh Queen's nurses 'paid 7517 visits to 321 cases'. By 1891 twelve other branches had been established in other parts of Scotland and demand for the nurses outstripped supply. By the time of the Queen's Diamond Jubilee (1897), 187 Queen's nurses were operating in Scotland.

This is not the place in which to give a full account of the Jubilee nurses, but the story of their establishment in Scotland is again an immense tribute to Christian and her friends. At the time of her death it was estimated that Christian had raised no less than '£20,000 for the work of the Institute in Scotland' a figure which, in the context of the times, can only be described as amazing, particularly when it is remembered that all the while she was devoting a huge part of her energies and resources to sustaining and developing the School of Cookery.[97]

In Christian's view, of course, her activities were all part of the same war and it is interesting that the School provided demonstration lessons for 'medical students', although it is not known whether the latter were male or female, or whether they were training to be doctors or nurses. Their classes were conducted in the large theatre of the Royal Infirmary and included instruction on the preparation of such dishes as a 'nourishing' soup, roast partridge and bread sauce, potato pudding, barley gruel, calf's foot jelly, claret jelly, savoury omelette, arrowroot souffle pudding, wine whey, and 'invalid's pudding'.[98]

At the end of 1887 the Committee of the School combined with their counterparts of the Glasgow School to submit a joint memorial to the Scotch Education Department pleading for changes to be introduced to the Scotch Code of the following year. Their concerns were with the qualifications of cookery teachers, the time allotted to cookery classes in elementary schools and the grants available for day and evening classes in schools. Essentially they wanted to ensure that only teachers holding a certificate from a school of cookery recognised by the Department would be acceptable; and that a grant of 4s would be payable for any girl presented for examination who had attended a minimum of forty hours of instruction and who had spent at least twenty of these hours personally cooking under the supervision of a teacher and in a class of not more than twelve pupils. A smaller grant of 2s might be payable in respect of a pupil with only twenty four hours of instruction and twelve hours practical 'hands on' experience, and that was suggested because of the difficulty recognised in arranging for forty hours in the typical mixed schools of Scotland. The twelve pupil classes were advocated on the grounds of efficient teaching and because of the limited equipment in most schools.[99] It was an interesting effort, but the truth was that breaking through some of the resistance at school board level was still proving difficult.

Two years later there came a very interesting development when the English Board of Education agreed to examine cookery teachers trained at the School. What the Scotch Department thought of this is not clear, but it was an understandable development given the reputation which the School had built up all over the country and the fact that many of its former students actually pursued their careers south of the border. The regulations governing the Elementary School Teachers' Cookery Diploma were as follows. Candidates for training and examination, of between 18 and 50 years of age, required to be teachers in elementary schools, pupil teachers or students attending a training college, but they were not able to obtain their Teachers' Cookery diploma until they had become certificated teachers. The minimum training required was laid down as a) one course of ten demonstrations on Artisan Cookery; b) one course of six demonstrations on Plain Cookery; c) either two courses of ten practice lessons on Artisan Cookery or one course of practice lessons on each of Artisan and Plain Cookery; and d) lessons on cleaning and scullery work. The practice lessons required to be in classes of not more than twelve pupils and the training had to be received from 'a teacher trained in, and holding a first-class Diploma from, the Edinburgh School of Cookery and Domestic Economy; the National Training School for Cookery (London); the Manchester Domestic Economy School; the Glasgow, Leeds or Liverpool Schools of Cookery'. In addition, there were written and practical examinations.

> In these examinations, special attention will be paid to economy in cooking, to rendering coarse and cheap food digestible and nutritious, cheap and varied dietaries, the dietetic value of pulses, cereals, garden vegetables, milk, and etc, the influence of work, climate, age, and state of health on quality and quantity of food required; the composition, properties, and uses in the body of the chief compounds contained in food; the composition, properties, and uses, in the body, of air and water; the processes of digestion, absorption, circulation, and respiration.[100]

The process of establishing a good standard of qualification for teachers and of inserting cookery into the ordinary school curriculum must have seemed long and slow to those concerned, but in fact a significant advance had been made and in retrospect it is clear that a great deal had been achieved in a comparatively short time. Certainly in the fifteen years since the School had been founded many difficulties had been overcome and a secure foundation had been laid on which to construct the next phase of development. As far as Christian and her friends were concerned the time for further major advance was at hand.

At a wider level it seems also to be true that very much had been accomplished by 1890. Throughout the first years of its existence it is evident that the Edinburgh School had made a major contribution to the spread of knowledge which was necessary to bring about genuine, long term, improvements in public health and in standards of nutrition in the community at large. Obviously an element of the work had been to enhance levels of cooking in middle and upper class households; but (given the popularity of the early lectures) it also seems to be the case that Guthrie Wright and her staff were particularly successful in getting the subject matter across to lower income groups. Moreover, judging from the serious, scientific nature of her *School Cookery Book*, the information being imparted genuinely represented the 'state of the art' as understood at the time. This is a subject which could stand further research from the perspectives of food science and nutrition, but as far as the historian is competent to determine, it seems clear that a vital and impressive contribution had been made to disseminating information crucial to creating the foundation necessary to bring about authentic improvements to the diets of the population as a whole, not just in Edinburgh, but in many other parts of the United Kingdom.

CHAPTER THREE

Atholl Crescent, The First Phase 1891-1925

As the 1890s commenced Christian and the other members of the committee took stock of their position. In May of 1891 the lease of the premises in Shandwick Place was due to expire and, although there was no suggestion that they would be required to give up the property, the opportunity existed to consider its suitability for development and, in the process, to determine the future direction in which they wished to take the School.

One thing was clear. Those responsible for the School had demonstrated that, although they were ladies giving voluntary service, they were well able to operate within the business environment. In a memorandum of December 1890 they pointed out that in its fifteen years of existence the School had provided public and private classes at Shandwick Place, in local schools and institutions and in more than a hundred other centres up and down the country. In that time £20,762, 'including £576 subscribed to fit up and start the School', had been taken in by way of fees etc.

> The School has not only paid its way, but the Committee hold £1,900 of invested capital, realised for the most part during the early great demand for public demonstrations of cookery. They have also cash balances and goods to the value of £190; and furniture and fittings estimated at about £150.

Reviewing the prospects, the Committee had come to the conclusion that an institution which aimed at long term success would require to provide more sustained courses of study and to have possession of residential facilities for a proportion of its students. This view was based on an examination of similar 'schools and colleges of domestic economy in England, Germany and other places'. It is known that Christian did go to Europe in the summer of 1887 and it may well be the case that she spent some of her time enquiring into German schools and colleges during her travels. Moreover, it may also be true that this line of thought in respect of residential accommodation was also to be brought to bear on the affairs of Edinburgh University, for within a year or two the campaign to establish Masson Hall was under way.

As far as courses were concerned, the intention was to concentrate on providing

a thorough training in Domestic Subjects - Practical Housekeeping and Management,

Cookery, Laundry Work, Needlework, Dress Cutting and Making, Millinery, Bookkeeping, and Instruction in First Aid to the Injured and in Home Sick Nursing. To students taking the full course, and passing satisfactorily, it is proposed to grant a Housewife's Diploma.

This was, of course, in addition to the traditional individual courses and to the training of teachers of cookery.

To give effect to these plans, the committee proposed not to renew the lease on 6 Shandwick Place but instead to purchase and equip a new, more suitable location with scope for future expansion. Their estimate was that the property and furnishings would cost about £4000 and to raise that sum they suggested forming a limited company, with an initial capital of £3000 - £2000 of which would be subscribed immediately in the form of £10 shares. They proposed also to borrow about a further £2000 on the security of the house. Any additional expenditures they hoped to cover out of their existing resources of £1900.[1]

The subsequent arrangements quite closely followed the pattern outlined above, except that five hundred and fifty-five shares of £5 were issued initially, with a further forty-five being issued in 1893. The total issue capital was therefore £3000 on which the Company paid a dividend of three per cent down to 1904 and four per cent for a few years thereafter.[2]

Early in February 1891 suitable accommodation for the School had been identified at 3 Atholl Crescent and Christian wrote to William Fergusson Pollock Esq offering on behalf of the Committee '£3500 for the house, stable and grounds.....Let me have an answer to this letter in the course of tomorrow if possible.' The School's agents in this matter, as in many previous instances, were Messrs Blair and Finlay of St Andrew's Square.[3] Four days later the deal was concluded and Christian wrote to confirm termination of the lease at Shandwick Place.[4]

With entry to the School's new home due to occur in May there were many plans to be drawn up and carried out and Christian quickly fired off letters to contractors setting out what needed to be done and demanding estimates for a huge list of conversions. The building had, of course, to be altered from a residence into a somewhat unusual educational institution and great attention was paid to the various requirements for teaching cookery and the other domestic subjects as well as the arrangements for housing some staff and students. As forecast, a loan was taken out on the security of the house and ultimately the full bill for purchasing and adapting the premises amounted to over £7,000.[5] That the new company had been able to raise the funds speaks volumes for the regard in which its leaders were held by the community. That Christian, Louisa and the others were willing to take on such a burden and challenge says a great deal not just for the self confidence which they had gained over the years, but about their belief in the future of the School. This was an aspect of the matter which, many years later, still inspired admiration and comment on the part of the generation which followed the founders.

When the conversions were being accomplished considerable care was taken to ensure that the external appearance of the front of the building was not disturbed and this was because several of the neighbours were hostile to the School's arrival. They apparently considered that the School would reduce the prestige of the Crescent which, of course, contained some of the finest town houses in the city.

The move took place in May 1891 when many of the alterations were still being carried out. 'As there were workmen in every room of Number 3 Atholl Crescent it was a scene of discomfort and dirt'. Christian herself seems to have spent much of her time carrying various articles from Shandwick Place to Atholl Crescent, and in the process she succeeded in losing a valuable ring. Nevertheless, it was a most exciting event and she presumably enjoyed its symbolism more than anyone.[6]

When the new company, The Edinburgh School of Cookery and Domestic Economy Limited, was created, more than simply the business form was altered. At the very head of the School there were changes. H.R.H. Princess Louise now became sole patron. The Marquis of Lothian became President and fifteen other leading figures, including the Duchess of Buccleuch, the Duchess of Roxburghe, Lord Advocate Robertson and Sir Douglas Maclagan, became Vice-Presidents. These appointments were obviously about maintaining the status of an establishment committed to female education, but the day-to-day business end of the structure concerned what now became the Board of Directors. Indeed, from now on it is interesting to note that members carefully referred to themselves as Directors, as if consciously demonstrating, not just their interest in educational matters, but their business prowess and position. Christian remained as Honorary Secretary, but the new Honorary Treasurer was Miss E Dalmahoy. At first the Board was composed of nine women and two men, the latter being Sir Alexander Christison and Mr N.J. Finlay, one of the Company's lawyers, but effectively the women ran the organisation themselves and, after a little time, Louisa Stevenson was appointed to be Chairman. The other members in 1891 were Miss C Campbell, Mrs Cathcart, Miss Christie, Mrs Aukland Geddes, Mrs Robinow and Miss M J Urquhart, and they were all close friends.[7] Within a few years the Board had become entirely female.

At this time the staff were typically on year to year contracts but most of the 'highly qualified' teachers were retained. A new appointment, however, was the new Lady Superintendent and Housekeeper, Miss Leith, and she was accorded a salary of £50 with full board plus £4 for laundering. She was also to undertake some further training in London during the summer and before the school re-opened in the autumn.[8]

The School year was now broken into two sessions, from mid September to mid February and, with a five day break, from February until mid July. The new Housewife's Diploma course extended over a twenty week period and included courses in Artisan Cookery, Plain Cookery, High Class Cookery, Cleaning utensils etc, Special lessons on Plain and 'Fancy' Bread, Laundry Work, Dressmaking, Measuring and Cutting, Millinery, Cutting out Underclothing, Patching and Mending Bed and Table Linen etc, Knitting, Swiss Darning and etc, Bookkeeping,

First Aid, Home Sick Nursing, and Housekeeping, House Work and General Management.

The fee for this course was £20 and if the student was in residence there was an additional charge of between £1 and £1.10s., which did not include 'laundry, church seat, medical attendance, or fire in bedroom'. The residential accommodation was intended for students undertaking the Housewife's Diploma, although other students could also be accommodated.[9] The regulations for boarding students indicate that board included breakfast, tea and supper and that a fire could be had in the bedroom for a charge of 6d per day or 4d just for the evening. A bath could be provided in bedrooms daily at a charge of 1s per week or, alternatively, once a week for 3d, but three fixed baths with hot and cold water were also available in the house and there was no charge for using them.

> The bell will be rung at 7am. Morning Prayers at 7.45: Evening Prayers at 9.30. The gas must be extinguished in bedrooms at 10.30. Boarders requiring light after 10.30 are required to provide themselves with candles, or to obtain them from the Superintendent.[10]

The first boarder arrived in September and she had to spend the first fortnight by herself, but within a few weeks there were five or six in residence. At first

> the housekeeper in charge would not allow them to go out until she was free to chaperone them. After a week they rebelled and one, older than the others, was allowed to take them out in her charge. Quickly the number of pupils and boarders increased and soon the hopes of those who started the new venture were fulfilled.[11]

The establishment of the new School was widely reported in such publications as *The Lady, The Truth* and *The Christian World* and there is little doubt that publicity was being sought in magazines which might be read by the parents and young ladies to whom the School wished to appeal. Indeed, *The Lady* actually indicated that the boarding facilities were 'for the benefit of lady students coming from the country'. The other reports were perhaps somewhat more mocking in style than had been anticipated.

> Just fancy, Amy, dear, some one has started a Company for turning out a constant supply of good wives, perfectly competent in every branch of domesticity, and guaranteed, so far as a diploma can guarantee them, to accomplish every particular of home duties in unimpeachable fashion. To Edinburgh belongs the credit of this happiest of inspirations. A school of cookery there has developed into this grand scheme. Charlie declares that the shareholders ought to have first choice of the successful students.

This was the account given by *The Truth,* and the *The Christian World* similarly suggested that the School would be wished well by 'every bachelor with matrimony in prospect'. It reported that

> after fifteen years of successful experience, the institution has just been converted into a limited company, having among its shareholders Lord Rosebery, the Countess of Aberdeen, Sheriff Thoms, and the leading ladies and gentlemen of the Modern Athens.

Slyly this item concluded by pointing out that while they were learning all the housewifely skills the students would be able to stay in a boarding-house 'where they will be 'done for' at from £1 to 30s'.[12]

Not the least interesting point about these reports is that far from being crumpled up and tossed into the basket, they were carefully cut out and pasted into the scrap book along with all the other pieces on the School. More significantly, however, these cuttings reveal quite clearly the fundamental nature of the change which had taken place. Previously much of the School's energies had been consciously advertised as being directed towards working class women and girls, although it also always had been operated by and for women from better-off backgrounds. But now in certain respects it was becoming much more deliberately a post-school institution intended for the daughters of the upper and middle classes. It would never, of course, entirely lose its social conscience so long as its founders were in control, but the focus of some of its activities had shifted in order to provide a more genuine form of post school education for the daughters of those who possessed the necessary money and interest. Given that the School was intended not only to be self financing, but profitable, there was probably no other option.

Most of the young women enrolling for the Housewife's Diploma could, therefore, in the normal run of things expect to have reasonable financial support. However, the School Directors did retain their concern for women, compelled for one reason or another to make their own livings. As a consequence a few years later the Lady Housekeepers Diploma was introduced. This covered similar ground, but was specifically intended as a qualification for women who wished to obtain employment as housekeepers. This course also quickly proved popular which is perhaps not surprising given the large number of women in domestic service of one kind or another in the Edinburgh area. Most of the entrants to the course were young, but there were always a few older women, widows and so on, for whom the course was a considerable boon. Miss de la Cour remembered the oldest such student as being over sixty years of age and happily she not only successfully passed her examinations, but also obtained employment in consequence of doing so. Subsequently much of the training for the two diplomas tended to merge.

In October 1891 the new School was formally opened by Princess Louise who was accompanied by her husband, the Marquis of Lorne. The Princess first dined at the city chambers at a lunch given by Lord Provost Boyd and attended by a host of dignitaries, including no less than five peers and their ladies, and both Christian Guthrie Wright and Louisa Stevenson. Thereafter Princess Louise drove to Atholl Crescent where she met the various vice-presidents of the School. She then inspected the premises, visited some of the classes and spent some time discussing the work with members of the teaching staff. It was the Princess's first recorded visit to the School and to Christian and her colleagues it was undoubtedly a landmark in a significant relationship.[13]

The School, of course, still maintained its interest in useful public lectures and in 1892 it was announced that programmes of lectures would be delivered by Dr Drinkwater on 'The Chemistry of Food' and by Dr Henry Littlejohn on 'Hygiene of the House and Household'. Littlejohn was Scottish Medical Officer of Health and it would have been hard to recruit a more prestigious speaker. His course extended over six lectures and dealt with such matters as the positioning and foundations of buildings, water supply and drainage, servants' accommodation, kitchen, scullery and sanitary arrangements, ventilation and 'slop disposal'. He devoted particular attention to the requirements of tenement dwellings. On 'houses of the poor' he concentrated on what householders could do to help themselves and the remedies which they could obtain from local public officials to deal with 'defects, remove nuisances, and to isolate infectious disease, including fumigation and disinfection'. The course apparently included a trip to visit the City Water Supply Company and to other locations of interest.[14]

The fame of the School and of its principal leaders had spread not just within the United Kingdom, but to many other countries. Indeed, a riffle through the pages of the original visitors' book shows how many distinguished guests, from England, from various parts of the Empire and from other countries, came to see for themselves what was being attempted. The first entry in the book, dated August 18, 1891 is by the Duke and Duchess of Westminster and they were followed by that doyenne of the womens' movement, Frances Mary Buss, founder of the North London Collegiate School for Girls.

Contacts were also established with North America and in 1893 Louisa Stevenson prepared a paper on the campaign to secure university education for women in Scotland which was read on her behalf to an Educational Congress in Chicago. Moreover, one of the best contemporary descriptions of the School is given by an un-named American visitor who, in July 1893, wrote a full account for *The Baltimore Daily*.

> The fine hall for demonstration and practice lessons has seats for the pupils modelled after the best university plan. It is furnished with a first-class range, a large gas stove and a stove for heating irons, and all the other equipment of a thoroughly equipped kitchen.

It was explained that the students were composed of 'all sorts and conditions of womankind' and this was partly achieved by attracting ladies for courses or single lessons and by providing training for their cooks and scullery maids. However, 'most in the regular classes are working for diplomas, as the demand for certificated teachers in cookery and laundry work far exceeds the supply'. After outlining the various courses and lectures on offer the article notes the twenty-week 'Housewife's diploma'. 'This is especially for upper middle-class girls, such as the daughters of clergymen, etc, who in a home-household of servants cannot acquire the practical knowledge necessary for the mistress of a household'.

The author noted that the teaching staff had given lessons in thirty locations outwith Edinburgh in the previous year and that sometimes private lessons would also be given to ladies at their own homes. In addition, instruction was provided to pupils or students coming from other institutions and a session for fifty students

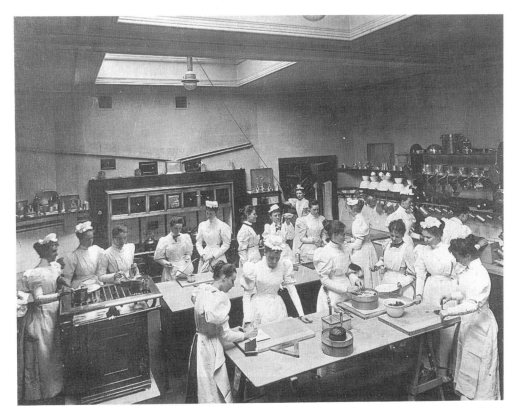

Kitchen c1890. Note the range and ovens to the rear and large gas cooker in the left foreground.

from Moray House Teacher Training College was witnessed. These students were being instructed in artisan cookery and worked in pairs in classes of no more than twelve; and the lesson that morning was on 'the making of a treacle (molasses) pudding'.

> Another class further advanced took up the making of bread-and-butter puddings of scones and plain tarts. The little puddings looked light and palatable as they were turned from out the small white bowls in which they were boiled on the hot ashes - which is Scotch for platter.

The prepared food was apparently bought by the pupils at a price which covered the cost of materials and this was held by the visitor to be an admirable arrangement, particularly for the boarding students who had to provide their own food.

> I observed several pairs who, after viewing their joint pudding with gratified eyes at its success, divided it into two parts and, sitting down together, ate it on the spot, thus securing their lunch at a small rate.

The visitor much admired both the demonstration and practice lessons and believed that such education must become universal in order to promote a proper degree of respect for the provider of household services and to defeat ignorance and disease. She particulary enjoyed one demonstration given by Miss Jack and has left us with a very vivid account of that occasion.

> But here was a woman with all the implements of her work set in orderly array before her, as they might always be in any kitchen. She herself was attired in the neatest of white gowns, a white apron and cap - the most easily washable of costumes. She handled her implements as skilfully as an artist his brush or chisel, giving all the time instructions in an agreeable voice and in clear, terse grammatical English, her words as exactly weighed and measured as her materials.
>
> She taught not only the more artistic forms of cookery, an aspic jelly, ornate meats and puddings, but first of all gave detailed instructions for the clarifying of dripping. Dripping seems to be the great corner stone of British cookery of the plainer sort. It fills the place that butter holds in our wasteful land. It butters much of the bread. And when you come to think of it, good beef and pork and mutton dripping is infinitely better eating than questionable butter.

The visitor was also delighted with the various forms of needlework and garment making which she encountered. She noted that dressmaking was taught via a chart and this was almost certainly a 'Eureka' chart supplied by Tate & Co of Birmingham. Specimens of needlework were admired and in a glass case 'a sampler hung .. exactly like that of my New England grandmother, done in cross-stitch, best of all marking stitches for underclothing'. Indeed, the array of needlework seems to have been particulary impressive and included demonstrations of the repair of various fabrics. 'In the advanced sewing course, which includes the marking, old German and Venetian, and embroidery, drawn threadwork, Holstein and other fancy stitches are taught.'

Comment was also made about the various classes held outwith the School buildings and the most important of these were mainly for 'factory girls', seven hundred of whom had attended during the previous winter session. These courses had principally been in cookery, although a few dressmaking classes had also been given. In addition, cookery lessons were given to medical students and hospital nurses at the Royal Infirmary. 'An Edinburgh physician, an officer of the Royal College of Physicians, told me he had to take the lessons in sick-room cookery and highly valued the knowledge he acquired'.[15]

Miss Florence Jack, the cookery teacher whose class is described above, was one of the first members of staff employed by the School who had also been trained in the School. She had qualified with a first class diploma in July 1888,[16] and was currently one of the better paid lecturers, earning a basic salary of £80 per annum to which were added allowances when teaching away from Edinburgh and her meals when in School.[17] The main teacher of needlework, and who had evaluated the Eureka chart for use in the School, was Miss Shaw. The salaries of the staff had to be upwardly reviewed in 1892 as a consequence of the improved rates being offered to cookery teachers by a few county councils.[18]

The classes for working class girls held in the old town represented an important innovation. The Edinburgh School Board was still proving to be unsupportive so far as the full introduction of cooking for school girls was concerned. However, in

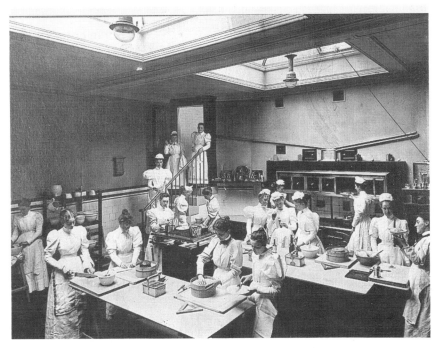

Atholl Crescent Kitchen c1890.

session 1892-93 the city's Town Council decided to intervene by offering the School an annual grant of £1,000 to lay on free classes of instruction for girls belonging to the city who were fifteen years of age (by which time, of course, they had left school). At first these lessons were given at 3 Chambers Street, but a more permanent location was found by obtaining and equipping the India Buildings in Victoria Street. The member of staff put in charge of this development was Miss Crawford, (who was eventually to become the first Inspectress of Domestic Science at the Scottish Education Department). The Town Council's intervention was, of course, hugely welcome to the School and it is tempting to think that Princess Louise may not have missed the opportunity to press the case with the Lord Provost during their meeting a few months earlier.[19]

1893 was noted as a year of 'special prosperity and of unexampled strain upon the teaching resources of the School', and it is clear that the pressure for rapid growth built up swiftly following the establishment of its new base. Not only had the branch been set up in the old town, but so overcrowded had the Atholl Crescent building already become that the Directors had to sanction the construction of an additional classroom out into the backyard and this became known later as kitchen number two.

The 1890s generally were years of sustained progress and there was a steady increase in the receipts accruing to the School. Despite expenditures to permit expansion, as early as 1895 the Directors were able to repay £1000 of the original

Laundry at Atholl Crescent, c1890.

loan. The pressure on space, however, was almost unending and in 1896, for example, an extraordinary arrangement had to be made in order to provide a room, apparently called the 'speed-the-work room', in which staff could relax, hold meetings or conduct interviews. 'This room was made by lowering the ceiling of the pantry and raising the floor of the room above and was, therefore, telescoped between floors'.[20] The staff, not surprisingly, were strictly warned that they were not to attempt to hold any classes in this apartment.

But such Heath-Robinson measures could not provide more than temporary relief and in 1898 the neighbouring house at 4 Atholl Crescent was leased and partly fitted as a Laundry. Three years later this house was purchased outright and extensively altered and this was achieved via a further loan of £3,500. Still the pressure was maintained, however, and in 1906 the Company's capital was extended by another £1,000, which was quickly fully subscribed. This, together with a mortgage of £2,000, enabled number 6 Atholl Crescent also to be bought and reconstructed. Meanwhile extra classrooms were being leased in such places as Rutland Square, Toll Cross and 11/13 Walker Street, as the School continued its expansion throughout the early years of the twentieth century.

One of the reasons for this growth was the significant extension of teacher training which had become possible as a result of the English Board of Education taking on the responsibility of examination. As Miss de la Cour, who joined the staff in 1896, noted, 'the training of teachers took a great spurt when the School moved to Atholl Crescent. ...The English Board ... appointed inspectresses .. because there was no examining body in Scotland'.

In 1898 the process of producing competent teachers was eased and aided when a committee of the Edinburgh School Board chaired by Mrs Anne Kerr and including Flora Stevenson in its membership, agreed arrangements to permit student teachers of Cookery and Domestic Economy from the School to undertake practice sessions in the Board's schools. The students concerned had to have completed training in Artisan Cookery and no more than two could be placed in the one school at any one time. In addition, they had to be given advance notice of any meal which they might require to demonstrate so that they could practice the lesson at Atholl Crescent before presenting it to pupils.

> Miss Guthrie Wright, Honorary Secretary, and Miss Melvin, Honorary Assistant Secretary, of the School of Cookery and Domestic Economy, Limited, who were present, intimated to the Committee that (they) .. would do everything in their power to make the arrangements work satisfactorily.[21]

This was an important step forward and the interest of the School Board now developed a little more helpfully, particularly with the introduction in Edinburgh schools of what were called continuation classes. These were intended to provide some on-going education for older teenagers who had left school. As continuation classes increased, of course, so the Town Council felt less need to maintain its sponsorship of free public instruction for fifteen-year-olds, and the grant for this purpose gradually reduced as the Board took over the task of supplying post school education in this area. Similarly, as the output of teachers coming from the teaching colleges, but with some training provided by the School (and indeed, by its Glasgow counterpart) expanded, so more and more elementary and normal schools were able to employ teachers with a little knowledge of Cookery and Domestic Economy, hence the need for the School to provide 'out' classes in certain areas diminished. It is arguable, indeed, that the Town Council's initiative had been a deliberate and perhaps not unsuccessful measure designed to prod or shame the Edinburgh Board into action. However, it should be understood that specialist systematic instruction in cookery was still not available to girls in many schools in the city and elsewhere in Scotland.

By this stage Miss Jessie Melvin had been appointed as Christian's assistant secretary and Miss Melvin was one of a number of writers who subsequently left some account of life in the School in the years around the turn of the century. Writing of the Directors' fortnightly meetings, for example, she indicates that these were held in the dining-room of the boarding house.

> Miss Louisa Stevenson ..as Chairman, sat at the head of the long table, observant of everyone and everything. Miss Guthrie Wright, as Hon.Secretary, was next to her and Mrs Robinow, the senior member, sat on the other side. Beside her was Mrs Aukland Geddes, who was Convener of the House Committee, and whose admirable knowledge of household matters enabled her to deal more especially with the housekeeper, boarders and servants and to bring their views and requirements before the meeting. Miss Elizabeth Dalmahoy acted as Treasurer, and was subsequently succeeded by Miss J. H. Wright.

Meetings were typically held at 11 o'clock and the room had to be vacated in time for the students to lunch at 1pm. Servants often had difficulty in getting in to prepare the table and apparently the method of persuading Miss Stevenson to bring matters to a close was for one maid to arrive bearing a tray of silver and glass 'jingling delightfully'.

According to Miss de la Cour one of the unofficial rules was that each member of the Committee should themselves hold the School's Diploma or some equivalent qualification. Christian, of course, had qualified in Cookery at the National in London, but Louisa Stevenson was also a qualified teacher of needlework. 'Miss Guthrie Wright felt that members must bring something to the School'. Accordingly, each member was given a specific department or function as her specialist area of interest. Mrs Geddes, for example, watched over the Boarding House and the brilliant Margaret J Urquhart, a fine classical scholar, concerned herself with needlework and dressmaking. 'She came so charmingly attired, she was the fashion plate and envy of many a less fortunate sister'. As far as Miss Melvin was concerned simply being a member of the Committee 'was one of the most liberal educations a junior could have'. Moreover, the general atmosphere seems to have been excellent and all of the memories which were recorded by various people at the time convey an impression of enthusiastic achievement by a group of thoroughly admirable women.

> There were many happy incidents. Nowhere could a point have been grasped more quickly or more pleasure obtained from a joke. If a post fell vacant the letters of the candidates put on the short leet were read and handed round, photographs were not encouraged as they were thought to be misleading; handwriting was commented upon, commas and stops noted, every member was invited to express her opinion.

Miss Melvin was very anxious that people who had not known the principals should understand that they were in every sense genuinely feminine in character. She was concerned that, because of their capacity for hard work and public campaigning, they might be thought of as lacking somehow in womanliness. The contrary, she maintained, was the truth. 'It was far otherwise. No one could have dressed more charmingly than Miss Louisa Stevenson...' Both the latter and Miss Guthrie Wright paid great attention to their personal appearance and it was as if they were conscious of publicly representing women in their dealings with the world.

Another to leave memories of this period was the needlework teacher, Miss A Pearce who had joined the staff in 1891. Her admiration for Christian was great and she described her as 'wonderful. I feel sorry for those who came too late to know her. She took a share in everything and an interest in each member of the School'.

Miss Pearce's memories are interesting, partly because of the comments which she makes about the difficulties of needlework in respect of female garments at the end of the Victorian age. The students had, for example, to be able to master the intricacies of a tight bodice, whether they intended to wear one or not, and apparently it involved 'eleven curved seams' which were 'full of opportunities for mistakes'. In addition, each seam had to be 'boned and good boning requires skill and practice', and 'the front opening had to meet closely, but never gape, over a waist of 22 inches'. Evidently few students would ever admit to a greater size of waist and the staff, therefore, became unwilling to accept anyone's account of her own measurements.

Apparently also the heavy tweed skirts of the day could weigh as much as five pounds and yet they were standard apparel for long walks or for playing tennis.

> But the greatest abomination in the way of dress was undoubtedly the trained skirt for outdoor wear. Cookery students had to have their trains fixed up with safety pins before they commenced to work. I think there is nothing at the present time (1925) which can compete with that long skirt for discomfort and dirt. Think of going out on a wet day holding a parcel, a train, and an umbrella.

Miss Melvin shared Miss Pearce's admiration for Christian, but also gives us an insight into one of her sources of advice and support.

> It was an unwritten law that any new project or alteration which might be the outcome of enthusiasm should not be carried out without Miss Guthrie Wright first consulting her friend and adviser Mr Patrick Blair, whose sagacious counsel was always accepted as final.[22]

Blair was one of the partners in the legal firm which had represented the School from its earliest days and without making any charge for its services. Apparently this was because of Blair's belief that the School 'would benefit the city', but also because of 'his friendship with Miss Guthrie Wright.'[23] Curiously, however, when the School Company was formed in 1891 it was Blair's partner Finlay who was appointed as a Director. Nevertheless, when the Blair/Finlay firm broke up in September 1897, and Blair formed a new partnership with Mr H F Cadell, the Directors unanimously agreed to stay with him, despite Finlay's evident willingness to be the School's agent. Undoubtedly, Christian had great confidence in Patrick Blair and it may well have been the case that she did look to him for business advice, particularly after her father's death. Blair sometimes took a leading role on official occasions and, for example, he chaired the formal reopening of the School after the acquisition of 4 Atholl Crescent in 1901. His wife also appears to have shared his interest in the School, since she was one of those presented to Princess Louise when the latter visited it a few weeks later.

In these years Princess Louise was a fairly frequent visitor to the School. As was mentioned earlier, she had performed the opening ceremony in 1891, and she returned with her husband in October 1895 and again in 1897. By the time of the 1901 visit her husband had succeeded to the Dukedom of Argyll, and on this occasion the Princess not only inspected the new premises and met the members of the Board and staff, but presented certificates to a group of bursers from George Square College for Young Ladies who were being trained at the School. In view of Queen Victoria's recent death the Princess was still formally in mourning and therefore her dress was black. It had a 'cape' or a 'collar of black velvet, a little white was seen on front of the bodice, in which, near the throat, was placed a small broach, which looked like a large Scotch pearl surrounded with diamonds'. After the presentation ceremony the formal thanks to the Princess was proposed by Flora Stevenson, who was present on behalf of the Edinburgh School Board, of which she had recently become chairman. It must have been quite a day for the Stevenson sisters because Louisa, as Chairman of the Directors, had been in charge of the proceedings and had, together with Christian, received the royal party and other guests.[24]

On an occasion such as the one described above, of course, everyone was thoroughly rehearsed for the great day.

> Before a visit from H.R.H. Princess Louise Miss Guthrie Wright would come in dressed for the occasion, invite criticism, tell where the grandeur had been got and then would hurry down to the kitchen to act as H.R.H., not with any thought of herself but that both teachers and students should be prepared to make their curtsey in the approved manner and all in one moment.

The Argylls came again to the School on the 5th December 1904 and Princess Louise was in Scotland on that occasion principally to receive an honorary LLD from the University of Glasgow. This was bestowed on her in recognition of the fact that she had been President of Queen Margaret College, Glasgow from its inception in 1877 until its recent absorption within the University. This College had always been directed towards securing the provision of university level education for women and after the Scottish Universities finally opened their doors to admit females the College authorities took the decision in favour of incorporation within the University, hence it gave up its separate existence. However, its name is perpetuated at the University through the Queen Margaret Union. Incidentally, this must have been a considerable day for Glasgow University, for not only was Princess Louise honoured, but Lord Kelvin, the great scientist, was installed as Chancellor.[25]

As a glance through the reference section will indicate, two of Miss Guthrie Wright's letter books of correspondence in connection with the School have survived. Her letters were blotted on sheets of tissue paper and these sheets provide an important source of material on the events and concerns of that period. The second book becomes progressively more simply a record of staff matters, formal letters of appointment and so on, and gradually it was less used by Christian and became rather more the province of Miss Melvin. Nevertheless, both books give very interesting insights into the attitudes and levels of conduct of the early pioneers. What comes across most vividly and above all are the scrupulous standards which were applied and the rigorous determination to put the interests of the School above everything. Despite the undoubted affection in which Christian and Louisa were held by staff and colleagues, there is no question but that they could be very strict and severe when necessary, although at all times they seem to have been guided by an innate sense of fairness and impeccable courtesy. There is no example of anyone being treated in a manner which lacks justification.

For instance, Christian could be very hard on students who were inadequately prepared and her reason was that she was determined to uphold the reputation of the School and of Cookery teachers by only qualifying students who matched the high standards laid down. On one occasion Mr Watt, the secretary of the Free Church Training School (Moray House), protested at the decision to fail sixteen of its students, and for his pains he received a long letter in which Christian set out the detailed reasons in each case as to why the candidates had been failed. Interestingly, in several cases the main factor was the student's inability to maintain discipline in the class room, although lack of preparation and poor 'arrangements' were also problems. Clearly there was a great determination to ensure that those who went out into schools bearing the imprimatur of the Edinburgh School could acquit themselves effectively.[26]

But the staff were subject to the same standards and at times were also treated with severity. Usually teachers were appointed subject to undertaking some additional training and thereafter proving themselves to be satisfactory performers. Quite often they did not achieve the necessary level and were accordingly discharged or required to take some further instruction. Just to give one example, in 1893 Miss Harrison was appointed as a cookery and health studies teacher, with the condition that she received some extra lessons in cookery. She was already reasonably qualified and was appointed on a salary of £100 per annum which, at that time, indicated that she was to become one of the senior teachers. However, a year later Christian terminated the appointment, writing that 'the quality of your cookery work and teaching ... are not such as to warrant .. employing you either to teach cookery or to judge of test lessons. Therefore with great regret they (the Board) instructed me to give you the required three months notice.'[27]

Another senior teacher who was dealt with firmly, but fairly was Miss Rotheram. She had been appointed as a Cookery teacher in 1891 and by 1895 was being offered a salary of £110 per annum which indicated the regard in which she was held. However, she was also asked to move from the Atholl Crescent residence and accept a room at 7 Rutland Square. This she was unwilling to do and demanded an increased salary to accept the change, failing which she would resign. Christian calmly responded that since she had declined the terms offered her she had effectively already resigned. Miss Rotheram now hastily back tracked claiming that she was entitled to a further three months' notice, but this was briskly rejected and to the letter with which was enclosed the teacher's settlement cheque Christian added a private note in which she said

> I fail to see why you did not at least make a trial of the room at 7 Rutland Square .....I do not see your difficulty as to cheaper rooms at some distance, because of the expense of travelling. Tram fares are now reduced and you can travel long distances for 1d. If however, you should wish to withdraw your refusal, it must be done promptly as I have already lost valuable time in making the winter arrangements.

Needless to say Miss Rotheram's resignation was withdrawn by return of post, the new terms were accepted and the young woman seems to have gone on to a long and valued career with the School. Christian's laconic response to her letter withdrawing the resignation includes not the slightest hint of emotion.

> I duly received your letter of yesterday. As requested by you I have withdrawn your letter of August 8th which can now be considered as cancelled ... I shall expect you at the School for a class in the morning of Monday 16th September.[28]

An interesting story about Miss Rotheram, by then Head Teacher of Cookery, is that one Easter she and Miss de la Cour were sent to Paris in order to pick up ideas for the High Class Cookery course. Their instructions were to dine at a different restaurant every night. 'We were very generously supplied with money so we could walk past the cheaper restaurants and just concentrate on the expensive ones'. Not surprisingly, much later Miss de la Cour remembered, 'we thoroughly enjoyed that holiday!'

Another excellent member of staff who received a kindly, but magisterial rebuke was Miss Harriet Horne. The latter joined the staff in 1892 and she became the trusted Superintendent of the Boarding House. On one occasion in November 1900, however, some function organised by the 'young ladies' seems to have 'got out of hand' to some degree. What the nature of their offence was we shall never know, but Miss Horne appears not to have secured permission for the particular event to go ahead and had to write to the Directors making suitable apology. In a letter on behalf of the Board and signed by both Christian and Louisa she was told

> ..you now understand that the whole government and arrangements of the House must have their approval and sanction .. They take this opportunity of again conveying to you their appreciation of your endeavours to secure the comfort and happiness of all in residence in the House. But in an institution of this kind everybody connected with it - individual Directors, officials and teachers - can only act with the authority of the Directors as a body.[29]

No lasting damage was done to Miss Horne's reputation and when she resigned eighteen months later to take another appointment the Board voted her a gift of £50 'in view of your happy relations with those who have been resident in the House.'[30]

As far as the students were concerned, they had a Representative Committee functioning from October 1905 and it was set up to enable discussions to take place formally with the secretaries and Directors 'about training and other matters'. It had six committee members, none of whom could be first term students, and included one from each of the main subject areas.[31] A Student of these days remembered her 'months at Atholl Crescent ..(as) .. very happy ones... Living conditions were good - in doors by 10pm, but no difficulty in getting late passes which I frequently applied for being an enthusiastic theatre-goer'.

The first male member of the teaching staff appears to have been Mr Calderwood, a lecturer in the Theory and Practice of Education. He was with the School from 1892 until 1906, although it is not certain that he was a full-time employee. However, when he sought an alternative position he was given a glowing testimonial from Christian. He was said to have 'raised the standard of teaching in the School and .. inspired both staff and students with high ideals of a teacher's aims'. He had qualities of 'kindness, calm judgement, even temper, justice and courtesy' which 'made it a pleasure and a privilege to have him as a co-worker in this School'.[32]

Another male teacher was Mr Stewart, lecturer in The Science of Common Life (Chemistry) from 1902 until 1905. Five years later the first lady Chemistry lecturer was appointed and she was Miss J Marjorie McLeish MA (Hons), BSc,DipEd, of Glasgow University. She arrived at the School in 1910 and was immediately required to undertake training in Cookery, and she duly obtained a first class diploma. Her assistant in the School was Miss (later Dr) Grace Macdonald BSc.[33]

In 1902 the School made its first attempt at the training of students who wished to enter hospital nursing. The course offered was of two months duration and was a preparatory course for students who would experience their main professional instruction within a hospital. The syllabus included lessons on the Structure and Functions of the Human Body, Sick Room Duties, Sick Room and Plain Cookery and Cleaning and Scullery-work and the examiners included Dr C J Lewis and a 'Trained Nurse'.

The Annual Report for 1901 summed up the position of the School at the start of the new century. Throughout the previous session staff teachers had given 3,290 Demonstration and Practice lessons on the standard range of subjects and had heard and criticised 154 Test Demonstrations by Teachers in training. Nine students of Cookery had been awarded first or second class diplomas after inspection by the Board of Education Inspectress, Miss H Deane. She had reported, 'Edinburgh - The students were charmingly neat and dainty in their practical work, but inclined to waste time ...The knowledge shown in the theoretical worked papers was above average.' Apart from the nine Cookery students

> during the Session 45 Teachers' Diplomas were issued by the School:- 14 students gained the Laundry Work Diploma, 7 the Dressmaking, 5 Elementary School Teacher Dressmaking, and 19 Needlework. 14 Lady Housekeepers completed their training during the Session; 47 students were training for the Housewife's Diploma. 20 completed the course during the Session, and of these 3 were awarded the Silver Badge, having obtained 75 per cent in every branch. A student gained a Diploma as a Popular Health Lecturer, and as a Lecturer on Sick Nursing.

Classes had been provided for such other Edinburgh institutions as George Watson's College for Young Ladies, Queen Victoria's Jubilee Institute (District Nurses), Moray House Training College, and James Gillespie's School. In addition, the Town Council's public classes for fifteen year olds were still functioning and 429 pupils had been given instruction at the India Buildings, a little less than half of the pupils studying Cookery and the remainder needlework or laundrywork. As far as the School premises were concerned, 'since the last addition to the accommodation .. there has been a steady increase of students applying for classes. Not only have the class-rooms been crowded, but many applicants were disappointed.' (This, of course, was the background to the purchase of Number 4 Atholl Crescent.) After allowing for twenty per cent of the cost of buying and fitting out the new accommodation and paying a dividend of £90, the revenue carry forward for the year was £285.[34]

As can be seen, therefore, the School began the new century as a thriving and viable institution performing a useful function within the city. However, it is also clear that the number of specialist cookery teachers being produced was still small and that Christian and the others who shared her point of view had been quite unable to secure a full place for Cookery within the standard curriculum for school girls in Scotland. In some schools and under some school boards a degree of penetration had been achieved to 1900, but it was patchy and obviously the resistance in certain quarters was still severe. Typically the opposition seems to have come from male dominated school boards, but it also appears to be true that not all women were convinced of the need for cookery teaching in school and many believed that mothers were well able to provide the necessary instruction themselves. The majority of the teachers being qualified by the School therefore held qualifications in other branches of domestic education such as needlework.[35]

This background to the School's activities, however, was now about to undergo a fundamental adjustment and it is appropriate to examine this in a little detail. The years since the School had been established had seen a huge change in school education in Scotland and in the position of female teachers. Although women had not yet broken through into the senior promoted posts within schools and were still being significantly undervalued by many school boards, the fact is that the structure of teaching staffs in many parts of Scotland had been transformed. Although prior to the 1872 Education Act there had been many female teachers in Scotland, the majority of the teaching profession was then made up of males, which was not surprising given the limited post elementary educational opportunities open to females. By 1901, however, there were more than 17,000 women teachers and they represented about seventy per cent of the Scottish total. Not all of the latter were by any means in favour of extending cookery classes in schools, but as has been explained, many of the student teachers coming from institutions such as Moray House had had some training in domestic subjects and certainly the influence of women within the education structure had greatly increased in many parts of the country.

In the early years of the twentieth century there was a sharp growth in the demand for more systematic instruction in cookery and the other domestic subjects. Part of the reason for this was a direct consequence of the war in South Africa (1899-1902) which produced a fairly appalling picture of the wretched physical condition of many of the young men volunteering for military service from British urban communities. In Manchester, for example, 8,000 out of 11,000 volunteers had to be rejected as unfit for active service and other cities reported a similar situation. The inevitable assumption was that poor physical condition could not be confined to male members of the population and the various investigations which were initiated in the period drew attention to the still high infant mortality rates. In England the death rate among infants in 1900 stood at 146 per 1000 births, which was a barely perceptible improvement over the 1860 figure.[36] And if the Scottish figure of 124 was better, it actually showed a deterioration from the 118 per 1000 births which was the comparative total for 1860.[37]

At this time there was a considerable interest among certain sections of the community, including many doctors, in the subject of eugenics, and they articulated particular concerns in respect of the causes of high infant mortality, declining fertility rates and the evident poor physical state of many young people. Environmental factors were identified as being responsible and a particular focus was on the role and conduct of women within the household.

In Scotland in 1902 a Royal Commission was set up to investigate physical training in Scottish schools and this enabled attention to be directed not just to the immediate subject of study, but to the condition of Scottish children and to the role of schools in promoting the health of on-coming generations.[38] One of the most influential witnesses before the Commission was Dr W Leslie Mackenzie, formerly Medical Officer of Health for Leith and recently appointed as Medical Inspector at the Local Government Board for Scotland. Mackenzie emphasised that the primary causes of ill-health among Scottish children were such factors as poor housing, overcrowding and lack of adequate nutrition. In his view, 'lack of proper nourishment' was a critical factor and he urged the necessity of girls being given instruction on domestic skills and on the properties and preparation of food. The Commissioners were impressed by this evidence and, in view of the absence of statistical information on such matters as the height and weight of children from various social backgrounds, they invited Mackenzie to undertake some comparative investigations. This he did studying 1,300 children from different locations in Edinburgh and Aberdeen in an attempt to establish whether or not there was a clear variation between the condition of children from poor working class areas and those from wealthier middle class homes. The evidence was inescapable with the working class children typically being smaller, lighter and obviously less well nourished. Moreover, the Commissioners were also confronted by information which suggested that astonishingly high proportions (more than 90 per cent) of working class children had significant medical deficiencies. Mackenzie called for the introduction of the systematic medical inspection of school children and the training of teachers in matters of health and hygiene.

In the light of this investigation a conclusion was that it was essential for the Scottish education authorities to develop closer links with the Cookery Schools. This, of course, highlighted the unsatisfactory nature of the training of teachers of domestic subjects, in that the Cookery Schools were independent voluntary organisations, the Scottish Education Department still was not formally involved and there was no direct provision of official funds for the training of teachers of cookery and related subjects. In other words, voluntary institutions such as the

Edinburgh School were doing their best, but the S.E.D. and many school boards were giving little help and beyond the modest inspection of cookery student teachers provided by the English Department of Education the system was virtually unregulated. Following this report, however, board schools were inevitably going to be given a central role in boosting the physical well-being of children and this meant that the role of women teachers and the particular education of school-girls were to become matters of major importance in subsequent legislation and the Cookery Schools would be brought formally into centre stage.

Not the least interesting point about this episode is that Dr Mackenzie's wife, Helen, a teacher in Aberdeen before her marriage, was an occasional lecturer within the Edinburgh School in the years prior to the First World War, and later she was to become a member and then subsequently Chairman of the College Council. She, in fact, was a major collaborator with her husband in his investigation of the health of school children. She organised the inspection of 600 Edinburgh children for the Royal Commission on Physical Training and probably also participated fully in her husband's study of children in Aberdeen where, no doubt, her knowledge of the schools was useful. Jointly she and her husband were responsible for a series of publications at this time on the health of school children and on the need to provide better training and support for Scottish mothers.

It would be a mistake, however, to assume that this was purely a Scottish phenomenon. The same sort of forces were at work south of the border for so concerned was the Government about the poor physique of young men that it established an Interdepartmental Committee to investigate the problem. The Report of this Committee published in 1904 argued that the general health of the population was improving, but that in congested inner city areas standards were extremely low. Again, much of the blame was laid at the door of domestic incompetence and the ignorance of many women in respect of nutrition, hygiene and the care of infants. Many of those who gave evidence blamed the inadequacies of the elementary school training provided for girls and it is interesting to note that one of the witnesses was Mrs Mackenzie, Secretary of the National Union of Women Workers. She stated in her evidence that 'where the working woman's condition breaks down .. is that they have no home training, their time is spent in doing education which is not suitable for them'.[39] (Lack of biographical information has meant that it has not been possible to establish definitely that this lady was Mrs Helen Mackenzie, but it certainly seems highly likely.)

In its final report the Committee called for major educational reform to provide a better training for girls. The report recommended that adequate courses of instruction on cookery and household management should be delivered in the ordinary work of board schools, ideally to girls in the later stages of their school careers, and that there should be proper official inspection to ensure that good standards were maintained.

As this investigation was being conducted the Board of Education initiated a series of enquiries into the education provided for girls in other countries as well as into the quality of cookery training in England. As far as the latter was concerned, the study by the Chief Woman Inspector, Maude Lawrence, revealed a situation which was far from satisfactory in many areas. Even where courses were being supplied children were often given very little 'hands on' practice and teachers tended to concentrate on inappropriate fancy 'high-class' foods, or on 'saleable' commodities such as toffee or buns, presumably to restrict the financial burden on school boards. Much of the training was categorised as a waste of time and money. The Code of 1906 attempted to remedy some of these problems in England and arranged for more systematic inspection.[40]

If the subject of Cookery in schools caused concern, so too did the question of the infant mortality rates and English Medical Officers of Health were equally demanding in their calls for the proper training of school girls in infant care and hygiene.

It will be seen, therefore, that in the early years of the twentieth century the climate of opinion was swinging rapidly and decisively in favour of the views of Christian and the other leaders of the Edinburgh School. Their arguments in respect of the need for instruction in cookery, health and hygiene to be provided to working class girls in the ordinary schools, for pupils to be given the opportunity to actually practice the required skills, and for teachers of cookery to be thoroughly trained in the selection and preparation of appropriate foods, seem all to have been vindicated by the various investigations which occurred at that time. Today this is a somewhat contentious subject since modern feminists sometimes take the view that the reorientation of the school education of girls which occurred in this period tended to reinforce gender role divisions and to make it more difficult for girls to compete with boys in the mainstream elements of education. This, it is argued, seriously disadvantaged the next generations of girls in respect of subsequent careers.[41] From a later perspective this argument may have some kind of validity. However, an education system presumably is shaped in an attempt to deal with the requirements of society at the time in question and the evidence seems to point clearly to the view that the British education systems were adjusting in response to the advice being given to legislators and administrators by doctors and particularly by the increasingly influential medical officers of health. Given that there seems to have been a consensus among the latter about the levels of ignorance prevailing in many households, and in view of the relatively limited channels of public information available at that time, it is very difficult to be too critical of the educational legislators of the day. Indeed, the fact is that from this point on levels of infant mortality began to improve rapidly and while this can probably not be explained purely in terms of educational reform, it would be perverse to suggest that improved levels of knowledge of food, health and hygiene among successive generations of mothers did not play a key part in the transformation which almost halved the death rate among Scottish infants by the late 1930s. Moreover, the same period witnessed a sustained improvement in the health of children with, for example, the incidence of rickets among Scottish youngsters falling from 9 per cent in 1910-1914 to just 1.5 per cent by 1937.[42] It is difficult to accept, therefore, that the educational reformers of the first decade of the twentieth century owed anybody many apologies.

Sadly neither Christian nor Louisa were to be involved when the key changes were introduced. In 1905 increasingly poor health forced Miss Stevenson to take a less active part and she therefore decided to retire. Christian succeeded her as Chairman with Miss Melvin becoming Honorary Secretary. By this time, however, the real merits of these pioneers were being recognised in many quarters and various honours began to fall to them. In 1903 Flora Stevenson received an LLD from the University of Edinburgh and three years later there was great pride among her former colleagues when Louisa Stevenson was awarded a similar doctorate.

By the time of her graduation, painful illness had taken a very heavy toll of Louisa and she was extremely frail. However, she heard Sir Ludovic Grant pay suitable tribute to her, particularly, of course, for her 'signal efforts' in bringing about the admission of women to a full education at the university. He described her as being

Strenuous in action, tenacious of purpose, and of high moral courage ...

When the Commission on University Education met here, the evidence given by Miss Stevenson produced a profound impression by its clearness, and the intimate knowledge and grasp of principles which it exhibited ...

.. It is fitting that one who was so instrumental in bringing university degrees within reach of women should herself receive our highest degree.

After her death in 1908 an old friend wrote to her neices 'of the extraordinary influence (which) she exercised over so many' people. Her secret lay in her 'intellectual and moral energy', her single minded sense of purpose, 'the force of her intellect, and her faculty of grasping almost intuitively the facts and

Louisa Stevenson

possibilities of a situation'. If she lacked the balanced judgement of her sister Flora, 'there was a fire of genius in Louisa' which made her a 'commanding personality'; and if, in her determination, she was sometimes 'too sure she was right' .. 'her sweetness and courtesy almost always disarmed her opponents' .. and she was greatly blessed by her sense of fun. Her friend, Miss McLaren, concluded that Louisa 'was a born leader ... always a fighter ... She .. had more zest in life, and joy her own powers and achievements ... than almost anyone I have ever known'.[43]

Despite the fact that she had been Chairman of the School's Board from 1891, Louisa Stevenson was not the leading force behind its existence and development. All contemporary commentators agree that the main drive and initiative was provided by Miss Guthrie Wright and Miss de la Cour, for example, describes Louisa as being among her 'colleagues and helpers.'[44] Nevertheless in evaluating her contribution it has to be said that she was far from being an ordinary helper. Specifically, her enthusiasm, her business instinct and her confidence on the public platform seem to have made her an invaluable and key asset over these difficult early years. Moreover, as with her sister, she provided an ideal role model to the following generations of Edinburgh women in general and to the School's staff and students in particular and this is clearly reflected in the respect which they accorded her. To describe her as Christian's principal lieutenant, therefore, is in no sense to belittle her immense contribution.

Christian was never publicly honoured, either academically or by the Crown, but this was probably partly because of her premature and unexpected death. Following a short illness, which was not at first believed to be serious, she died in February 1907 at the age of sixty-two. *The Scotsman* was fulsome in its tribute.

> A lady of remarkable activity and great breadth of sympathy, she also had a capacity for sound judgement, a keen and unbiased sense of justice in the affairs of life which penetrated through the conventional to the essential, exceptional powers of initiative, and resourcefulness. Her interest in the progress and welfare of women-kind in general found an embodiment in a substantial and practical form. Miss Guthrie Wright was above all a womanly woman; and her activities have been displayed in those channels which have been the recognised province of women.

The two achievements for which the newspaper thought she would be most remembered were the formation of the Jubilee Institute of Nurses in Scotland - 'the extraordinary success and the important position which this institute has now attained was in large measure due to her efforts' - and the creation of the Edinburgh School of Cookery and Domestic Economy. It was suggested that the School, in particular, would 'serve to perpetuate her memory'. It

> has from comparatively small beginnings grown steadily into an important educational institution whose influence is felt all over the country. It is a training school for teachers of cookery; and also has departments for laundrywork, housewifery, needlework and dressmaking ....The diplomas qualified for in the School of Cookery are now recognised by the Board of Education in England and the Scottish Education Department: and a

Christian Guthrie Wright

large proportion of the teachers of cookery in various centres throughout this country have qualified for their positions as a result of the tuition they have received in Edinburgh.

It was pointed out that the School, which was entirely financially self supporting, also provided invaluable domestic training to many women and girls from the Edinburgh area and that no less than 2,000 pupils had received instruction at the School in the previous year.[45]

Christian's funeral took place from St Mary's Cathedral on the last day of February 'amid every manifestation of the respect and esteem in which she was held by the citizens of Edinburgh and the public generally'. *The Scotsman* reported that Louisa Stevenson represented HRH Princess Louise at the funeral and that the latter had sent a telegram on behalf of Queen Alexandra expressing the Queen's sympathy and sense of the loss sustained by the Institute for Nurses. For herself Princess Louise wired

> Please convey to the Council of the Institute and to the directors of the School of Cookery Her Royal Highness's sorrow at receiving the news of Miss Guthrie Wright's death. Her Royal Highness feels her loss irreparable to the Queen Victoria Institute and to so many Scottish institutions to which she gave her invaluable services.

The Princess also sent a beautiful wreath 'In Grateful Memory'. Moreover the former Liberal Prime Minister, Lord Rosebery telegrammed, 'I am most truly grieved to hear of the death of that excellent woman and dear friend, Miss Guthrie Wright'.[46]

With the benefit of historical perspective there is not a great deal to be added to the assessment of her contemporaries. They appear to have understood perfectly well the value of the contribution which Miss Guthrie Wright had made within and beyond her city of residence. She was, of course, the product of an age which believed firmly in the voluntary principle rather than in State directed solutions to the problems of the day. While she believed passionately that board schools should take on the responsibility for the instruction of girls in domestic knowledge she was not prepared to wait while those concerned made up their minds. Moreover, where the needs and interests of women were concerned, she was fundamentally at all times a believer in personal Christian action. She devoted her life to the cause of women and provided the dedication and hard work necessary to unite and focus the efforts of the talented friends who gathered around her and who invariably seem to have worked in harmony with her. Moreover, she understood the need to change attitudes, to win over hearts and minds to advance the interests of women, and she was outstandingly successful both through her ability to attract the public support of leading members of society and in developing and maintaining a flow of helpful publicity.

The College obviously does, in some ways, represent a memorial to its main founder. However, as was pointed out at the time of her death, her influence extended all over the country, in Scotland and England and, indeed, through the work of her students, to many other parts of the world. As has been shown, from the earliest days teachers from the Edinburgh School gave instruction up and down the land until such time as local people felt willing and able to organise and take up the task in their own communities. This was obviously particularly true in Manchester, but it was also the case in other towns and cities. It would, therefore, be interesting to know just how many modern educational institutions have their roots in public lectures given by the young women sent out from Edinburgh by Christian Guthrie Wright.

Christian's unexpected death was certainly a severe blow to the School, but not the least tribute to her is that it was able to continue to grow and flourish even without her. Indeed, in an increasingly favourable background it shortly entered a period of swift progress and change. In session 1907 - 1908, the last before major transformation, the School staff numbered twenty-two teachers and they gave instruction to approximately 2,300 students.

For a time Miss E.G. Dalmahoy took over as Chairman, but the leadership was largely in the hands of the Honorary Secretary, Miss Melvin and her assistant, Miss Ethel de la Cour. The first principal change occurred later that year when these two met with Professor Darroch and other members of the Edinburgh Provincial Committee for the Training of Teachers and Mr Scougal and Miss Crawford of the Scotch Education Department. Their task, about which negotiations had previously been commenced by Miss Guthrie Wright, was to agree the regulations for the training of school-teachers of Cookery and Laundrywork. It is extremely interesting to note that to guide and advise them at that meeting Miss Melvin and Miss de la Cour were accompanied by Christian's friend Miss Paterson of the Glasgow School of Cookery. All of the key points for which Christian had struggled were conceded. Intending teachers had to be educationally well qualified, they had to obtain 'the Diploma of a recognised School of Domestic Economy', they had to undertake instruction and practice in teaching methods and in hygiene, they had to undergo training in the methods of teaching their specialist subject (the School would develop a particular 'Mistress of Method' to ensure that this was done), and the procedure would be monitored by the Provincial Committee which would arrange for the school boards to pay the appropriate fees. Moreover, teachers recognised by the Provincial Committee, both those qualified by the teaching colleges and university graduates, who wished to secure additional qualifications to teach Cookery or other domestic subjects, would be able to undertake an additional course within the School which would be funded by the school boards via the Committee. This was obviously an effort to rapidly expand the numbers of appropriately qualified teachers in order to quickly increase the volume and quality of domestic education in schools in eastern Scotland.[47]

The fundamental change took place in the following year with the passage of the 1908 Education (Scotland) Act. Under this Act school boards were given the duty of medically inspecting the children in their schools and of taking action against parents whose children were 'verminous' or unclean. They were also required to feed children from the homes of the poor. Finally, however, the authorities took a direct responsibility for the domestic education of school girls and the Schools of Cookery in Edinburgh, Aberdeen and Glasgow were to be brought under the ultimate control of the Scottish Education Department by being turned into Central Institutions. (In Glasgow at this time the West End and Glasgow School of Cookery were amalgamated to form the Glasgow College of Domestic Science).

As far as the context of women's education is concerned, the first suggestion of the concept of a central institution appears to have been made by Elizabeth Wolstenholme-Elmy as far back as 1869. Writing of the lack of resources in provincial towns and of the inadequacies and unsuitability of large boarding schools, she had suggested 'the establishment, in various country districts, of ... a central institution, that is to say, with its complete staff of teachers and profes-sors.....By some such plan the economical and social advantages of collective instruction (would) be secured.'[48]

In Scotland the concept had been introduced by the Scotch (Scottish from 1918) Education Department in the area of technical education in the period 1901-1902 when the first four Scottish Technical Colleges (now the universities of Strathclyde, Heriot-Watt, Robert Gordon's in Aberdeen, and Abertay in Dundee) were designated as central institutions. They were so named in consequence of 'past achievements, because they were well staffed and equipped for a considerable variety of work, and because they were situated at the natural centres of population'. They were intended to make technical instruction available for residents of the surrounding communitites.[49] Having developed the idea in this manner so recently it is not, therefore, surprising that the Department should turn to the same model for the delivery of domestic education.

Obviously the proposed change meant a certain loss of independence and the winding up of the existing School Company. In June 1909 the Secretary wrote to shareholders explaining what was being planned and pointing out that under present circumstances, because it paid a dividend to shareholders, the School was unable to receive direct grants from the Government. Since Government assistance was essential to bring about the required development it was necessary to reconstruct the company in such a way as to protect the share capital then subscribed while allowing the Scottish Education Department to take over responsibility for much of the subsequent financing of the School. Effectively shareholders received Debentures bearing interest at three and a half per cent in exchange for their ordinary shares and the constitution of the School was transformed so that it became a company without share capital and limited by guarantee. With these changes approved the old company was voluntarily wound up in June 1909 and application was made to the Scottish Education Department for the School to be recognised as a Central Institution in terms of the Act of 1908. Such recognition was duly granted on 15th October 1909.

In consequence of these changes the small group of women who had effectively controlled the School as a Board of Directors were replaced by a much larger School Council of Management. Individuals were invited to contribute two guineas in return for which they became Life Members of the School. Life Members were empowered to elect fifteen people to the new Council, but as many as nineteen other representatives were appointed by Edinburgh University, the City Council, the Edinburgh Merchant Company, the Edinburgh Education Authority and the Education Authorities of eleven counties ranging from Berwick in the south to Perth and Stirling in the north and west. Hence the School had become a central institution in the sense that it was intended to serve the needs of schools throughout a large 'province' of eastern Scotland.[50]

From this point on the close day-to-day supervision which had formerly been

Miss Ethel de la Cour, the first College Principal. (From the Edinburgh School of Cookery Magazine, 1914.)

provided by the old Board was impossible. As a consequence a professional leadership was appointed and Miss de la Cour became the first Principal of the School. As far as the Council was concerned, Professor Alexander Darroch, the nominee of Edinburgh University, became Chairman with Miss Melvin as his deputy and the faithful Mr H.F.Cadell was appointed Clerk and Treasurer. One result of these changes was that for the first time many men became involved in the School's governing body, although those elected by the Life Members ensured that women were still in the majority. Among the latter two notable members of Council were Mrs Leslie Mackenzie and Mrs (later Lady) Haldane.

On one matter the Education Department had to depart from its normal arrangements and make a special dispensation and this was to enable HRH Princess Louise to continue as Patroness.

As has been noted, these changes were largely to enable government funding of a further radical expansion of the School and this now took place mainly through the acquisition of number 5 Atholl Crescent and the subsequent reconstruction of the premises. 5 Atholl Crescent was a large house in the terrace and was one of those which had been purchased by the Town Council at a time when it was thought that the Usher Hall might be built on the site of the Crescent. When the neighbouring number 6 was purchased in 1906 the Council had been unwilling to sell Number 5, but with the take over by the SED the Council now felt compelled to co-operate and the house was sold to the School for £3,900. Thereafter a huge development was initiated. This included building out at the back of the various houses, blocking off the doors to numbers 3,4 and 6 and making the doorway at number 5 a fine main entrance with a stone porch and Ionic columns and capitals. To give access to the other parts of the building corridors were cut to left and right and the whole building was divided into sections appropriate to teaching and residence.

> On the basement floor the back greens have been built over to form classrooms & etc lighted from the roof. These include a lecture room, large laundry, kitchen for the teaching of children, large new kitchen and circular demonstration hall capable of seating 200 students. There are in all nine kitchens and four laundries for teaching purposes. Lined with white tiles, they have a light and cheerful appearance.

At the rear various cloakrooms, recreation rooms and other facilities had been constructed and the stables at number 7 had also been bought with the intention of creating a modern chemistry laboratory. Residential facilities for some members of staff and students had also been extended and at the opening of the new session in 1910 forty-eight students were boarders. Interestingly, among the facilities was a model three-roomed 'working man's house' which was intended to be used for teaching housewifery to children. These very extensive alterations to the properties had involved the removal of walls and the introduction of heavy beams to support the superstructure, and the opportunity had been taken to equip the premises with electric lighting, internal telephones and central heating. *The Scotsman* informed its readers that the result was that the

Main lecture hall c1911. Miss de la Cour and other members of staff are in the front row. In the foreground there is a good view of a gas cooker of the period. It appears to be very similar to the one designed by Dorothy Scott in 1888.

School as now reconstructed is the largest and most complete School of Domestic Economy in Great Britain, and the appreciation by the public of its usefulness is shown in the increasing numbers of pupils. The enrolments for the ensuing session are greater than ever before, and notwithstanding the large additions the whole accommodation is already fully occupied.[51]

The S.E.D. had supplied a grant of £4,500 to purchase the new building and gave a further grant of £5,500 towards the expense of the alterations. These in fact cost £12,340 and the School was expected to raise the revenue itself to provide the balance.

However, as the report above notes, the new accommodation was already creaking at the seams and as early as 1912 further premises had to be purchased in the shape of numbers 1 and 2 Atholl Crescent. Again the Department gave a grant of £3,500 towards reconstruction costs, but £4000 had to be raised by means of borrowing in expectation of future revenues and by an appeal to the public. This phase of rebuilding was accomplished in 1913-1914. These changes all meant, however, that the School now commanded an imposing frontage along the Crescent.

Students of 1913. Evidently this photograph was taken on the roof of one of the extensions at the rear of the School.

In launching the 1912 appeal for funds mentioned above, the School Council noted that the School was one of the largest of its kind in Britain and that its work was 'most important'. 2,584 students had been enrolled in the previous session and the staff had given more than 7,000 lectures and demonstrations, mainly in the School, but also in various parts of Edinburgh. In addition, they had provided lectures in many other parts of eastern Scotland on such subjects as 'Home Sick Nursing, Hygiene, Care of Infants and Maternity'. The School was said to give instruction on all aspects of domestic science while also training teachers in these subjects.[52]

As explained, the School was now required to provide assistance to an education 'province' which essentially covered eastern Scotland from Berwick to Perth and which was subdivided into six 'Districts'. In 1910, at a meeting with Dr Struthers and Dr Macdonald of the Scotch Education Department, which was ostensibly to work out the financial support required to adapt the new premises, the opportunity was taken to discuss the services which the School was expected to provide outwith Atholl Crescent. In the course of this discussion Dr Struthers indicated that the

School should enable the Provincial Council to support the supply of proper instruction in domestic subjects throughout the area as its main task, while the training of teachers would be an important but secondary duty. In this discussion the School was represented by Professor Darroch, Mr Darling, Mr Cadell and Mrs Haldane and this demonstrates how far the control of the School had altered in a very few years.[53]

Shortly thereafter the details of the system were agreed and various members of staff were designated as district superintendents with the duty of advising school teachers of domestic economy subjects within their appointed district on the preparation of courses of study and in the best methods of delivery. Grants to maintain this system of support were provided by the Department which now also supplied bursaries for student teachers. If the need arose the School could take over the job of recruiting suitable teachers to assist a school board or secondary education committee which asked for special help.

For intending teachers the courses were now expanded to give a thorough training and they were grouped into Diploma 1 - Cookery, Laundrywork and Housewifery, and Diploma 11 - Needlework, Dressmaking and Millinery. The Cookery course, for example, now took 840 hours of instruction and practice over a forty-two week period, and the full Diploma 1 course took three years to complete and Diploma 11 two years. Candidates for admission were expected to have passed the university local examinations or alternatively to have successfully completed an entrance examination in English and Arithmetic or to be in possession of secondary Leaving Certificates in these subjects. Demand for places on the full-time course soon became very high. In addition, however, the training could be undertaken concurrently with a university or teacher training college course. The School also provided teaching qualifications in various individual specialisms such as, for example, in Popular Health and Sick Nursing.[54]

The changes introduced at this time were by no means confined to Domestic Subjects or to the School's activities. Similar training was being made available to teachers of other specialist subjects and the intention of the S.E.D. was essentially to eliminate untrained teachers from the teaching professions. In summing up this period Helen Corr concluded that the 'entire organisation of teacher training was transformed'. By the outbreak of the First War in 1914 the 'majority of women teachers were certificated and trained', which was still far from the case in England and Wales.[55]

If teacher training was now important, it was still a subsidiary activity and the main business remained to provide training in all domestic subjects at whatever level was required by the community. One new diploma course introduced at this time was in Social Work and two years' training was required to secure the full qualification. The course was aimed at health visitors, welfare managers, sanitary workers, factory inspectors and voluntary workers. The lecturers involved in this course included Professors Darroch and Lodge from the University of Edinburgh, Dr Ker, from the City Hospital and Mrs Leslie Mackenzie, Miss Christie (qualified at Cambridge and later to go on to a position at the London School of Economics) and several other members of staff. They dealt with such subjects as Social Psychology and Philosophy, Local Government, Industrial Law, Infectious Diseases and so on.[56]

Another notable new course was for 'Princess Louise Nurses for Children'. This was a course for what would now be known as nursery nurses and it was commenced in conjunction with the Edinburgh Day Nurseries Association. At first the course was operated in connection with a creche run in St Bernard's Crescent, and with the students receiving their theoretical instruction within the School. However, this arrangement was not satisfactory and eventually some stables at the rear of the School were pulled down and a purpose built nursery suite was constructed on the site. From 1912 there were two day nurseries, eight night nurseries, 'splendid bathroom accommodation', a dining room, kitchen, bedrooms and a sitting-room for the matron and her assistant. The training settled down to a six month course and about thirty nurses, for whom demand outstripped supply, were qualified each year.

The infants and young children below the age of five years cared for within the School came from various backgrounds. Some were the children of parents living abroad in climates deemed to be unsuitable for children; some were children placed in the school while their mothers recuperated from illness; some were children who needed special care; and there were usually a few there because their mothers had died. Sometimes children remained in the nursery only for a matter

The nursery, 1930s.

Westminster. August 18. 1891.
A. Westminster.

Frances M. Buss —
N. Lon. Coll. School for Girls
London

Louisa Buccleuch
Feb.y 6th 1899

Katharine Scott.
Feb. 6th 1899

Constance Scott.
Feb. 6th 1899.

Louise
9th December
1901.

Argyll

John Cowan

Flora C. Stevenson

Mary R
July 10th
1920.

Mary.

Margot Asquith Dec. 19th 1911.

Mary Trefusis

Mary Minto

June 17. 1936.

Edith S. Haldane
Chairman.

George R.I.
July 29th 1943

1934.
May 28
Monday.

Helen Leslie MacKenzie.

Elizabeth R
July 29th 1943

18. Sept. 17. Fanny L. Calder M. A. Liverpool.

From the visitors' book.

of weeks, but others stayed for years. At least one little boy is known to have spent the first six years of his life in the School and he was sadly missed when finally he went on to boarding school.[57]

In the year that the Princess Louise Nurses course was commenced the Princess made her first visit to the School since Miss Guthrie Wright's death. Indeed 1911 saw various interesting guests arrive and they included Margot Asquith, the Prime Minister's wife and, a little earlier, members of a Canadian Royal Commission on Industrial Training and Technical Education.[58]

One of the innovations resulting from designation as a Central Institution was that members of the teaching staff now qualified for a superannuation fund. Essentially staff were required to contribute £6 per year for a thirty-six year period at which point, from the age of fifty-seven, they became entitled to a pension of £78 per annum. It may not sound much today, but it was an amazing change from the conditions which had confronted many women when the School was first established.[59]

Early in the First World War, for the information of the Principal of the National in London, Miss de la Cour summarised the pay and conditions offered by the School. She herself had an annual salary of £300 and, as with all teachers, she had two meals per day in the School. The starting salary for a fully qualified teacher without experience was £80 and rises were typically of £5 per year up to £110, beyond which any further increases were purely at the Council of Management's discretion. Several staff teachers actually received salaries of £125-£130. As far as Head Teachers were concerned, there seems to have been a definite hierarchy. The Head Cookery Teacher was best paid with a salary of £190 and the lowest were the Heads of Laundry and Housewifery who each had £140. The Heads of Dressmaking and the Nursery Nurses both had £150.[60]

From its earliest days the School had employed many non-teaching members of staff including maids and so on. Some had some curious titles. For example, in April 1914 Miss Allan was appointed 'Foreman of the Steam Laundry' at a wage of 25s per week with breakfast, dinner and tea in the School. At about the same time Mr Watson was given the job of Porter and Engineer with £1 2s 6d per week together with his meals.[61]

By the outbreak of the First War, therefore, the School had undergone a remarkable transformation in the years following Miss Guthrie Wright's death. In that period with the support of the Department it had blossomed into a formidable institution with fully developed courses and making a major impact on the lives of women and school girls all over its 'province' in eastern Scotland.

Inevitably the War brought its own changes. Much of the normal work continued although many of the students eventually found themselves going on to initial careers which were very different from what they might have expected. Many years later, for example, Mrs Agnes Forbes wrote recalling her experiences.

About ten days after the First War broke out I became a student at Atholl Crescent.

The poster of Kitchener's pointing finger and the words 'Your King and Country need you' was prominent in Edinburgh as our period of training was ending - Easter 1917. Four of us volunteered to go to York Barracks as 'scrubbers' ...I was sent to King's Bridge Camp, Anglesey, as Head Cook in charge of personnel (about 10 women): at the end of a few months the W.A.A.C. was formed and I got a commission and was posted to many different parts of England.[62]

As can be imagined, and as is inferred by this letter, qualified students from the School were in great demand during the war and the same was true in respect of members of staff. Many of the latter gradually left to undertake war work and it became something of a problem to retain sufficient of the younger teachers to maintain the full programme of standard courses in addition to the extra work which had to be taken on as a consequence of the war. Indeed, Miss de la Cour herself took a very active role both within the School and on various official committees as a result of which she was offered a position in France. She appears to have turned this down presumably on the grounds that her work in Edinburgh was as important as anything which she might have done elsewhere.[63]

As the war developed so food became rather more scarce and this was particularly true following the sharp increase in submarine activity in the second half of the war. Partial food rationing was not introduced until 1917 and at first the Government relied heavily on voluntary restraint by members of the public. Institutions such as the School, therefore, had a vital role in advising and encouraging members of the public to be frugal and efficient in their food practices, and later the object was to help people to get the most out of their food rations.

Led by Miss de la Cour, staff took on these duties in a variety of ways. For example, they produced a series of pamphlets on war-time cookery and they mounted appropriate courses and demonstrations. In 1915 they ran courses on the feeding and care of children under prevailing conditions, and later that year they gave special open demonstrations of cookery which included an explanation of how to cook with a 'hay-box'. By 1917 this work had assumed an increasing urgency and the various special courses were being provided under the auspices of the 'Edinburgh Food Campaign Committee'. Again several 'saving contrivances' including the 'hay-box' and 'multiple-steamers' were demonstrated, and guidance was given on such matters as food alternatives to meat and on substitutes for wheat flour. These included rye bread, maize meal cakes, maize flour pudding and oatmeal roly poly. Among the various items offered were mock chicken cutlets, curried tripe, rice flour short crust, and something called allies pudding.[64] Apparently it was very difficult to get Scottish housewives to accept maize flour and the staff went to great lengths to devise recipes which made it more appealing.

These demonstrations were not confined to the School and Government grants were provided to enable them to be delivered to the widest possible audience. Shops around the city were taken over for daytime demonstrations and, of course, the products were sold over the counter at the end of each lesson, which was probably not the least of the inducements to attend. In addition, staff travelled all over Scotland doing similar work and special short residential courses for school teachers of cookery were laid on to enable them to bring themselves up to date before returning to pass on the instruction within their own communities. The latter courses were apparently first offered in 1915 on the suggestion of the 'Patriotic Food League' and the instruction was available to teachers free of charge, although they were expected to contribute to the cost of residence. They were also expected to offer voluntary instruction to the public in their own schools and to adapt their classroom syllabuses. In a letter describing this course Miss de la Cour indicated that the various dishes demonstrated had been planned by senior staff in consultation with 'Dr Chalmers Watson, the well known authority on food values'.[65]

By the latter part of 1917 partial rationing had been introduced and Food Control Committees had been established. At the request of the Edinburgh Committee the School mounted a Food Economy Exhibition demonstrating a full week of three meals per day based on an assumed household of one man and three women. Although the portions were undoubtedly small it represented a balanced and imaginative diet.[66]

In February of 1918 *The Scottish Gentlewoman* carried an account of the exhibition in the form of a letter to 'Dear Rosamund'. The display showed that a meatless diet need not be injurious to health and that it was possible to have adequate nourishment on 'less than the proposed scale of rationing'. The scientific exhibition was particularly informative and it illustrated the food values of various items such as lentils, oatmeal and cheese. 'All sorts of unsweetened 'sweets' are displayed in another room, and for those who care for them, nineteen varieties of potato scones, potato bread, potato puddings, & etc are of interest'.[67] This month long exhibition, which had been opened by Lord Strathclyde, demanded a considerable amount of work since exhibited food had to be freshly prepared each day.

Valuable though such activities undoubtedly were, the School's concerns were not only about food. During the war years there was obviously a vast increase in the numbers of women going into factory employment and this was particularly true in respect of industries engaged in the manufacture of munitions. Moreover, some of the companies concerned, particularly in the Glasgow area, suffered from a great deal of labour unrest. This was partly associated with the rising cost of living in the early part of the war, but other problems related to the pressure on traditional working practices which involved dilution of labour and which were sometimes associated with the arrival of women in the work-place.

To address these matters an Edinburgh and Glasgow Joint Committee for the Training of Munition Welfare Supervisors was established and, from 1916, Miss Christie and her colleagues delivered two-week long courses of instruction in the School and these were accompanied by a period of practical training within factories in Glasgow. The lectures dealt with such things as 'Women's Industrial Problems', First Aid, Welfare Work, Factory Law, and so on, and the resulting qualification was recognised by the Ministry of Munitions.[68]

Throughout these years, of course, the normal courses continued and one student who studied for her Teacher's Diploma in the period 1915-18 was Mrs Martha E.R.Coggins. She remembered that her final Cookery exam involved preparing a seven course dinner 'perfectly cooked, presented and timed'. One wonders whether the dishes reflected the war-time austerity about which the School had become so expert. One of her contemporaries was Mrs Jessica Clarke who arrived in 1917 ill prepared for the tasks with which she was to be confronted.

> The first day I presented myself for what I thought was a lecture on Kitchen Equipment, and as I had been asked out to tea later I wore a white blouse and light skirt. Imagine my horror when I was given instruction on cleaning flues followed by an effort at doing it. Although I wore an overall, I emerged more like a chimney sweep.[69]

One of the real problems during the war was the business of paying for the food used in classes and in the boarding house accommodation. For the first three years the SED provided grants to cover a deficit in excess of £3,000, but curiously the Department declined to accept the bill incurred in 1918-19, hence the School finished with a debt in this area of £851.[70]

The war record of the School was therefore valuable and distinguished, and this was perhaps reflected by yet another visit from HRH Princess Louise on 7th December 1918. (An interesting guest a year earlier was another of the very early pioneers, Miss Fanny Calder, founder of the Liverpool School of Cookery.)

The pace of activity slackened somewhat towards the end of the war, but thereafter it picked up sharply as the requirement to assimilate service women back into civilian life imposed new demands from 1919. This process was supervised by the Central Committee for Women's Employment and the School's role was to provide suitable training particularly for women coming out of the W.A.A.C. or the Red Cross. At the same time the demands placed by an increasing flow of school leavers stretched resources to the limit. As a result, the process of expansion soon resumed.

In 1919 7 Atholl Crescent was purchased and a year later Number 16 was leased for the use of Housewifery classes. In 1921 Number 8 was purchased, but there were still acute problems. One difficulty which had been felt for many years was the lack of a suitable main Hall. Eventually, in 1922-23, two of the back gardens were excavated and a former Y.M.C.A. hut was purchased and erected on the site. It proved to be 'a handsome hall' and was a considerable boon to the School, since it served as a dining-room for the ever increasing numbers of day students. Moreover, it provided a facility for recreation, dances and other entertainments for boarders. To purchase this hall various fund raising efforts were embarked upon, including an exhibition of students' work, but an appeal to former students also brought in generous donations. On this occasion, however, no government grant was made available and the School was forced to resort to borrowing more than £3,000 and, in so doing, deepened its cumulative debt to almost £22,000. In 1925, Mr Cadell, the Treasurer calculated that the School buildings had cost a total of a fraction less than £100,000. At that date the accommodation of the School included a large Demonstration Hall, thirteen practice kitchens and four house kitchens; eight practice laundries and a steam laundry; for sewing, dressmaking, millinery, and upholstery, eight rooms are provided. There is also a science laboratory and a lecture room. In the Boarding Houses there is accommodation for 150 resident students. The large .. Dining Hall .. and beside it a Day Students' Sitting Room.

In addition there was the nursery suite which accommodated the matrons, twelve nurses and fourteen children, and housewifery students had the use of the three flats leased at 16 Atholl Crescent.[71]

Former students were by now taking an active interest in the affairs of the School. The Old Students' Guild was actually founded in 1914 and it offered members the opportunity of an annual reunion in the form of a Guild Social and lectures, normally given by a distinguished invited guest speaker. By the 1920s the Guild commanded a typical membership of about 650 and this is a measure of the appreciation and affection with which the School was regarded by its former students.[72]

Much later that level of respect and interest was still obvious from the number of individuals who retained their membership of the Guild and from some of the reminiscences set down by members. For example, Mrs Margaret Gardner, who qualified as a Cookery teacher in 1922 wrote, 'I was lucky enough to train with Miss Lindsay for cookery and Miss Armour for teaching, both of whom were outstanding'. In July 1920 Queen Mary and Princess Mary were due to come to the School and Mrs Gardner was one of the students prepared for the Friday visit. Through some mis-chance the Royal party failed to arrive and 'we sadly cleared everything away'. However, to make up for the disappointment The Queen insisted on coming on the Saturday and the boarding students were hastily dispatched to fetch in their colleagues living in digs around the city.

> My partner and I made an aspic mould decorated with truffles, lined with tomato puree and filled with sweetbread puree. The bright colours may have attracted the Queen for she came over to ask how we had done it.

But it was not only the former full-time students who reflected on these days with affection. Mrs Isabel Merrill, who was then a pupil at Bruntsfield School, walked each Tuesday and Thursday to Atholl Crescent with another seven girls to receive Cookery lessons.

> The ladies there ..(taught) ..all the very best ideas how to be thrifty and at the same time cook nourishing meals....Needless to say we used to eat our cookery on the way home if it was something we liked....We had very happy days, I shall never forget all they taught us.[73]

In 1925 the standard qualifications issued by the School in the period since 1912 were summarised as follows. Diploma 1 in Cookery, Laundrywork and Housewifery had been gained by 700 student teachers and of these 83 and 358 respectively had secured additional Endorsements in High Class Cookery and Needlework. Diploma 11 in Needlework, Dressmaking and Millinery had been obtained by 216 teachers. The Housekeeper's Diploma had been given to almost 1,700 students and a very similar number had received the Housewife's Diploma. Certificates in Plain and High Class Cookery had been awarded to 792 students and 20 Laundry Manageresses had been qualified. Finally 186 'Princess Louise' Nurses for Children had successfully completed their training. This obviously ignored all that had been done as part of the war effort, but it was a very considerable output and indicated the formidable service which the School was now contributing to Edinburgh and, indeed, to Scotland. Apart from anything else, a powerful regiment of Edinburgh trained teachers was now at work in schools all over country.

In 1936, reflecting on a long life devoted to the cause of women, Sarah Mair, now Dame Sarah Mair, DBE,LLD, had this to say.

> Seventy years ago education, compulsory and free did not exist. There were no school boards, no university education for women, no women doctors, no Jubilee Nurses, no School of Domestic Economy in Edinburgh, no Ladies' Clubs even; no women sat on Town Councils and no women voted in Parliamentary elections or sat in Parliament.[74]

It is a remarkable list of achievement and progress, but it also gives a perfect illustration of just what the School had come to mean and to symbolise to her generation of Edinburgh women.

CHAPTER FOUR

1925-1962 : The Wingfield Era

A few months before it celebrated its fiftieth anniversary the School sustained another severe blow through the sudden death in 1924 of Professor Darroch, the Chairman of the Council of Management. Darroch had given important leadership to the School particularly at the time of the negotiations which resulted in it becoming a central institution. Although the process had begun before Miss Guthrie Wright's death, nothing had been concluded and the prospect of having to accept the burden of maintaining the funding of an independent institution may have been daunting and deeply worrying to the senior members of staff. Darroch was, therefore, in Miss de la Cour's words, 'a great friend at this time', and in a sense he deserves as much credit as anybody for navigating the School through the years from 1907 until his death. He was succeeded as Chairman by Sir Malcolm Smith.

The School's Jubilee was marked in various ways, including the publication of a commemorative version of the School magazine, which paid suitable tribute to the founders, and by an exhibition of students' work which was opened by the Secretary for Scotland, Sir John Gilmour. Princess Louise, who had recently been unwell sent a message to say that she was 'exceedingly proud of having been their patron for so many years and frequently quoted the activities of the School and the advantages it afforded to young women in Scotland'.[1]

On 24th October of that year a large reception was held to mark the retirement of Miss J.G. Crawford, the first Women Inspector of Domestic Subjects at the Scottish Education Department. The attendance on that day was practically a 'Who's Who' of Domestic Education at the time and there is no doubt that all concerned were very proud of Miss Crawford's achievement. She had been a former student and lecturer at Atholl Crescent and had been recommended to the S.E.D. by Miss Guthrie Wright and the Stevenson sisters. From 1902 until 1910 she had been solely responsible for monitoring and guiding the development of domestic subjects in Scotland. Thereafter two other Inspectresses were appointed to cover the Western and Northern Divisions of Scotland under her supervision and her duties had involved the oversight of the three Domestic Central Institutions, all schools in Southern Division and the development of appropriate school leaving certificates. To the generation which met to honour her in 1925 she was

Miss J.G.Crawford. She had been a student and then member of staff in the School, and had run the continuation classes in the India Buildings before becoming the first women Inspector at the Scottish Education Department.

undoubtedly one of the key educators of her day and she richly deserved the sapphire and diamond ring and pearls which were presented to her by Miss Melvin on behalf of teachers from all over the country.

Also on that day Miss Christie of Dollar, one of the early directors of the School, unveiled a memorial tablet. This was made of oak and was designed by the celebrated artist, Sir Robert Lorimer. It was located in the entrance hall and contained the following words.[2]

> On the 50th anniversary of its foundation, this school recalls the wisdom and zeal of its founders, and in particular of Christian Eddington Guthrie Wright and Louisa Stevenson,LL. D.:
> For their work continueth,
> Broad and deep continueth,
> Great beyond their knowing.

Sir Malcolm Smith served as Chairman until 1929 when he was succeeded by the loyal Miss Melvin. Sadly she died within a few months of taking the senior position and there is in the College records a touching death-bed message which she relayed via Mr Cadell, the Treasurer. Miss Melvin had been on the governing body for approximately thirty-five years and she told how 'she looked back with happiness to her long connection with the School'. She urged the staff to retain their spirit of unity and loyalty which had always 'been one of the great features of the School ... This was the spirit which Miss Guthrie Wright always tried to instil and encourage'.

Miss Melvin's appeal for unity may have been coincidence. On the other hand it may be that she sensed that, by 1930, all was not well and that a difficult period now required to be negotiated. Miss Melvin was followed briefly as Chairman by Dr T.G.Naysmith.

In 1929 Miss de la Cour intimated her intention to retire. She too had had a long innings, having served the School since 1896, first as Assistant Secretary and then Lady Superintendent, before becoming Principal in 1911. She was another key individual through the critical years and there was indeed great general pleasure when she was awarded the OBE in 1929 in recognition of her distinguished services. Ten years' earlier she had been awarded the MBE for her notable work throughout the First War, but this new honour was clearly in recognition for her contribution to domestic education and she was believed to be the first person to have been so recognised for work in this area, hence the jubilation within the School and among former students and colleagues. Princess Louise was among those to telegraph her 'warmest congratulations',and again indicated her pride in the School and its 'great traditions'.[3] Fortunately Miss de la Cour's interest in the institution did not wane with her retirement and for much of the remainder of her long life she continued to contribute at appropriate times and through the Old Students' Guild. Nevertheless her departure in the summer of 1930 signalled the start of an uncomfortable period.

The new Principal, Miss Geraldine Croft, at thirty-four, was comparatively young to succeed to the Principalship. However, she had an outstanding war record as a V.A.D. with the Red Cross, having seen service in both Italy and Germany. Moreover she had qualified in Sociology at the University of London, had been Head of the Women's Evening Institute of London County Council 1924-28, and had lectured at Rhodes University, South Africa in 1928/9.

At this range of time it is difficult to know precisely what went wrong, and the various relevant minutes are typically discreetly worded. However, it is obvious that Miss Croft was a somewhat unconventional character who probably found it difficult to adapt to the culture and traditional ways of the School. Very soon there was something of a spate of resignations among members of staff, but one of the first to go was the Council Chairman of a few months, Dr Naysmith and he resigned in January 1931. How far these matters are connected, it is impossible to say, but before her second term had expired Miss Croft's own resignation was being sought by the Council and it was made clear that if it was not forthcoming she would be dismissed as a result of 'difficulties which have arisen at the College'. At this time Miss Croft appears to have been considering returning to London in any case, but the situation may simply have been becoming intolerable to all concerned, including herself. However, when she asked the Clerk, Mr Cadell for a note to be used in support of an application for another post he communicated the fact to his fellow Council members and this may have been the last straw which resulted in the decision to require her resignation. But the episode was traumatic to say the least, and no fewer than six resignations from Council were intimated to the meeting of 17th April 1931 before the decision was taken. Finally, it is worth noting that after ensuring that proper procedures were followed, the S.E.D. gave its full support to the Council.[4]

At the time of this upheaval and for the next few months the leading role seems to have been taken by Helen Mackenzie (now, following her husband's knighthood, familiarly known as Lady Leslie Mackenzie), who, among other things, took over the chair at the critical meeting, and Mr C.W. Allan, JP, who was thereafter appointed Chairman. These two seem to have been particularly instrumental in calming the situation and securing the support of senior staff. They also organised the immediate strengthening of the Council and one of the methods by which this was achieved was through the temporary return to membership of Lady Haldane.

After this experience the Council was determined to proceed with caution and to make sure that everything was done to obtain the right person to fill the senior executive position. Therefore throughout the rest of 1931 much of the main burden fell on Miss Jean G.B.Cunningham and during the hiatus she was appointed Head of Cookery and Acting Principal. Miss Cunningham, a student in the School in 1910, had returned to join the staff in 1914, and was therefore fully familiar with the School and its ways.

In November 1931, after a careful selection procedure, the Principalship was offered to the redoubtable Persis L. Wingfield who was to exert a dominating influence over the next three decades. She too was comparatively young, but as Assistant Secretary and Treasurer of Somerville College, Oxford, she was thoroughly experienced in the operation and activities of an established women's college. Her salary was £600 rising through annual increments to £750.[5] At this point Miss Cunningham became the College's first Vice-Principal and she proved to be a staunch friend. According to Miss Wingfield, she could not have 'found a wiser, fairer, more far-sighted and loyal colleague' than Jean Cunningham, who was 'the originator of many a new policy, many a fresh development and the College owes her ...far more than can ever be recorded'.[6] The duties of the two were clearly delineated, with the Principal being in overall charge and responsible for the organisation of the College and its hostels, and the Vice-Principal for supervising courses and the operation of classes.

One of the first problems with which Miss Wingfield had to deal was an instruction from the S.E.D. which had arrived almost at the time of her appointment to the effect that all staff salaries had to be cut by 7.5 per cent. This, of course, was a period of extreme economic depression and the order was part of a Government effort to restrict public expenditure by a general reduction in the wages of teachers and other public employees. Although there were obviously staff concerns and some anomalous situations resulted from the process of implementing the reductions, the whole business seems to have passed off fairly peacefully and this was probably at least partly because staff were accustomed to a situation where salaries were subject to annual review. Miss Wingfield proposed to Council that in future it should move to a system such as that applied to her own remuneration, namely salary scales with annual increments and this was accepted.

The Atholl Crescent College.

In 1930 the name of the institution had been changed; it ceased to be a 'School' and became instead the Edinburgh College of Domestic Science. Such a title had been suggested as far back as 1908 during the negotiations to become a central institution, but it had then been vetoed by the Department on the grounds that 'good work was being done under an unpretentious name and there was no need for a change'.[7] By the 1930s, however, there was still concern that cookery teachers in schools were being treated somewhat as the 'cinderellas of the profession' and there was a desire to do what could be done to enhance the status of diplomates. The new title was therefore adopted with such an aim in mind. (The first choice proposal in fact was The Royal College of Domestic Science, and Princess Louise actively pressed for the adoption of that title, but, perhaps to avoid an outbreak of hostilities with Glasgow, the Department blocked the use of the word Royal and substituted Edinburgh.) In the mid 1920s the numbers of students being recruited for training as cookery teachers had been restricted because it was felt that too many were seeking too few job vacancies and this was enabling education authorities to pay cookery teachers less than some of their colleagues. Moreover, it was decided to stagger the sessions so that qualified teachers were not all being turned out at the same point in the year. (A few years earlier an unsuccessful attempt was made to persuade Edinburgh University to validate a degree in domestic science, again in an effort to end some of the discrimination against cookery teachers.)

By the mid 1930s the position in respect of teachers seems to have been a little easier in that the College had relaxed some of its restrictions, but it may be that part of the solution had been to encourage more students to seek their first employment in England. Certainly, of the 61 Diplomates qualifying as teachers in 1933 whose first appointments are noted in the magazine for that year, 34 are listed as having jobs in England, 2 in Ireland and only 25 in Scotland. Similarly, in 1936 the returns indicate 45 having secured positions in England, 20 in Scotland and 1 overseas. In this period, of course, far larger numbers of students were studying for Institutional Management or Household Management qualifications, presumably because it was easier for such students to obtain employment, but also perhaps because the courses were somewhat less rigorous.

In fact College students seem to have had a fairly good record for obtaining jobs. The period 1929-1933 was the nadir of the inter-war recession yet in the year to March 1931, 394 full-time students leaving the college registered themselves as having successfully obtained positions, 125 of these being as teachers and the remainder being in 'administrative and children's nurses posts'. The same report from which these figures have been extracted also indicates that at the time the College employed sixty members of staff, forty of whom were lecturers of one kind or another.[8]

In 1937 some modifications were made to the teaching courses. Needlework training, hitherto optional, was added to Diploma 1 so that students securing this qualification were enabled to teach both of the main aspects of domestic subjects. Similarly, Diploma II was extended to be a three year course, with the addition to

"Ayton, Edinburgh"

Students' Union Committee, Spring 1936.

the syllabus of crafts such as weaving and cane-work. Far more students undertook Diploma I than Diploma II, since the former enabled its holder to teach cookery in schools. However, the shift towards a more 'industrial' dimension in Diploma II was indicated by the appointment of a teacher of design, at first on a part-time basis.

A modest growth area of the 1930s was in Institutional Management. Towards the end of the 1920s financial conditions encouraged the College to look to ways not only of augmenting the educational experience of students, but also of adding to revenues. The result was the establishment of a Catering Department which produced hot meals for sale and distribution in containers to firms and individuals around the city. This enabled students to be given some training on a commercial scale. Miss Wingfield indicated that demand for this service became somewhat erratic and consequently it was discontinued in 1932.[9] However, there may have been rather more to this episode than Miss Wingfield admitted since the then College driver, John MacDougall, who delivered the prepared food to customers, remains convinced that the real problem concerned complaints from commercial caterers that the College's activities constituted unfair competition.[10]

As a consequence of the termination of this business venture, the Catering Department was renamed as Cake Sales Department and, as the name implies, concentrated its attention on a more modest bakery operation. In this it seems to have functioned fairly successfully until it was eventually shut down on instructions from the Ministry of Food during the Second World War. Its activities did provide for the training of students in commercial baking, but an alternative had to be found to provide large scale cooking experience and this was accomplished from 1933 by sending students out on placements to hospitals, hostels, factories, hotels and so on all over the city. At this time the Institutional Managers course of training extended over one year to which was added the one term work experience placement.

It was at this time too that the College first became involved in the emerging profession of dietetics. A department for the training of dietitians was established at the Royal Infirmary as the Edinburgh School of Dietetics and a close relationship developed between it and the College. Students who had qualified in domestic science within the College could become hospital 'dietists' after completion of an additional six month course at the School.

Most of the other courses then offered by the College have been noted previously, but a curious one which also deserves mention was the course which first introduced male students to the College. This was a course for 'Sea Cooks' and it was operated to enable students following careers as cooks on merchant ships to obtain their Board of Trade Certificate in terms of the Merchant Shipping Act of 1906. The course was introduced in 1923 and continued as required down to 1949. The syllabus was as set out by the Shipping Federation and included provision for different grades of qualification. Typically courses lasted for a fortnight and included from eighteen to thirty men at any given time, drawn usually from ships docked at Leith. Their presence in the College occasionally involved something

A study bedroom, probably in Melvin House.

of a culture shock, particularly when many of the men came from far afield. Loud whistling in the College kitchens, for example, was not something calculated to appeal to Miss de la Cour. Miss Wingfield was struck by the range of tattoos displayed on the seamen's arms. 'A pierced heart on the right arm might accompany hands-across-the-sea on the left. Tombstones were popular and we were assured that a woman on the right arm and a snake on the left had no bearing on the qualities of our teaching staff nor on the discipline they exercised'.[11]

With Miss Wingfield's appointment the process of the development of the College premises resumed. From 1933 to 1935 Numbers 1 to 8 Atholl Crescent were again largely reconstructed. Corridors were created from end to end, kitchens were grouped on the ground and 'garden' floors and sewing and laundry-rooms on the first floor. An additional laboratory, a lecture room and some test dining rooms were formed and, in 1933, the house at Number 16 Atholl Crescent was purchased and allocated to the Housewifery Department. Extra staff facilities were also produced in the shape of work-rooms, a staff common room and cloakrooms. Similarly a Students' Union was established in 1932 which, within a short period, extended to include two large club rooms, a library, a committee room and a pantry.

These years also saw the considerable extension of the residential accommodation. At that time the availability of suitable boarding facilities for a significant proportion of students was vital to the success of the institution. Many middle-class parents of the day would have been deeply reluctant to have permitted their daughters to fend entirely for themselves hence the provision of absolutely

The Library, Melvin House.

respectable 'supervised' dwellings can be said to have made a significant contribution to the College's survival and success. The development and expansion of this aspect of the facilities enabled the College to market itself effectively to potential students literally from the whole of the UK although, of course, the great majority tended to come from the various corners of Scotland.

Guthrie Wright and Stevenson were the two hostels located in Atholl Crescent and between them they could accommodate 168 residents. In 1932 Melvin House was opened as a result of the purchase and conversion of Number 3 Rothesay Terrace and the neighbouring top flat of Number 2 and this new hall had a capacity of from fifty to sixty students. In the older houses much of the accommodation was in the form of 'cubicles' and some double bedrooms, but it was decided now to provide more individual study bedrooms, a change which was greatly approved by students. One of the latter, Mrs R.M.Marshall (Rosemary Gregory) remembered that at Stevenson House 'we had an elegant common room and it was very convenient being above our place of work, (but) we were not so happy in our 'cubicles'. To move to a new hostel where we all had our private rooms was very much appreciated'.[12]

Another development of this period was that students in halls were given rather more opportunity to involve themselves in the running of their residences. They were encouraged to organise social activities such as dances and so on and the new

Lacrosse 1st XII, 1933-34.

mood was perhaps symbolised by the change in the designation of residential supervisors from 'wardens' to 'housekeepers'.

In 1933 a fourth house was opened at Drumsheugh Gardens to house yet another 52 students and this was the new hall in which Mrs Marshall became one of the first residents. At the suggestion of HRH Princess Louise, this hall was designated Lorne House, taking her title at the time of her marriage. The first resident housekeeper at Lorne was Miss Mary Knox and she recalled that to assist her she had 'eight maids, two tablemaids, three housemaids and two kitchenmaids'. Lorne House, being the most modern in arrangements was used as a training centre for Institutional Management classes.

It will be seen, therefore, that in the 1930s the four halls could between them accommodate some 280 students which, for an institution of its type, was a very considerable asset.

Skimming through the College magazines of the period reveals many little glimpses of the lives of the students of the day and among the most vivid examples is a piece submitted to the 1934 edition by a student whose initials were C.C. and who had just completed her Diploma 1. She described her experience as follows.

A taxi draws up in front of a row of sombre , grey houses. The new student alights, and her heart sinks. On entering questions are asked, 'What course are you taking?' 'Are you a T.T.?' (Teacher Training) 'You are brave.' 'You don't know what you have let

Cricket Team 1937. Back row, L. Keltie, B. Henderson, M. Hewetson, M.H.Fraser. Middle, S. Wiseman, B.Anderson, M.Barnes, N.Watson, C.Austin. Front, B.Doig, P.Spear.

yourself in for.' 'Where do you come from?' Students come from many places in England, Scotland or Ireland; some to have a good time, others to escape boredom at home, others to train for a job. T.T. is here for three long years. Soon, however, life becomes less strange and confused, the uniforms look odd no longer, such terms as P.C., H.C., K.13 are intelligible and the maze of passages is less bewildering. The T.T. begins to enjoy herself. It is true that there are many horrors in front of her, dress shirts for instance, examinations, test dems., and children's classes, but even the two latter are not without humour, particularly for the onlooker. How often in cookery classes will she hear a well-known voice, 'Students, I smell something burning!' and vainly attempt to reach the oven without being seen! But besides work there are such things as hostel parties, attended in weird and wonderful fancy dress, college dances, pyjama parties at which she eats fruit-salad from a saucer or a soap dish with equal relish. There are games, perhaps walks over the Pentlands, or long days at Gullane, when the trials of A.C. seem very far away. Or evenings at the theatre that begin with tedious waiting in a queue, followed by a wild rush upstairs to the front row of the 'Gods' from which she can see everything and can make witty remarks about the bald heads in the stalls.

And so the three years pass and she wonders whether in the future she will agree with other old students who have said that were it possible to come back, they might almost return and begin their three years' training again.[13]

Other contributors expressed their impressions and feelings more poetically. One such might indeed have been the same student but on this occasion the initials at the foot of the piece are G.C.C.. The poem is called Test Dinner Fever and was written with apologies to John Masefield:

I must go and stir that soup again, or the bone will be high and dry,
And all I ask is a clean bowl and a spoon to skim it by,
And a hair sieve and a hot tureen and luck with the pepper and salt
And a pleased gleam in Miss Cunningham's eye to show that nothing's at fault.

I must go and look at that tart again, for the smell of a burning pie
Is a wild smell and a clear smell that you may not deny;
And all I ask is a clear brain while round the kitchen flying,
And a quick hand and a light wrist, and the heart to go on trying.

I shall think back to these days again, to these hours of my College life,
To the good days, and the bad days when the 'crit' cut like a knife;
And all I ask is the power to learn from every chance-met rover,
And a quiet sleep and a sweet dream when the long tuck's over.[14]

During one of the various changes to the College premises the Nursery was moved from Atholl Crescent to Numbers 11 and 13 Walker Street where it remained throughout the 1930s. However, the Princess Louise Nurses course was one of the first 'victims' of the outbreak of the Second World War in 1939. For a time children and students on the course were evacuated to Lady Haldane's house at Cloan, Auchterarder, but thereafter the decision was taken to 'suspend' the course for the duration of the war, though in fact after 1940 it never resumed.

At the end of 1939 the College mourned the death of Princess Louise. For some years she had not enjoyed good health and had been unable to visit Edinburgh, but her messages from time to time made it clear that she had not lost any of her interest, and of course, she represented one of the last links with the founders. The editorial in the College Magazine looked back 'with gratitude' to the support of 'one who took a foremost place among the pioneers of women's education', and Miss Wingfield, who described the Princess as being 'practical and helpful', also wrote elsewhere of the general sense of loss at the death of a 'beloved patron', which certainly suggests that the College remained very proud of its association with the Princess.[15]

The hunt for a successor did not last many months and early in 1940 HRH Princess Alice, Duchess of Gloucester, agreed to become the new patron. Princess Alice (Christabel), was a granddaughter of Louisa, Duchess of Buccleuch, who had been one of the original four joint patrons of the Edinburgh School of Cookery, hence she was an appropriate choice, particularly since Princess Louise had had no children. In 1935 Alice had married HRH Prince Henry, Duke of Gloucester and younger brother of George VI. As a result of the war several years were to pass before the Princess was able to visit the College for the first time.

Even more than had been the case in 1914-18, the Second World War was a

WHERE GIRLS LEARN ALL ABOUT DOMESTIC SCIENCE

OUR photographer visited the Edinburgh College of Domestic Science in Atholl Crescent, and obtained these pictures of the activities of the students. The college, which was established in 1875, provides instruction in all branches of domestic science.

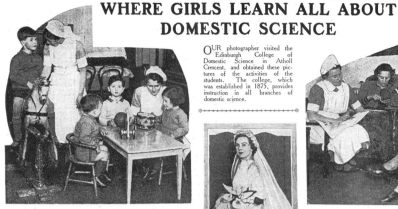

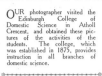

TRAINING NURSES.—A section of the college is at 11 Walker Street, where " Princess Louise " nurses are trained to manage children.

A CORNER in the Students' Union common room at the college.

HIGH-CLASS WORK.—Here are two girl students at work on high-class cookery—fancy cakes, &c.

A " BRIDE " at the college. One day she may wear this dress which she has made at the college.

HAT MODELLING in the millinery class at the college.

IN THE LAUNDRY, where students are trained in all processes and the effects of chemicals on different material.

DRESSMAKING.—These girls at the college are at work in the making of dresses and models.

THEIR OWN WORK.—These charming evening dresses which the girls are wearing were made at the college by the girls themselves.

COOKERY STUDENTS obtaining and weighing their supplies from the storeroom.

Scenes from Atholl Crescent in January 1936, as captured by the *People's Journal.*

civilian's war. Partly this was because bombing literally brought the physical conflict home, but also because of the manner in which government was forced to intervene in detail with the lives of citizens almost from the very beginning. Inevitably, therefore, the College, as an institution specialising in the practical matters of everyday life, had a part to play and it is worth spending some time recalling this period. Much later Miss Wingfield set down some of her memories and the account which follows draws heavily on her notes.

In the uneasy months before the outbreak of the Second War the College found itself drawn into the preparations by being invited to organise lectures on such matters as the feeding of children, canteen organisation and on large scale cookery, all subjects which would assume an increased degree of import-ance within a matter of months. Similarly staff attended for instruction on survival in the event of gas attacks and on what to do if there were air raids. On the whole, however, in the period between the Munich crisis of 1938 and the start of the war business went on much as usual. In fact it was at this time that the Institutional Management Association was formed to create 'a recognised national qualification in management and large scale catering'. Another initia-tive of the period was the organisation of a Pre-Nursing course for school leavers intending to enter the nursing profession, but who had not yet reached the then minimum entry age of nineteen.

Early in 1939 the College hosted a fortnight long visit from Miss Akre, the Principal of The Oslo College of Domestic Science and she urged the Edinburgh College to take a lead in the activities of the International Federation for teaching Home Management. This organisation was due to hold its quinquennial congress in Oslo in August and a largish representation from the College was due to attend. However, in May the Secretary of the Scottish Education Department was sum-moned to London to discuss questions of 'Food Control' and consequently the increasing international tension became very obvious within the College. As a result it was decided that Miss Cunningham should go to Oslo by herself. As it happened the congress was abandoned after just two days and the Norwegian ship on which she attempted to return to this country was recalled to Norway when war was declared on September 3rd. Fortunately she did manage to get back to Scotland several weeks later.

The declaration of war occurred three weeks before the autumn term was due to commence, but Miss Wingfield's war began immediately when a distraught father from London arrived on the door-step with his daughter. He had been posted to Canada and she had been due to attend hospital that day for an operation, but he had not been prepared to leave her in London with the imminent risk of air raids. The Principal therefore had to find accommodation for the student and the College doctor duly arranged for her to have her operation in Edinburgh.

Apparently Mr Cadell, the Treasurer, and other members of the Council had been reluctant to spend money on war preparations and prior to the start of that first term of the war Miss Wingfield had to make emergency arrangements.

I had now.. to buy up hurriedly all the black cloth and paper I could find and to call the staff back from their holidays to employ their ingenuity in covering every chink through which light might escape. Balancing on steps with drawing pins, safety pins, hammers and tacks, they worked heroically. Shutters long since screwed up, were wrenched open. Passage windows and skylights were painted dark blue, and red bulbs were fitted into every socket. This produced a blackness from the point of view of our air wardens or any marauding enemy air-craft. So, for the duration of the war, daylight was unknown in any of our corridors.

With the use of sandbags the basements of the hostels and of the main College were turned into air-raid shelters, and in the case of the latter were at least theoretically capable of housing the 900 people who could be expected to be in the College on any given day. The shelters in the hostels were fitted up with tiered bunks so that students could sleep in reasonable comfort when they had to be used. These arrangements were evidently not without their discomfort and there was some embarrassment when the lack of ventilation resulted in a most un-Atholl Crescent like proliferation of black beetles. 'Ultimately we were fitted with a somewhat primitive air-conditioning, which came on with such a blast that we thought ten thousand bombs had fallen'.

A student at that time, Betty W Young, wrote an account of life in a hostel during the war. Previously she had been inclined to sleep in, but now 'in the early hours of the morning resounding crashes all along the corridor awaken me, and inform ..(me).. that my less slothful companions are putting back their shutters'. When the 'wretched siren' sounds

> it is with admirable restraint that the long file of girls go to the shelter, clad in a variety of costumes, varying from the glamorous siren-suits to the 'common or garden' pyjamas and dressing gown.
>
> ... There are three choices, top, middle or lower bunk. But whichever storey one obtains one is struck by the dignity of the remarks passing to and fro. Someone is heard to say, 'Kindly remove your toe from my mouth.' 'With pleasure!' comes the quick reply. Here is no panic, no hysteria. The very spirit of which Mr Winston Churchill is so proud. Few of us realise that we are making College History as we settle down to our shelter life, for never before have the basements of Hostel contained such original sleeping accommodation.[16]

Miss Wingfield had written to parents prior to the start of the war making clear the College's intention to continue to operate even if war broke out, hence there was no break in activities. However, at first families from northern Scotland were somewhat nervous about the potential safety of Edinburgh. By contrast, parents in England looked on the city as a safe haven and were very keen to send their daughters to the College. In the event, there was comparatively little physical danger and most air-raid warnings occurred when enemy planes flew over en route for the shipyards of Clydeside. On the first occasion that warning was given 'half of Edinburgh's sirens ... failed to sound the 'all clear', and many angry people sat up all night quite unnecessarily. But a drunk man sat down in the middle of the road and sang 'Rule Britannia'!'

1st Hockey XI, 1939-40. Back row, M.McDonald, M.Mitchell, M.Le Page, R.Rimmer, M. Thompson, M.Kemp. Middle, H.Buchanan, D.Barron, D.Ross. Front, K.Jones, H.McKenzie.

Some of the staff soon left to join the forces, but given the support of the S.E.D. there was never any question of the College interrupting or suspending its activities. In this apparently it was unique 'since ours was the only domestic science college which was not evacuated or seriously disturbed in other ways'. But a consequence was tremendous pressure for places and, in particular, demand for hostel accommodation as families from the south sought to enrol their daughters. Indeed it was the scarcity of accommodation that resulted in the transfer of the Nursery in order to permit the Walker Street premises to be converted into another residence from 1941. Moreover, with Government direction of labour in operation it became impossible to obtain resident maids, so students had to be used for cleaning and so on.

With rationing food was also a problem. At one level some households which formerly had been able to rely on cooks and servants, now found themselves in urgent need of guidance on how to get the most out of their food allowance and the College did its best to provide suitable classes. More serious, from the College point of view, however, was the problem of obtaining food for instruction purposes. For example, the allowance for class kitchens was 2d worth of meat per student per week and 'the rations of other commodities were even smaller. Realising that a student could go through a three-year course without once having an egg to crack, we began keeping hens on all our flat roofs.' The eggs thus obtained turned out to be expensive because an old man had to be paid to look after the hens. The only real solution, of course, was to use the residential kitchens and the rations of the students for teaching purposes, but that meant that the students staying in the hostels were the only ones who got to eat the prepared food and their local colleagues must often have felt more than pangs of hunger.

> The cookery staff went through our syllabuses and arranged that foods in short supply should be used in demonstrations in order that students should at least see, for example, a chicken though they might never handle one. I caught the Vice-Principal one day about to slaughter one of our precious roof fowls. A demonstration on game and poultry had been advertised and nowhere in Edinburgh had she found a hare for soup, a pigeon for pie, nor any bird - not even a chicken.

Indeed, the innovative pursuit of food resulted in one of Edinburgh's epic disasters of the war. Vegetables became very expensive as a consequence of transport problems, hence the brave decision was taken to cultivate some of the College's hockey pitches at the games field at Succoth Avenue. Incredibly the tractor driver hired to do the job went to the wrong place and instead ploughed up Watson's School's best cricket pitch. What the Watsonians thought of this act of sabotage is unrecorded in the College records, presumably because it was unprintable.

Also rationed, of course, was clothing and the College commenced 'Make Do and Mend' classes which were much appreciated by many hard pressed women of the city. In a similar vein, twenty-six members of staff gave up much of their Christmas holiday in 1939 to produce what was known as the *Atholl Crescent Alphabet*. This was a series of pamphlets covering a host of economical ways of living. Titles in the series included, *All about food, Economics for Needlewomen, Hygiene in the Home, Nothing Wasted, Scottish Fare,* and *Zeal.* The complete set was sold at 2/9d and proved to be very popular.

Requests also came from various groups for urgent assistance. One such was a territorial battalion of the King's Own Scottish Borderers. Made up of soldiers who were part-time volunteers in peace time, the battalion had relied on local women to prepare food, but when it became clear that it was about to be posted south and that none of the men could cook, the College was asked if it could turn nine men into an operational kitchen unit in just four days. The task was attempted and was not helped by frequent visits from officers anxious to see what progress was being made. 'Every time they appeared the privates sprang to attention, scattering knives, spoons, bowls and food in all directions. I had to call a halt to Army Regulations.' Apparently their brief training did make a difference to the efforts of the soldier cooks, but the College was distressed to learn soon that their friends were all lost at the time of the fall of France in 1940. (The soldiers may well have been from the 5th Battalion of the K.O.S.B. which was attached to the 52nd (Lowland)

Division. During the retreat the Division managed to fight its way to Cherbourg and from where the remnants of the battalion, 'scampering in at the last moment', were able to escape, but evidently without their cooks.)

Other calls for help came from a local factory where round the clock war production was threatened by the collapse of its catering organisation; from the Ministry of Labour concerned to train groups of women to cook for squads of workers being sent to construct airfields and other such facilities in remoter parts of the country; from the Ministry of Agriculture pleading for staff and students to provide emergency cooking for harvest workers; and so on, and usually the task was completed one way or another. For example, throughout the war the College apparently organised nightly meals for the local Home Guard and it was also prepared to cook for large numbers of people in the event of Edinburgh citizens being bombed out of their homes. Fortunately the city was never really attacked and only on one occasion was it necessary to provide emergency feeding for 150 people. Another strange and sombre task was in the summer of 1940 when College residences were used to accommodate children who were about to be evacuated to Canada. Sadly Miss Wingfield noted that some of the ships carrying the children were torpedoed.

Early in the war the students in hostels decided that it would be a good idea to 'adopt' some unit to which they would give their particular care and attention. Guthrie Wright House, for example, adopted a ward in the military hospital at the castle, Melvin House worked for an Anti-Aircraft Battery, Lorne House gave its attention to a Polish submarine, *Wilk*, and Stevenson House gave its protection to the minesweeping trawler *The Goodwill*. In fact Stevenson claimed to be the House which initiated this kind of activity, but all joined enthusiastically in knitting 'comforts', sea-boot socks, jumpers and so on and gathering other suitable presents to make life easier for those concerned. Great was the anguish of the residents of Stevenson when their little trawler was sunk in 1941, but they promptly adopted another Polish submarine called *Sokol*.[17] This kind of activity was maintained throughout the war and when H.M. Submarine *Urtica* wrote pleading for someone to adopt her none of the various student organisations was immediately available. Determined that the sailors should not be disappointed the Old Student's Guild decided that the boat would be their particular concern and so royally was her crew treated that when she was decommissioned after the War *Urtica's* pennant and crest were entrusted to the College.

Another to come seeking help was the Lord Provost, Sir Henry Steele, and this was in 1941 in connection with the first of the Ministry of Food's British Restaurants. This was located at Fountainbridge and it was not really yet properly equipped or staffed and was in no condition to open its doors. However, the Provost confided in Miss Wingfield that the King and Queen were coming to visit the restaurant. Under war conditions of secrecy about the movements of the monarch the city had received little warning and, if the College could not help, all round embarrassment was inevitable. Mrs Masson and a squad of students were sent immediately. A member of the party was Honor Brooke.

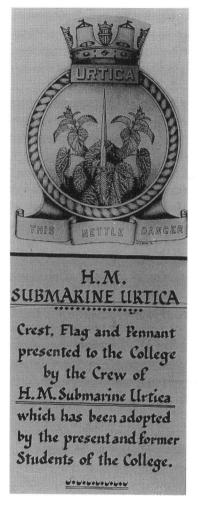

URTICA

THIS NETTLE DANGER

H.M. SUBMARINE URTICA

Crest, Flag and Pennant presented to the College by the Crew of H.M. Submarine Urtica which has been adopted by the present and former Students of the College.

The crest of HM Submarine, *Urtica*. This boat was 'adopted' by former students and when she was decommissioned at the end of the war her crest, flag and pennant were presented to the College.

On arrival at the scene of action, one look around told us that a great stock of energy and determination would have to be summoned. The restaurant - due to be opened the following afternoon - was a seething mass of workmen. Paint was wet, linoleum half-laid, cooking apparatus incomplete, and artistic efforts still in progress. The mess .. was inconceivable, but our manageress was an inspiring person. Under her expert direction things were sorted out as if by magic ..[18]

'The Neebor's Tryst', as the restaurant was called, duly opened on time and received the Royal party in the first afternoon. So impressed was everybody by Mrs Masson's efforts that the Town Council asked for her secondment for the rest of the war to run the city restaurants which were subsequently established in various parts of Edinburgh.

In the first part of the war another of the tasks which fell to the College was to provide training for servicewomen, particularly for those who were going to be

H.M. Queen Elizabeth presenting prizes, 29.July,1943. In this picture the senior winner, Brenda McLean of Gillespie's High School is being congratulated. (The Times,1943)

cooking or undertaking similar duties on military or Air Force camps. WAAFS attended College for six week courses in cookery, but it was quite impossible to bring all the people concerned to Edinburgh hence College staff were dispatched all over Scotland to give their instruction wherever required. Later in the war, of course, the Services established their own training facilities, but in the first year or so much effective work of this kind was done by hard pressed lecturers.

A fairly frequent visitor to the College in these days was the Secretary of State, Tom Johnston. He was above all responsible for the well being of the people of Scotland and one of the methods by which he sought to fulfil that task was by encouraging people to make as much use as possible of indigenous resources and, in particular, to eat home produced foods. Accordingly he instructed the schools of Scotland to organise local heats of a national competition in the use of oatmeal, herrings and potatoes. Twenty thousand pupils entered the contest and the finals were held in the College in July 1943. Remarkably the King and Queen attended and Queen Elizabeth presented the prizes. The audience was made up not just of students, but of parents of the finalists and some of the farmers and fishermen who had provided the raw materials. Some of the herrings had been rather too long in transit, but it proved to be a memorable day. According to Miss Wingfield

> delighted excitement prevailed.... The competing children spent the morning cooking. They were allowed to compose their own recipes. Their Majesties arrived punctually at

3.30pm. Among those presented was Miss Cunningham, the then retiring Vice-Principal. We were all so pleased that the Royal visit should coincide with her last official day in College.

Johnston evidently was delighted with the outcome and it seems to have been an exciting occasion for all concerned. Later he told the Principal that the King and Queen regarded their afternoon at the College as the happiest event of their tour in Scotland. One student, M.C.L., recorded some of her impressions.

I felt the accolade of knighthood had been conferred on our College, that the building itself had received a new dignity..(from the Royal Standard flying from the College flag-pole).

The Queen wore lilac. Her simple dress and jacket of heavy silk crepe were embroidered with silver and lilac sequins, which formed a bow on the bodice of the dress and two rings below the elbow of the bracelet length sleeves. .. The Queen had a diamond bracelet on her left wrist and wore the badge of the Royal Scots pinned high on her left shoulder.

... The King turned to Lady Leslie Mackenzie and we heard him say 'They wanted to send me somewhere else, but I said no, I was coming here, I like this kind of thing.'...Our College colours of blue, green and silver looked very lovely on the shining box of home-made oatcakes which our Principal, Miss Wingfield, presented to Her Majesty.

The whole picture was a most historic one ... Streaming through the window in the background the sun's rays caught up these golden words, 'For their work continueth -

Another prize-winner of the Scottish Produce competition (Eileen Clarke of Frederick Street School, Aberdeen?) receives her award. (29 July, 1943) (*The Times*, 1943).

Broad and deep continueth - Far beyond their knowing.' Never before have the words on the Memorial Tablet erected to the memory of the Founders of the College been more applicable.[19]

Moments like that in the dark days of the war were important, and not just to young students. Indeed, the episode and the descriptions capture perfectly the role of King George and Queen Elizabeth during the war and the popular response which they attracted.

Another Royal visitor in October of that year was the new patron, HRH Princess Alice. 'The Duchess was looking charming in a dress of cinnamon brown fine wool, with a tiny matching hat ..'

It was fitting that on both of these occasions the hostess was the venerable Lady Leslie Mackenzie who had become Chairman of the College Council in 1943. By this time she was in her eighties, but even in old age she retained all her mental vigour and capacity. When she died in 1945 the obituary notice in the College Magazine referred to her 'vigorous common sense, her shrewdness, her trenchant comments, her energy, her humour, her sincerity'. She had been a fine teacher, but the 'work that was nearest her heart, was that in connection with Public Health, in which she was associated with her husband, the late Sir Leslie Mackenzie.'[20] For her efforts in this area she had been appointed CBE and, in 1937, Edinburgh University also honoured her by the award of an LLD. A close friend and associate of Dr Elsie Inglis, Lady Mackenzie was one of the truly great Scotswomen of the early twentieth century and she had a superb record of achievement not only in connection with the health of school-children, but also in the promotion of mental health care and rural district nursing. She had been a key figure in the College for more than thirty years and she was greatly admired both for her practical directness and for a splendid down to earth sense of humour.

One of the most remarkable episodes in the College's war occurred in 1944 when Miss Wingfield was contacted by the Secretary of the Scottish Education Department. Evidently the war cabinet was in something of a dilemma and Tom Johnston had suggested that the College might be able to help. The origin of the problem was that the bomb damage in London was very severe and was being added to by the ongoing attacks from flying bombs. Unless damaged houses could be repaired before the onset of winter there would be considerable distress to the population and some civil disorder was possible. Workmen had been drafted in from various parts of the country, but because no adequate provision had been made for their accommodation and feeding they were returning home. Accordingly Miss Wingfield was asked to send a party of students to London at once to organise some essential catering. She pointed out that parents had sent their daughters to the College and were paying fees, partly because Edinburgh was perceived as being safe. In these circumstances she would have to obtain parental permission before discussing the matter with senior students. She was given twenty-four hours to come up with an answer. Telegrams and telephone calls produced an almost unanimous agreement from parents, which was admirable, particularly when it is noted that London was sustaining some very heavy attacks at the time.

While initial preparations were being made, Miss Wingfield dashed south to choose from several hotels one which the contingent would take over and run as accommodation for the workmen. She was fairly horrified by the condition of some of the suggested establishments, but eventually selected the Royal Palace Hotel as being 'the least bad'. Unfortunately the underground kitchens were prone to flooding, but that was only discovered after the group was in residence.

The students were volunteers, but the Principal then had the tricky task of selecting

a member of staff, of the right temperament and experience in large-scale cookery, to go with them. Was I sending her to her death? I chose Miss Meiklem and, apart from the working conditions, the worst shock she had was to wake up on her first morning to see a mouse sitting on her sheet contemplating her.

The group received a remarkable send off from Edinburgh with bagpipes, cheering crowds, press photographers and the Secretary of State no less, all at Waverley Station to wish them 'God speed'. The first task was simply to clean the filthy hotel from top to bottom, but the students then quickly settled down to the job and the Manager was soon delighted with their cheerfulness and the change which they accomplished. They worked in two shifts, from 5am until 2pm and from 1pm until 10pm, and for their pains they were paid the princely sum of 3s per day. On one occasion they were taken on a sight-seeing tour of the bomb-damaged city and this included a visit to the House of Commons where, strangely enough, a

Secretary of State Tom Johnston visiting the students at the Royal Palace Hotel, London. (Associated Press, 1944).

debate was 'in progress on the muddle regarding the very workmen they were to serve'. Not surprisingly, the students would have loved to have been able to contribute their thoughts on the matter. In due time a second group was dispatched to relieve the first and later they were followed by students from other Colleges.

Miss Wingfield concluded her notes on this incident with the words, 'I was told that when Mr Churchill heard that our students were coming, he dropped his head on the table and wept with relief'. Well, perhaps not, but what cannot be doubted in view of the circumstances is that the College group had made an important and useful contribution when it was badly needed.

Of all the war-time episodes involving the College, the one which, in retrospect, touched Miss Wingfield most concerned a party of F.A.N.Y.s (First Aid Nursing Yeomanry) for which the College was asked to provide some instruction and to keep them occupied for three or four weeks.

> They were a group of highly intelligent women and we were requested to ask no questions ... Never have we had a bunch of such eager students. They worked hard and were delighted with all we could offer them. Each said that she would return for a full training after the war. Not one did. There were hazards in being parachuted behind enemy lines, torture and the gas chambers and there were lonely heroines, who gave all in resisting the evil which threatened the world. To have had those splendid girls with us was perhaps for us the greatest privilege of the war.

The College, then, in its inimitable way had done a lot of useful things and in 1945 Miss Wingfield was deservedly rewarded by being appointed OBE. She saw this honour as an 'appreciation of the wonderful work done by the Staff and the old students of the College', and she received her medal at the hands of the King during an investiture at Holyrood House on his Victory visit to Edinburgh.[21]

The return to peace brought no slackening in activity and in the early post-war period various pre-demobilisation courses were provided for service women to prepare them for the return to civilian life. The object was partly to help the women concerned to readjust to looking after themselves and their families. Many of the women were married, but were awaiting the return of husbands from abroad and had had little or no experience of running their own homes.

As was noted earlier, in 1943 the Vice-Principal, Miss Cunningham had retired and she was succeeded for the remainder of the war by Marjorie H Craig. In 1945 she in turn was followed by Isobel E Nettleship. A number of the wartime staff had obviously carried on past normal retirement age and there were many others whose marriage plans had presumably been delayed. In addition, there seems to have been some desire to make room for people returning from the services. Hence there were many staff changes in 1945-46. Among those leaving was the redoubtable College engineer, William Tucker - 'with the good wishes of generations of staff and students who will miss their friend' - and those returning included Regimental Sergeant Major William Martin, who took up the position of Head Painter.

After the war several of the new members of staff who joined the College had considerable experience of large scale catering organisation and they were particularly helpful in enabling the establishment of a three year course in Institutional and Catering Management leading to the award of an Institutional Management Association Certificate.

In 1947 another of the key individuals in the history of the College died and this was Hew Francis Cadell. He had served the institution since 1892, as its law agent, and had been its Treasurer and Clerk since 1908. A long obituary notice was contributed to the College Magazine by Miss de la Cour and she wrote that Cadell had interpreted his responsibilities in the 'broadest way', being interested in everything which went on. He was particularly involved in the various phases of the physical development of Atholl Crescent and typically dealt with the questions of finance and reconstruction.

> He never spared himself, his interest never flagged and he never counted the cost to himself of the work and service he gave the College. ... Those who worked with him can testify to the great debt of gratitude owed him for his services to the College and for his foresight and power of taking the long view in his policy.[22]

From 1947 to 1952 additional accommodation was purchased in Atholl Crescent and this included Numbers 12, 15 and 17 and thereafter 15, 16 and 17 were gradually amalgamated to form a unified Housewifery Department.

Hew F. Cadell, Honorary Law Agent to the School and Clerk and Treasurer, 1908-1947. (E.C.D.S. Magazine, 1947)

The years immediately following the Second War were difficult years of reconstruction and austerity, and rationing, for example, was not fully removed until 1951. In these circumstances the skills of prudence in domestic economy were still in high demand and it may be suggested that in the period until the later years of the 1950s the College reached something approaching its apogee as a model institution of its type.

In 1950 the seventy-fifth anniversary was quietly celebrated and a party of journalists was among those to be shown round. *The Scotsman*'s Scotswoman's Diarist was impressed, but found the tour 'bewildering'. 'The realisation of the number of courses available to the students, the variety of activities engaged in, and the amount of work covered was somewhat overwhelming'. Various classes in cookery, needlework and millinery were visited and the courses and qualifications were described. These included the diploma courses, but also short craft classes and public lectures, because, as Miss Wingfield explained, 'we try to do whatever we are asked to do'. The journalists were also given examples of student 'assignments' and one suspects that the founders seventy-five years earlier would have been quite comfortable with tasks such as - '*How would you plan an after-theatre supper* and *what preparations would you make before going out to the theatre?*' and '*If you were the wife of a miner on night shift, with three children of specified ages, how would you arrange your morning work between the hours of 8 and 12 o'clock?*'[23]

The College Patron, H.R.H. Princess Alice visiting Atholl Crescent, November, 1948. Miss Wingfield accompanies the Princess. (Evening News, 1948)

In 1950 two of the things which were done to mark the College's anniversary were the design of a formal college crest or badge and the adoption of a motto. For several years apparently an informal motto had been intermittently suggested, but it was thought appropriate at this time to identify a phrase which could be formally approved by the College Council. Among the astonishing suggestions considered were such curiosities as 'Wha Tholes Succeeds'; 'Guid Foresicht furthers the Wark'; 'An ill cook should hae a guid cleaver'; and 'Vitae praecepta beatae' (which evidently can be interpreted as 'the secret of a happy life', or 'Feed the Brute'). Eventually 'With Heart and Hand' was regretfully forgone since it was 'the motto of a well known family', and instead the phrase which was finally adopted was 'Head, Heart and Hand'.[24]

In August 1953 the College's pre-eminent position among its peers was indicated when it acted as Britain's host institution for the VIII International Congress on Home Economics. The College, of course, lacked the facilities to accommodate the 1200 delegates from 47 countries who attended and the plenary sessions were therefore held at the McEwan Hall. Atholl Crescent, however, was fully utilised for residential and social events and to house many of the associated exhibitions, and Miss Wingfield, with her 'commanding presence', was absolutely in her element. The reports of the Congress are fascinating because of the insights which they give into the attitudes of the day.

Typical 'rag-day' scene of the 1950s.

Broadly, the delegates seem to have formed themselves into two camps. The first of these followed in the tradition of the founders of the Edinburgh School and looked to the education of women to maximise the 'civilising' impact of the home. The most vivid example of this perhaps came from Mrs V Pirkovic, a Yugoslavian delegate who told Congress that at the end of the war seventy-four per cent of women in Yugoslavia were found to be illiterate and that the standard of health among children was appalling. Accordingly, domestic education, concentrating on female literacy, hygiene, health and nutrition, was being given major priority. Other delegates spoke in favour of this traditional position, arguing for school based domestic training supported by adult classes. Some agreed, but also urged the need for enhancement of the status of home economics and Mrs K S Dongerkory of Bombay, for example, explained the need for the subject to be made available at degree level, as was happening in a few Indian universities. This group was, therefore, less concerned with employment, other than in teaching and domestic service, and was much more interested in focusing on progress within the home. They were largely responsible for securing passage of a resolution which drew attention to the task of home economics teachers as being vital to 'individual and social progress'. They also emphasised the critical role of the housewife in maintaining standards within the home, partly by leading the involvement of all family members. 'A woman who does not give this opportunity to the family to use their gifts for the good of the home will not fulfil her task nor her civilising mission', the resolution added.

The second group was typically represented by some of the delegates from the United States. It is interesting that the congress had Home Economics rather than Domestic Science within its title, a clear sign that in some ways it was following North American practice. Women's education in parts of the United States had progressed rapidly in the late 19th Century, perhaps flourishing in a more progressive and democratic environment than was commonly found in contemporary Europe and a trend towards a more academic tradition had taken root at a major conference at Lake Placid in 1902. At that time Home Economics was defined as 'the study of the laws, conditions, principles and ideals concerned with man's immediate physical environment and his nature as a social being, and specially the relation between those two factors'.[25] This, of course, was to move the field of study well beyond domestic skills. In many North American educational institutions thereafter Home Economics became the portfolio for a range of social, economic and scientific studies which, in the UK and elsewhere in Europe, tended to remain rather more discrete academic disciplines.

The different traditions were quite distinct at the 1953 Congress. Delegates such as Miss M Horton, executive secretary of the American Home Economics Association, Washington, directed her attention to the many career opportunities which existed for people qualified in Home Economics. She said that 'careers in education, health and hygiene, business, public relations and information services and community services were all available to women trained in home economics'. She and others argued that it was not enough simply to concentrate on the home, but that the lessons must be applicable within the wider working environment. An-

Delegates at the 1953 International Conference on Home Economics gathered outside the McEwan Hall.

other American delegate, Dr K Holtzelaw, had studied home economics teaching programmes in twelve European countries, and she concluded that it was important for teachers to develop much more of an economic perspective. They 'should develop a programme which took into consideration the conditions and resources of the community'.

At one level there was no real difference between the delegates and undoubtedly as a social event the Congress was a huge success. The opportunity to exchange ideas and experiences was immensely valuable and the chairman, Mr Joseph Piller of Switzerland, was easily able to identify the enthusiasm of delegates who 'would carry away unforgettable memories of the Congress, and a better understanding of the permanent values which Great Britain represented in the world.' Summing up, the Edinburgh Director of Education, Mr J B Frizell said

> you have seen what we are doing for the children of this country. You have seen the quality of the work of the training college. You have talked ... about the art and science of your craft, a craft which is doing so much to help the happiness of home life as the foundation of our human society.

At another level, however, the tension between delegates was clear. As described above, the traditional domestic focus represented by the Edinburgh College was under a pressure, which was soon to increase in intensity, for forms

Diploma Day 1955. The man being congratulated had successfully completed the '151' Cooks' qualification. The Vice Principal, Miss Nettleship, and Miss Wingfield are standing to the right. The student seated second from the left in the front row is Mary Graham, later a long serving senior lecturer in the Department of Home Economics

of education which were less purely concerned with the home and more in tune with the needs of the oncoming generation, and particularly for an educational experience which would open doors to a wider range of career opportunities. In a sense, therefore, the contributions to the Congress represented both the past and the future.[26]

In retrospect, it seems clear that major changes were going to affect the College sooner or later. As the community prospered in the post war period, as the huge new housing programmes progressed, and as the modern buoyant consumer society gradually emerged, with its emphasis on the disposable and the convenient, so many of the traditional practices cultivated within the College were bound to seem increasingly dated and less and less relevant. New technologies and devices within the home would dictate their own changes. Specifically, the washing-machine and synthetic detergents, the refrigerator and freezer, the pressure-cooker and, ultimately, the microwave oven, formica and various plastics, synthetic fibres and stainless steel, and the multitude of derivative products and processes which they spawned, would bring about a complete revolution in the typical domestic kitchen. Most importantly, the changing requirements and expectations of women would present fresh challenges. As far as employment was concerned, for example, with the passage of time more and more women would seek occupations which could be followed whether or not they were married, and the College could no longer expect significant numbers to go into domestic service. Indeed, it is interesting to note that throughout the 1950s, for the first time, the proportion of married members of staff steadily increased, illustrating the contemporary trend. Education generally and the College particularly, inevitably, therefore, would have to reflect and respond to these and similar pressures.

For several years life within the College seemed to go on much as before. Added to the range of courses were technical courses for the hotel industry - instruction for apprentices leading to the '151' City and Guilds Examination in Cookery and, in 1954, to the creation of a College Diploma in the same area. On the other hand, a serious loss of the same period was the decision by the Royal Infirmary to discontinue its relationship with the College in the training of dietitians.

Throughout the latter part of the 1950s much of the full-time work of the College continued to be directed to the training of teachers, about 220-250 being in

A science laboratory of the 1950s.

training at any one time. However, as Miss Wingfield noted, 'during the whole of this period a threat hung over the College that the Aberdeen pattern might be arbitrarily imposed on the College and responsibility for training in teaching taken from it'.[27] By the 'Aberdeen' method she meant that teacher training would follow a period of academic or specialist instruction and, in Edinburgh, that would almost certainly mean that the teacher training would be done at Moray House. Such a change was, of course, eventually introduced in 1972, but in the earlier period it was strongly opposed by Miss Wingfield and her colleagues because it was bound to result in the loss of the fourth-year senior students.

Culling the records of this period one becomes gradually aware of individuals and, indeed, of an institution under steadily mounting stress. As the pressure from various quarters for change slowly intensified it is almost as if the initial reaction was to cling even more fiercely to the traditional ways and attitudes. Of course, the leaders of the College always had commanded undoubted authority, but this had been exercised easily and had been accepted by all concerned. Up to this point there are, for example, very few recorded examples of students or junior staff challenging the standard practices and procedures. However, it seems that in the 1950s the regime became for a time increasingly authoritarian and found great difficulty in adjusting to the demands imposed by the oncoming generation

Physiology lecture in the demonstration hall c. 1955.

of students. To give just one example, in March 1960 disciplinary action was taken against several students. Some were put 'on probation' for breaching 'house regulations' and one had her diploma withheld pending a satisfactory report on her first three months *at work*, because while missing some classes she had 'kept social engagements extending in some instances, into the early hours of the morning'.[28] In fact, in the 1960s this conflict between the traditionalists and the emerging students became increasingly serious. Many of the residences became significantly under-occupied as students sought alternatives by means of which they could avoid what they considered to be excessive restrictions. In these circumstances the residences became increasingly uneconomic and, remarkably, it was even suggested to Council that students should only be permitted to stay in accommodation inspected and approved by the College.[29]

One student of the late 1950s, who was later to become a lecturer, reflecting on the staff of her student days, laughed ruefully as she said, 'they were complete tyrants! Their way was the right way and God help you if you disagreed.' Yet she admits to a considerable affection for, and many happy memories of, the people concerned. The truth is that in many ways these years witnessed something more than a normal generation gap. Indeed, perhaps it is true to claim that the period marked a real watershed between two different cultures and the old was gradually having to give way to the new. The real question was increasingly not one of the 'right way' or the wrong way, but simply could the College adjust, change and survive in the emerging world?

Almost symbolic of the situation was a crisis in the summer of 1957 about the condition of the Atholl Crescent buildings. What was intended to be routine maintenance resulted in a survey which indicated serious problems in various areas. Eleven chimney stacks had to be reconstructed and extensive rot and decay was found in walls, roofs and floors. So severe was the problem in the day students' dining room behind 5-8 Atholl Crescent that it simply had to be taken down. The hero of this particular episode was Willie Martin, by now Clerk of Works, and the decision was made to award him a bonus in recognition of the many extra hours which he had put in to ensure that College could open on time at the start of the new term.[30]

The immediate cost of effecting repairs was almost £7,500. However, the longer term problem with the buildings could not be dealt with so easily and when the position was thoroughly investigated in co-operation with the S.E.D. it was realised that eventually either the College would have to be comprehensively reconstructed or a new College would require to be built on an alternative site.

The Atholl Crescent College always had been somewhat 'make -do-and-mend' in character, with bits and pieces being acquired and adapted over decades. It had not originated from a design with its basic purpose in mind, hence it is not really surprising that fundamental inadequacies should begin to catch up sooner or later. Physical deterioration presented some problems, but the other real disadvantage was that the structure lacked the capacity for development. Part of the reason for this was that the Scottish Unionist Association, which owned number 9 Atholl

Students line Atholl Crescent to welcome Princess Alice in 1958. Miss Grainger Stewart is walking beside the Princess. (*The Scotsman*, 1958)

Crescent, would not agree to sell the building nor would it accept a suggested exchange involving the College's Walker Street premises. This meant that the College's stretch of the Crescent was effectively divided and could not be fully inter-connected. More fundamentally, however, the sheer cost of reconstructing the buildings was believed to be prohibitive and some problems, such as the restricted potential for car-parking, would have been insoluble.

Moreover, there was a vague understanding that development and expansion would be required. In terms of educational content there is little evidence of any immediate concept of the forms of learning on which such growth might be based. However, those charged with considering the future talked about 'the bulge' in the potential student population arising from the post-war increase in the numbers of children, and thus realised that a College of greater size would be possible. Ultimately it was agreed that such growth could only take place on a new location and interestingly an initial, but very tentative guess, was that this might cost £600,000.[31]

In retrospect the structural defects which showed up in the old buildings in the summer of 1957 proved to be a blessing in disguise, because they forced the College authorities to confront at an early stage the question of a new site. Had that not been done it is arguable that terminal decline would have been probable and loss of independent status an eventual certainty. As will be explained later, the 1960s

Teachers in training, 1958.

were a period of immense expansion in tertiary education. Much of this was
concerned with growth in the university sector, but it is equally true that all over
the country there was an enormous increase in the numbers and size of further
education colleges controlled by local authorities. Having stimulated or created
such institutions there was the inevitable task of justifying them and of providing
them with courses and students, hence 'rationalisation' and reorganisation went
hand in hand with growth. As a consequence one by one the old domestic science
colleges closed or were swallowed up by the new institutions. In England such a
process was easy to accomplish since the local authorities controlled and funded
both the old and new institutions. In Scotland, central institution status provided
some protection, but the real saving grace in the case of Edinburgh was the early
movement towards a new campus. Even so, it was to prove to be a very close run
affair.

Much of the future development depended on personalities and by the spring
of 1958 three members of Council who were to be particularly influential were in
place. Mrs (later Lady) Hirst (a former H.M.I. in England) was Convener of the
College Committee, Mr G.D.Cheyne chaired the Finance Committee, and the
over-all leadership passed to Miss C.E.Grainger Stewart as the newly elected
Chairman of the College Council. Initially Miss Grainger Stewart was on the

Council as the representative of East Lothian County Council, but later, in 1964, she was able to continue in the Chair as a representative elected by the Members of the College. Of course there were other important players, but these three seem to have given essential leadership at critical stages. In many ways in their attitudes and outlook they were fully representative of the *ancien régime*, but they all understood the need to progress and were absolutely determined that the College should continue to flourish as an independent entity.

The major upheaval in terms of personnel occurred with the retirement in 1960 of the Principal, Persis Wingfield. When some months earlier she announced her intention to retire Miss Grainger Stewart commented that it was difficult 'to visualise the College without Miss Wingfield at its head', and certainly, having occupied the position splendidly for thirty years, she must have come to seem almost indispensable. The Chairman spoke for the whole College when she thanked her for 'all the years of selfless work ... for her wise leadership, for her enthusiasm and her generosity', and there is no question that the debt owed to Miss Wingfield was enormous. It was decided to mark her distinguished tenure of the Principalship by commissioning a portrait by the celebrated artist, Stanley Cursiter.[32]

Technically Miss Wingfield was young enough to have continued for a little while longer, but she emphasised that she did not wish to be asked to stay on and the suspicion must be that she hoped and wished that her friend and partner the Vice-Principal, Miss Nettleship, would succeed to the senior position. If that is the case it was a sad error and, with hindsight, it might have been a happier situation, not least for the Vice-Principal, had she also decided to withdraw at the same time. As it was, both the Council and the S.E.D. concluded that it was time for a change and in February 1960 46 year old Miss Bertha Danielli of Liverpool was appointed as the new Principal. Almost immediately, however, there was a foretaste of trouble when the retiring Principal objected to the terms of reference given to Miss Danielli. Miss Wingfield maintained that oversight of course development was the Vice Principal's territory and that this task should not have been specified for the new Principal. But the Council declined to give way and this does suggest that the need for fresh thinking in terms of course provision was understood by members.[33]

Miss Danielli's term as Principal was short and very difficult and a major factor was undoubtedly the tension between her and the old order as represented by Miss Nettleship. Miss Danielli's remit had been to introduce essential changes, but in this the Vice Principal provided a focus for resistance and opposition and it is evident that Miss Wingfield herself found it hard to resist the temptation for continued interference through her close friend. Ultimately matters came to a head in January 1962 when Miss Danielli decided that she had had enough and informed Miss Grainger Stewart of her decision to seek another position, giving as a main reason 'the absence of support and co-operation of the Vice-Principal which had prevailed from the outset'. Aware of the strained relations and 'of the ill effect that these engendered in the general administration of the College' the Chairman and a small ad hoc committee of Council arranged a meeting during which they attempted to bring about some form of reconciliation, but the only result was that Miss Nettleship too decided to resign.[34] When she attended her final meeting in July of that year she was thanked warmly for her great service to the College, extending over no less than thirty-five years, fourteen of which had been as Vice-Principal. Miss Nettleship's meticulous attention to detail and tireless efforts on behalf of the College were properly praised, but, before wishing her a long and happy retirement, the Chairman sadly concluded that 'it is a matter of the greatest regret to us all that your last two years have been such unhappy ones'.[35]

In fact, before that occasion Miss Danielli had also submitted her notice since in May she intimated that her application for an alternative position had been successful and that she had been appointed as the first Principal of a new College of Education in Liverpool.

In considering Miss Danielli's two year tenure of the Principalship, it seems clear that her position had indeed been made very difficult. However, it is possible to make rather too much of this dispute. The fact is that from the records she was very often absent from the College on visits to England, ostensibly studying developments elsewhere which might guide the planned future of the College. No doubt much useful information was gained, but the feeling persists that her heart may not have been in the task. When advising Miss Grainger Stewart of her decision to look for a position elsewhere she gave as her reasons not only the personal issue, but her 'anticipation of the withdrawal of the Teacher Training Course'.[36] Throughout these years there was obvious uncertainty about the future not just of the College, but of domestic subjects generally. For example, in 1961 there were various meetings between Principals and others reported by Miss Danielli where the appropriate title was under dispute. London (presumably the National, and now tottering on its last legs) apparently preferred 'Home Science' to 'Domestic Science', but others advocated adoption of American practice in the form of 'Home Economics'.[37] Moreover, so far as the College itself was concerned, for most of the period the numbers of students being recruited were falling.[38] In addition, for months the pursuit of a new location proved fruitless, while the problems of the old buildings remained a continuing worry. The suspicion therefore remains that, deep down, Miss Danielli had no real confidence in the long term future of the College and that she was not really reluctant to seek more promising pastures.

The search for a new location was far from straigthforward. For more than four years a variety of sites were contemplated and this included possible positions at Murrayfield House Estate, Ravelston House, Barnton Park, Crammond House, Inverleith Nursery and Abercorn Estate, but all failed for one reason or another. Some were quickly ruled out; others, such as Barnton Park troubled the Council for months, but the task of getting the S.E.D., Town Council and the potential seller of land all to agree, not to mention overcoming competition, seemed almost impossible, and there were many frustrations. Finally, however, in July 1961 the solution was almost literally handed to the College gift wrapped and courtesy of the building firm Messrs Wimpey.

Miss Grainger Stewart.

Following the death of the life tenant, the Clermiston Estate and mansion house was about to come on the market. The land extended to a total of 67 acres, which was more than could then be used for house construction. Moreover, the land was currently zoned not for building but as open space and the mansion house, although in poor condition, was a Grade 2 listed building. Wimpey's proposition was that the firm would bid for the whole estate on the understanding that, if it was successful, the College would guarantee to buy from it a twenty-five acre portion, including the mansion house, at a price later agreed to be £37,500. At the time that this deal was proposed neither Miss Danielli nor Miss Nettleship were available, hence Miss Grainger Stewart hastily assembled some of her Council colleagues, visited the estate, agreed that it was in many ways almost ideal, and accepted the deal in principle, subject to S.E.D. approval. By the following February most of the immediate problems had been overcome, Wimpey had secured the estate and had sold on the agreed portion to the College.

Whatever troubles lay ahead the College could now look to the future in the knowledge that it possessed a potentially fine new location on which to build. The question remained, could the possible lifeline be seized? Interestingly, on the very day that the successful purchase was intimated to Council, Miss Danielli reported on a meeting with other Principals in London 'when the difficulties being experienced in all Colleges regarding domestic administration had been discussed. The changing of the title 'Domestic Science' was also considered and there was no doubt that, at some date in the future, the College would have to be renamed'.[39]

CHAPTER FIVE

The Development of Queen Margaret College

BEFORE examining the history of the emergence and development of the modern college, it may be appropriate here to digress a little in order to reflect on some of the changes which were occurring in the educational context in the years in question.

As early as the late 1940s J.R Peddie, of the Carnegie Trust for the Universities of Scotland, (and Chairman of the College Council, 1945-47) had noted a facet of Scottish education which was both a weakness and a strength. He pointed out that Scotland had 'not developed any system of adult education comparable with what has been evolved in England'. By comparison with England, technical education, as represented by the handful of colleges in the C.I. sector, was severely underdeveloped and the reason for this, in his view, was that Scottish universities had succeeded in attracting a much higher proportion of the population interested in higher post-school study. He pointed out, for example, that while 1 in 473 Scots attended university, the equivalent figure for England was only 1 in 1,018.[1]

On the face of things this situation appeared to be to the advantage of Scotland. However, throughout much of the early post-war period many commentators frequently compared British education unfavourably with the education provision available in other countries and in the United States in particular. British universities, for example, were often held to be very traditional, too classically academic, insufficiently interested in scientific or technical education, and almost oblivious to the needs of industry and of the economy. An inadequate education system was held to be at least partly responsible for the evident comparative failure of the country's economic performance. Especially from a Scottish perspective, the traditional nature of post-school education was a serious problem.

Some of the earliest steps to address the situation occurred in the mid 1950s. In 1956 a White Paper on *Technical Education* was published by the Government. Its purpose was to promote the development in England and Wales of Colleges of Advanced Technology and, in Scotland, to stimulate a significant improvement in the existing central institutions.[2] At about the same time the Scottish Office announced its intention to promote the creation of a comprehensive system of local technical colleges.[3]

Over the next few years the S.E.D. established a series of Working Parties the reports of which ultimately resulted in a considerable reorganisation of Scottish education. One report which was published in 1959, for example, produced major change in the school curriculum and introduced the Scottish Certificate of Education. Another important report was entitled *From School to Further Education* and it appeared in 1963. Taking its popular name from its chairman, H.M. Senior Chief Inspector, Mr J.S.Brunton, the 'Brunton Report' recommended the development in schools of more 'vocationally biased' courses, urged that pupils should be given more effective career guidance from suitable teachers and proposed much closer links between educational institutions and industry. Central institutions and technical colleges were directed firmly towards 'practical' and 'vocationally relevant' fields of study.[4]

By 1960 pressure was mounting for an enhancement of technical education and for advanced post-school education to be made available to a larger proportion of the population. In December of that year the Government appointed the Robbins Committee 'to review the pattern of full-time higher education in Great Britain', and this remit provided one of the first formal statements of a concept of 'higher education' which extended outwith the university sector. By the time of publication of the Report, however, a further significant change had occurred in Scottish education. As early as 1960 *The Scotsman* had suggested that the Royal College of Science and Technology in Glasgow might be elevated to university status as a means of quickly expanding the university pool while giving an appropriate measure of prestige to the traditional practical fields of study of that institution. This idea was adopted by the Government in 1962 and a year later the first students were admitted for degree study. In 1964 the University of Strathclyde received its formal charter.[5]

Following publication of the Robbins Report in 1963 three further universities were created in Scotland. As with Strathclyde, Heriot-Watt was translated from central institution to university. In addition, parts of St Andrews University were formed into a University of Dundee and the completely new Stirling University was created.

As far as England was concerned at this time many of the Colleges of Advanced Technology similarly became universities with powers to award their own degrees. But the Committee suggested wide ranging reforms which would also concern many of the other technical colleges. For such colleges the Committee advocated that

> a new system for degrees should be established, covering business studies, languages and other subjects as well as science and technology. We consider that among what are now Regional Colleges there will be found scope for some further elevation of institutions to the status of universities.[6]

The Committee hoped that its various recommendations would result in fresh impetus being given to 'the development of vocational higher education in Great Britain' and would remedy the major weaknesses in the organisation and delivery of technical education and research. To supervise the development of the 'new system for degrees' the Committee proposed the setting up of a Council for National Academic Awards, and within a matter of weeks the Government had accepted the suggestion.[7]

It is quite clear that at the time Robbins and his colleagues anticipated a system which would enable many of the emerging technical colleges to develop themselves into universities. Later Robbins wrote that it was the intention of his Committee to encourage the creation of a 'more or less continuous spectrum in the developing system of higher education' and that within that spectrum there would be various institutions which would gradually reach university status.[8]

At the end of 1964 a General Election brought Labour to power and over the next few years some major political decisions resulted in a departure from the initial plan. Starting with Anthony Crosland successive Secretaries of State for Education emphasised their support for a binary system of higher education, with the autonomous university sector being clearly separated from a local authority organised system based on polytechnics and, for lower level work, further education colleges.

It has been argued that the decision to create a binary system flowed from Labour's strength in local government and a desire to protect the local authorities from the constant loss to the university sector of their leading institutions.[9] However, the decision may also imply a continuing doubt about the ability of the more traditional universities 'to respond appropriately to the needs of a rapidly changing society', as well as a belief that the polytechnics might well be able to deliver high level technical education more cheaply and, therefore, to a much wider section of the community. Whatever the reasons, the decision in favour of a binary system is 'central to the history of higher education from its elaboration in the second half of the 1960s', and there is no doubt that the division produced a number of critical tensions and distortions.[10]

By 1967 Crosland had designated twenty-eight new polytechnics for England and Wales. These were often formed through amalgamations of existing institutions and by taking over diploma level work abandoned by the new technical universities. With the assistance of C.N.A.A. the polytechnics rapidly turned their attention to the development of degree level work. In Scotland, with the formation of Strathclyde and Heriot Watt, there were no instant candidates for polytechnic designation. However, there was a considerable expansion in local authority further education colleges and two of these, Napier College in Edinburgh (formally opened at Merchiston Castle in 1965 and boasting no less than 6500 students in its first full year) and Glasgow College of Technology, (based partly on courses left by the old Royal College and the College of Commerce at the time of the formation of Strathclyde University) appeared likely to attain polytechnic standing in due time.

The changes described above devastated many of the small, older colleges in England and many of the venerable domestic science colleges, for example, were swiftly absorbed to support the growth of the new institutions. Similarly in Scotland rationalisation occurred in the sense that lower level craft courses were seen as belonging to the province of the further education colleges and central institutions were encouraged or instructed to hand such courses over. However, in one way the Scottish situation was different in that the mere existence of central institutions meant that the structure of post school education in this part of the U.K. was not binary, but had three distinctive elements.

With the creation of Heriot-Watt and Strathclyde Universities the Scottish Education Department had obviously relinquished what were virtually the jewels in the crown of the central institution sector. Moreover, the natural successors to these large institutions, Napier College and Glasgow Technical College, were under the control of the local councils of Edinburgh and Glasgow respectively. Under these circumstances one possibility must have been that the central institutions might have been absorbed into the further education structure and placed under local authority control. There was, however, absolutely no enthusiasm for such a step within individual colleges and reasonably it can be assumed that Departmental officials were equally keen to retain a number of institutions under direct Scottish Office jurisdiction. In any event, for the next few years the Department seems to have devoted a great deal of energy to the redevelopment of the colleges (including the teacher training colleges) which remained under its control, and it is clear that within this process the Edinburgh College of Domestic Science's location within the same city as St Andrew's House did it no harm at all. Certainly it seems to have been particularly cherished by H.M. Senior Chief Inspector Brunton who, at the end of the 1960s, was to become first a member and then chairman of the College Council.

To return to the specific history of the College, in the course of session 1962/63 some fairly crucial decisions had to be made. These in particular concerned the selection of a new College executive and the creation of an educational strategy to support and justify the development of the new campus at Clermiston.

One slightly earlier verdict which, in retrospect, must be regretted, was the decision to sell the games field at Succoth Avenue on Murrayfield hill. This eight acre field had been leased shortly before the First War and had subsequently been purchased and developed into an excellent facility which included twelve tennis courts (some grass and some hard courts), as well as a number of hockey pitches, a cricket pitch and a roomy pavilion. In the early years it had been extensively used by clubs organised and run by a Games Club managed by the students and, in 1925, it had been said that 'no more delightful spot near Edinburgh can be found on a summer day than the tennis courts with their clear view over to the Fife hills..'[11]

Fashions among students change, however, and by the later 1950s College Council repeatedly noted with disappointment that the sports field was not being used to any great extent. By this period, for example, it was believed that only about twenty students were playing on the tennis courts in the summer months. To take up some of the slack some of the courts were leased to local neighbourhood tennis clubs.

In February 1962 it was reported that the facilities at Succoth were in need of improvement, the pavilion was in poor condition and some of the courts needed repair and renewal. Not surprisingly the Council was not inclined to lay out funds for this purpose, particularly because a tennis court at Clermiston could quickly be brought into use for students and it was believed that there would be sufficient land on the new site to complete an acceptable sports ground in due course. Moreover, it was thought appropriate to redeploy the groundsmen to Clermiston. As a consequence it was decided to construct three courts at the new location in time for the autumn term and to sell the Succoth games field. Curiously, therefore, the first construction work done at Clermiston for the College was the preparation of the three tennis courts and this was a fairly botched job with the initial uneven surface having to be relaid by the contractor. After various manoeuvres to secure a change of planning use the Succoth sports field was eventually sold to the builder Mowlems Ltd in 1965 for a price of £40,000.[12] At face value it was a shrewd piece of business, because, of course, the College received more for its eight acre sports field than it had paid for its new twenty-four acre campus. On the other hand, with the benefit of hindsight, it has to be said that a satisfactory replacement for the old sports field has never really been found.

In 1962 the most pressing matter was to replace the College executive and the first temporary move taken was to promote Dr B M Henderson, Head of the Science Department, to be Acting Vice Principal, a position in which she was confirmed in the following year. The Principalship was more difficult, however, and there seems to have been an instinctive understanding that the appointment on this occasion would be particularly important. Despite an appeal, Miss Danielli was firmly held to the terms of her contract and the full six months of her period of notice were occupied in the careful search for a suitable successor. The choice fell on a figure of real stature and it is believed that members of the Council went to considerable lengths to persuade her to make herself available for selection.

Aileen King, a Yorkshire-woman, was one of the best-known figures of the day in the field of domestic science education. From 1948 to 1960 she had been Principal of Radbrook College where she had developed courses both in teacher training and in institutional management. From 1960 she had been an H.M.I. in England, hence she was fully familiar with the trends and issues of the day and was aware of the pressure to which the domestic science colleges were being subjected. Since she was in her late fifties at the time of her appointment it is clear that she was brought to Edinburgh with a specific and fairly immediate task, namely to make the arrangements associated with the transfer of the College to its new home. She was undoubtedly an inspired choice and it seems likely that not a little influence was exercised from within the S.E.D. to obtain her services. Moreover, it is perhaps true to suggest that in domestic science circles the Edinburgh College represented something akin to the inner citadel and the challenge of ensuring its

Mrs Aileen King, Principal of the College 1963-1971.

survival may well have appealed to Mrs King. She took up office in January 1963, within a matter of weeks of her appointment.

By the mid 1960s many of the College courses were coming under considerable pressure and there was difficulty in attracting sufficient numbers of students. One of the reasons for this was the opening of many new Colleges of Education in England which had led to the decision by the Department of Education that no grants would be given to English students who enrolled in Scottish institutions. The result of this was a sharp fall in the numbers of students from England coming to Edinburgh. In addition, however, the development of local further education colleges, and particularly Napier College, was also creating problems and one of Mrs King's first confrontations with the Department was over the probable transfer of the '151' Hotel Catering Course to Napier, where a Catering Department was about to open. In addition, the pressure on the teacher training courses was sustained with the various Scottish Colleges of Education pressing to take over the professional training of domestic science teachers.[13]

To address these matters Mrs King immediately opened up discussions with the S.E.D. to see if an agreed position could be reached and initiated bilateral negotiations with her counterpart at Moray House to obtain an accommodation on teacher training in Edinburgh. In the latter case she was successful and an agreement with Moray House and subsequent development with the help of the

H.R.H. Princess Alice, the Patron, arriving at the College, July 1965.

S.E.D. meant that Edinburgh was the only place in Scotland where the training of domestic science teachers continued through the 1960s on a concurrent basis. This was a key achievement since it meant that when the College moved to its new home in 1970 it was as an institution with a large proportion of its students still engaged in teacher training.[14]

Nothing could be done to save the Catering course, however, and similarly the short four-term Institutional Management course, with its emphasis on large scale catering was also lost. In addition, S.E.D. officials made clear their view that public demonstrations and the kind of practical advice day 'interest' classes which the College had provided over the years were not suitable for a Central Institution.[15] Consequently throughout the 1960s the craft courses and public lectures gradually disappeared from the College programme, dramatically reducing the numbers of part-time or occasional students. Throughout these years the numbers of full-time students also slowly continued to dwindle, for example, falling from 562 in 1963 to 469 in 1965.[16]

During this period Mrs King and her colleagues made vigorous efforts to work out a viable educational strategy and there were many visits made to institutions in other parts of the country and to various conferences in an effort to obtain appropriate ideas. Their real problem was that the context was still moving steadily away from the traditional type of course, yet no consensus had so far emerged as to convincing forms of replacement learning which would meet the needs of contemporary women, but also enable some of the essential ethos and culture of the old system to survive. Not surprisingly, members of Her Majesty's Inspectorate were frequent visitors and many suggestions were debated at length. For example, in May 1963 H.M.I. Brunton made some not particularly helpful suggestions about short courses, but he also raised the possibility of the development of a three year course in 'Home Economics', with entrance requiring two specified 'A' levels or three 'Highers'. This in fact was one way forward, but at the time the debate on the future of 'Domestic Science' / 'Home Economics' was far from being resolved. Mrs King co-operated with English efforts to develop a degree in Home Economics, to be validated possibly by Exeter and Sussex Universities, but agreement on a 'national' course proved elusive.[17] Similarly the 1963 Robbins Report on Higher Education seemed a sad disappointment and a Council sub-committee on the Report noted grimly the lack of reference to the Central Institutions (particularly the smaller ones), the need firmly to remind the S.E.D. of 'the importance of continuing the present identity of the College', and the need to develop a degree level course in Scotland in the general area of domestic science.[18] Interestingly, however, within a few weeks the Council thoughtfully reflected on the forthcoming formation of a Council for National Academic Awards and noted that 'it would be open to a College like Atholl Crescent to submit syllabuses of courses for the abler students, which might be regarded as suitable for an award by this National Council'.[19]

The latter possible life-line lay some way ahead, however, and one of Mrs King's more immediate, but vital initiatives was the decision to develop a four year

S.R.C. 1964-65, with Mrs King.

integrated Dietetics Course, combining three years of study within the College with one year of work in hospital. Edinburgh Royal Infirmary agreed to co-operate and the S.E.D. was persuaded to accept this idea, but the process was slowed down by some of the conditions imposed by the British Dietetics Association. This Diploma course emphasised catering rather than clinical dietetics, but when it commenced in 1969 it was an important initiative because it meant that the College had at least one four-year course with definite potential for development to degree level.[20]

Over the 1960s the main task for the leaders of the College was, naturally, to develop the new campus. On the advice of Professor Sir Robert Matthew it was decided to select a design via a closed architectural competition.[21] For this purpose the assessor who guided the Council was the well known architect, Mr G Grenfell Baines, OBE, and in April 1965 the competition was won from a field of eight submissions by a design proposed by Andrew Renton, a Scot trained at the Edinburgh College of Art, but whose firm, Renton & Associates was located in London.[22] Later the design was significantly altered to take account of the various requirements laid down by Mrs King and her colleagues and developed in discussions with the Department. In accordance with Mrs King's views the new College was built with the assumption that it would continue as a teacher training establishment. But as the decade passed this proposition remained in some doubt and until building work fully commenced questions as to the long term future must have remained in many minds. It must, therefore, have been a considerable relief when construction started and when, in a small ceremony on 7 June 1968, the College patron, H.R.H. Princess Alice, formally laid the foundation stone.

The new College buildings gradually emerged on the north and eastern portions of the twenty-four acre site and one of the reasons for the success of the basic design was the intelligent way in which the sloping land was used, enabling substantial areas of woodland and of the original gardens to be retained, but not dominated. One feature which was lost, however, was the old mansion house. As was noted earlier, it was a Grade 2 listed building, but when its poor state of repair was explained to the Royal Fine Arts Commission it was agreed by all concerned, including both the Scottish Office and the City Council, that the competing architects should be given a free hand either to include or exclude the mansion. In keeping with Renton's design, it was demolished. Its approximate position was on the site of the amphitheatre over-looked by Grainger Stewart Hall of residence.[23]

The main teaching block was located parallel to the northern boundary and it was intended to provide accommodation for subject departments along each of five levels, although use of the sloping land enabled the building to be constructed with no more than four storeys at any one point in its length. Originally Home Management was to be on the ground level, Catering and Cookery were on the next two levels, and the Science and Dress and Design rooms were positioned on the fourth and fifth floors respectively. The front of the building, in addition to the main entrance hall, provided facilities for the administration offices, the Principal's suite and what was originally known as the 'Council Room'. Further along the corridor and facing to the west (in what are currently information technology rooms) was the library. Leading down from the front hall was the main concourse which included a precinct provided with shopping and banking facilities. On the right was located the main lecture theatre, while the assembly hall was on the left. Along the rear of the concourse, in what is now the Staff Lounge, the Student Union Rooms were positioned, and the main Refectories were, as now, on a lower level to either side.

A key feature of the agreed design, which owed a great deal to Mrs King's personal insistence, was the arrangement provided for student residences. Linked to the administration block by a 'vennel' and facing the teaching wing, was positioned Guthrie Wright Hall, and this was planned on traditional lines to provide study bedrooms for 150 students who were intended to dine communally and share common rooms, pantries and laundry facilities. Set further to the south and connected to the main complex by a corridor under the vennel was Stevenson Hall. Here the intention was that single study bedrooms should be grouped into a series of terraced houses, each capable of accommodating up to thirty students. The over all capacity of the houses was intended to be about 140 and again a common dining room was provided. Finally, further into the campus and running parallel to the teaching wing was located Grainger Stewart Hall. In this case accommodation was planned for 134 students in the form of a block of three and four-bedroomed flats. The students in this case were expected to live independently. Mrs King explained to the *Scottish Field* that the various forms of accommodation were planned to reflect the development of students over their years of study. The flats of Grainger Stewart were intended for third and fourth year students and the latter could have visitors, who 'should be away by 11.30 pm during the week, midnight at weekends. There must never be night visitors, not even mums, and no pets, not even budgerigars'. Such accommodation was held to be unsuitable for the first or second year students. 'We don't think the 17 and 18 year olds are ready to live that very free life', hence the more traditional residences of the other two blocks.[24]

In addition to the buildings described above, a games hall or gymnasium was positioned beside the south refectory and a swimming pool was built close to the tennis courts. Squash courts were also provided and a games field of sorts was created on the western edge of the campus, although it was never adequately drained, particularly bearing in mind its position at the lowest point of a sloping site.

The main buildings were constructed on concrete frames and all the flat roofs and floors were also made of *in situ* reinforced concrete. The residences had load-bearing brick walls, but the finish to all the buildings was grey granite aggregate blocks with slate-black infill between windows. The over-all impression of the complex was, and remains, very much in character with the late 1960s early 70s, but at the time of its completion it was greatly admired. In retrospect, aspects of the design leave something to be desired, particularly the flat roofs which have resulted in frequent problems of damp penetration, and the black infill slats which are difficult to protect and tend to appear shabby. Nevertheless, the real saving grace of the design may be said to have been its sympathy with the superb parkland setting hence it remains a splendid modern campus with perhaps few rivals in Scotland. Its approximate cost of construction was £2.5 millions.

As was noted when discussing the residential accommodation, the history of the College was reflected in the names given to various buildings and, in the case of the residences, these titles have remained in use. But the theme was also originally repeated throughout the main complex. The Assembly Hall was known as De la Cour, the Administrative block was Persis Wingfield and the council decided to name the library after the Principal, Aileen King. Subsequent changes, including the construction of a new larger library on the western end of the teaching wing in 1976, meant that these latter titles quickly fell out of use.

By the end of the 1960s it was clear that a difficult period had been traversed and that the new College would soon come into existence. That it had survived successfully through the decade and had not, for example, simply been swallowed up by emerging potential competitors, was due in no small measure to Mrs King, and her successor is certainly of the opinion that without her it is very probable that the Clermiston College would never have been completed. Others seem to have shared that view and there was great general pleasure when she was rewarded by being appointed CBE in 1969. Her staunch supporter over these years, Miss Grainger Stewart, retired a year later, shortly before the move, and she too had made an important contribution at a critical stage hence it was appropriate that the memory of her connection with the College should be perpetuated by the attachment of her name to one of the halls of residence. She was succeeded by the equally significant participant, Lady Hirst. Finally, in these days it was not the custom to give much recognition to public officials, but it can be said now that without the support of the S.E.D. and of H.M. Inspectors such as Mr Brunton and his colleagues, the task of creating the Clermiston College would certainly have been very much more difficult. Brunton himself had by this stage retired from the inspectorate and had accepted office as a member of the College Council. He was to serve as Chairman from 1974 to 1976.

The move to the new campus took place in the summer and autumn of 1970 and the formal opening and dedication ceremony, conducted by the Secretary of State for Scotland, Gordon Campbell, MC, was held on 25 June, 1971. Mr Campbell paid tribute to 'everyone concerned with this tremendous project' and there is no doubt that there was a great sense of achievement all round. The journal, *Home Economics*, for example, wrote in its report of 'the beautiful new buildings', of 'the wonderful working conditions' and of the 'splendid' residential and recreational facilities provided for students. On the following day the College was opened to the public and no fewer than 3,000 people, many of them former students and staff, turned up 'all very pleased and proud of 'their' new College'. Yet there were also many backward glances, and at the ceremony the 'Head Student', Jill Wadsworth, expressed the sentiments of many when she spoke of 'the dear old rabbit warren' which had been left behind and to which so much history was attached.[25]

Front of present college.

The Clermiston campus.

Speech therapy tutorial.

Physiotherapists working in a human performance laboratory.

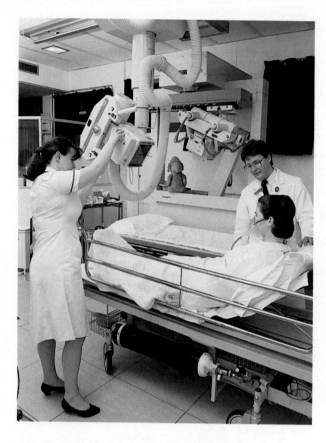

Radiographers preparing a patient for treatment.

In the college foyer.

The library.

The ubiquitous computer.

Food remains a key area of interest.

The old Leith
Academy building,
scene of the
next phase of College
development.

A modern lecture theatre.

The graduation ceremony, 1993. l. to r. Lord Provost Irons; Mrs M.Hall (Governor); Professor L.W.Rodger (Chairman of Governing Body); The Pro-Patron, The Rt. Hon. the Countess of Elgin and Kincardine; Vice-Patron, Professor Leach; Assistant Principal, Dr Austin Reid.

When the properties of the old college were sold in the winter of 1970-71 a total of £372,706 seems to have been raised. Numbers 1-8 Atholl Crescent yielded £185,500 and numbers 12 and 15-17 produced a further £75,017. The properties in Drumsheugh Gardens and Walker Street were sold for £67,000 and Melvin House in Rothesay Terrace brought in £45,189. The bulk of the money was simply passed on to the Department since, of course, most of the buildings had been purchased and maintained by public funds. However, 3,4 and 6 Atholl Crescent had been bought by the old School company prior to it becoming a central institution, and the College was therefore able to retain the £67,000 raised from these properties. Just over £50,000 of this was reinvested in the new campus, mainly to provide a swimming pool, and the residue of £16,650 was retained in order to form an Amenities Fund.[26]

(For a time the Atholl Crescent buildings were used for civil service staff training purposes, but later they were largely acquired for office accommodation and, behind the magnificent facade, the terrace was completely reconstructed in the early 1980s.)

Inevitably, moving out of the old buildings after so many years and leaving them in a state fit for sale was in itself a major task and Mrs King told the College and Hostels Committee of the sterling work which had been done by many of the staff during the upheaval. In particular she commended Miss Close, the Domestic Administrator, Mr Adams, the Secretary and Finance Officer and Willie Martin, the Maintenance Officer, for their unstinting efforts in clearing the old buildings at comparatively short notice.[27]

With the move fully accomplished Mrs King duly retired in September 1971. Some months earlier her successor, Miss Claudine L Morgan, M.Ed., had been appointed and to her now fell the task of leading the development of an educational institution worthy of the new physical setting. Miss Morgan was a Scot by birth, but had spent most of her life in England. After training in domestic science in Newcastle she had followed a teaching career in Durham and Yorkshire, before moving to the Elizabeth Gaskell College of Education in Manchester. She had gained her Masters Degree at the University of Manchester and for the four years prior to coming to Edinburgh had been Deputy Principal of the Manchester College.

The situation which confronted Miss Morgan was by no means straightforward. As has been noted, through the 1960s many of the traditional craft courses operated by Atholl Crescent were either abandoned as having outlived their usefulness or were deemed to be inappropriate for a Central Institution and were, therefore, handed over to further education colleges. Similarly, most of the old demonstration and interest classes were discontinued. Finally, the traditional domestic science courses were constantly under attack from (particularly) feminist educational theorists, while the teacher training element was to some extent coveted by the Colleges of Education. Consequently, when the new College opened in the autumn of 1970 it had no more than 489 full-time students in an establishment then equipped to provide teaching for 900 and with residential accommodation for no less than 450. Three and four year Diploma courses in Domestic Science, in Dietetics and Catering, and in Institutional Management, together with shorter ordinary level Diplomas in Hotel and Institutional Management made up the basic provision, but clearly the College was operating far beneath capacity and still lacked the educational foundation on which to develop.

Returning on the train following the interview with the selection panel, during which she had accepted the Principalship, Miss Morgan reflected on the obvious absence of strategic vision among those with whom she had spoken. 'What did they intend should be done in these great buildings?' Slowly she concluded that, quite simply, no one knew; and that fundamentally it would be her job to find the answer. Moreover she would have to do so in a city which boasted one of the finest educational endowments in the country and where competition was bound to be intense.

As if the problem was not severe enough, within a matter of months the decision was made by government to terminate the concurrent system of teacher training in Edinburgh and to bring training into line with practice elsewhere. The College was, therefore, instructed to bring to an end the three and four year Diplomas in Domestic Science. The main rationale behind Mrs King's planning had, therefore, collapsed more or less immediately.

The principal reason for this decision was perhaps that over expansion in the 1960s had led to over capacity in the Scottish Colleges of Education and this situation was now becoming clear. The Department felt that the transfer of some students would be helpful. However, it is also the case that the hostility to domestic science in certain educational circles was very strong by this period. A little later Eileen Byrne, for example, wrote witheringly of the girls' curricula in many schools which were 'still too often centred on a patronizingly trivial collection of domestic skills and consumer material based on their future homes, ambiguously labelled "Design for Living" or "Child and Home".' She pointed to the 1967 United Nations resolution which declared that 'equal rights in education at all levels, meant the same curricula' etc; and she argued for the replacement of 'the present domestically oriented skills' with fields of study which concentrated on preparing 'both sexes for the best jobs or careers' of which they were capable.[28] These were typical of some of the sentiments which were being expressed and, indeed, the Sex Discrimination Act of 1975 made curricular discrimination unlawful. The pressure to reform teacher training in this area was, therefore, formidable. From the College's point of view, however, future courses would now have to be designed to appeal to both sexes and the focus would have to be increasingly directed to preparing students for the world of employment rather than the home and for jobs in the business community rather than in school teaching.

The initial reaction to the decision to end the domestic science diplomas and concurrent teacher training was the rapid development of a three year full-time Diploma course in Home Economics to which students were admitted from 1973. This was an interim measure, but it allowed successful students if they so wished to go on to undertake a one-year teacher training course at a College of Education.

Obviously the loss of fourth year students was disappointing, but this change to Home Economics provided an important breathing space.

At this point another small helpful addition was provided when the College was invited to house a forty-eight week full time course for Health Visitors. This course was very much in keeping with an older tradition and those concerned were warmly welcomed when they transferred in from the City Public Health Department. Much of the initiative to secure this course was taken by Bailie Mrs Mansbridge, a former student and now a member of the College Council.[29]

A little more immediate help was also provided from an unexpected quarter. At the privately run Edinburgh College of Speech and Drama the students had become thoroughly disenchanted by some of their apparently very poor facilities and conditions. In February of 1972, therefore, led by Peter Marshall, they organised a series of sit-ins and demonstrations and petitioned the Scottish Office to be taken over by the new Clermiston College. Whether such an approach was instantly welcomed by the College authorities may be questioned, but the idea was viewed with sympathy at the Department, and from the autumn the Drama course was established. Initially, the numbers of students were not great, but they represented a useful little addition and they undoubtedly brought an extremely interesting extra dimension to the College portfolio.

With the ending of domestic science, of course, the earlier prediction of the requirement for a new name for the institution had been fulfilled and at a meeting of the members of College on 22 March, 1972 the decision was taken to adopt the title Queen Margaret College. It is impossible to say who first suggested the name, but at the meeting Miss Nettleship and Mrs Thomson spoke in favour of the change and the resolution was proposed by Lady Hirst, the Chairman of Council, and seconded by the former Principal, Miss Wingfield.[30] It was a good choice, because clearly if a new range of courses was to be developed it was useful to have a name which did not associate the institution with a narrow or specific field of education. Moreover, Queen Margaret, the eleventh century English princess and wife of King Malcolm, is not only one of the most romantic figures in Scottish history, but she is particularly remembered for her civilising influence and her support of the Church which led to her eventual canonisation. It is perfectly appropriate, therefore, that her name should be attached to the College.

Perhaps, however, the historian can be permitted to express a certain disappointment at this choice. If it was felt at the time to be an advantage to adopt a Royal title it is in some ways sad that the chance was not taken to link the College with the name of its original patron, Princess Louise, Duchess of Argyll. Not only had she been intimately connected with the College for some sixty-four years, but she was one of the real unsung heroines of the movement for women's education in the nineteenth century and she was particularly committed to the progress of Scottish women. She has now largely been forgotten and it seems a great pity that the opportunity was not taken to keep her name and her association with the College firmly before the public.

As the above episode indicates, many of the former staff and old students remained closely in touch with the institution, particularly through their member-ship of the College - which had given them the opportunity to make the decision on the title - and through the Old Students' Guild. It was good that they retained this contact and that a great figure from the past such as Miss Wingfield, for example, should maintain her interest on into her old age. Long after the move to Clermiston she continued to refer to the place as 'my College' and she struggled valiantly to attend meetings after she had become both frail and somewhat deaf. Once, when she had required to be helped to a chair, she barked at the head janitor, 'Henderson! You have waited all your life to order me about in my College. And now I must just do as I'm bid.' On another occasion she imperiously interrupted a graduation ceremony to insist that the volume was turned up to enable her to hear. Such incidents may have caused a little mirth at the time, but in truth they were warmly appreciated because they encouraged an invaluable sense of continuity in a modern setting where such feelings could so easily have been lost.

The loss of teacher training was a fairly devastating blow to Miss Morgan and she later confessed that, had she known in advance of such a decision, she might well have accepted an alternative position at the head of an English College. However, confronted with the situation she felt forced to search with even greater vigour for a viable strategy. One which was considered, for example, was the possibility of amalgamation with Heriot Watt University and there were some grounds for believing that such an approach would have been received sympathet-ically at the time. But the desire for continued independence was strong and the Department was not keen on the suggestion, presumably not being willing to see the fine new College withdrawn from the C.I. sector.

A very significant factor in the subsequent development of a plan flowed from the Government's *Central Institutions (Scotland) Regulations* of 1972, which required Central Institutions to establish an Academic Council which would draw in not only members of the College management, but members of the general teaching staff and perhaps additional co-opted members.[31] With the formation of Academic Council the old College and Hostels Committee was wound up and the new Council settled down to the task of preparing a detailed development strategy. In this members noted the 1973 White Paper, *Education in Scotland: A Statement of Policy*, which anticipated a considerable expansion in the numbers coming into higher education in the years through to the early 1980s.[32]

In addition to introduction of an Academic Council, the Government instructions to Central Institutions also produced new arrangements in the governance of colleges with the College Council being replaced by a Governing Body which contained a sharply reduced degree of representation by local councillors and an increase in members coming from the business community and other employers of students. This change was introduced from the summer of 1974,[33] and a few months later Academic Council reported to the new Governors that it had now formulated a 'Course Development Plan'. This plan contained proposals to develop to degree level the present courses in Home Economics, Dietetics, Institutional Management and Nursing and to produce new courses in Speech Therapy and Social Work. The intention was to attain a student population of 1290 by 1980-81.[34]

Essentially, therefore, a two-pronged strategy had evolved and this was aimed at developing both the quality and breadth of the educational programme offered by the College. In the first case, it was felt that if the College was really going to be able to compete it was going to have to offer potential students the possibility of following their studies to the highest levels of attainment. Inevitably, as the Principal told Council, it would be necessary 'to develop certain courses to degree level' and, indeed, in due time, to enable higher degree studies to be undertaken.'[35] In the second case, the objective was to develop a wider range of study within a rational field. Key requirements were obviously, as far as possible, to hold on to the College's traditional female 'constituency', while producing courses equally interesting to male students, and to create courses which were closely aimed at the world of employment. It was reasoned that studies in the caring professions were most likely to achieve such aims, hence the declared programme.

Broadly, the S.E.D. seems to have reacted favourably and supportively to the second element in the strategy, but to have retained a considerable measure of scepticism and doubt about the possibility of making a reality of the first part. Nevertheless, such was the approach adopted and Miss Morgan now gathered about her a team aimed at delivering the required programme. Dr Henderson, the Vice Principal, retired after having made an invaluable contribution through the difficult 1960s, and Mr Bernard Doherty, Head of the Department of Education and Dean of the Faculty of Community Studies at Manchester Polytechnic, was brought in as her replacement. The new Vice-Principal proved a key support, as did Robert Smith, who, in the capacity of Assistant Principal, relieved some of the administrative pressure on the College Executive and thus allowed the required level of energy to be devoted to development.

When the changes to the College's leadership structure were being introduced the student population was surveyed in detail and this study produced some interesting information. For example, in the autumn of 1974 places of home residence of students were recorded as follows:

17.2% came from Edinburgh
13.2% came from Lothian Region outwith Edinburgh
57.4% came from other Scottish Regions
12.2% came from other parts of the U.K. and overseas.

These figures clearly reflected the College's identity as a national rather than local institution and emphasised the wisdom of a strategic plan which aimed at attracting students from far afield to pursue their studies in Edinburgh.[36] However, the task of developing an appropriate programme at the required level was not easy and imposed some very considerable burdens on lecturers. It is apparently the case that when the transfer was made from Atholl Crescent into the new campus only seven members of the staff had degrees and these individuals were almost all concentrated into the Science Department.[37] Obviously a gradual programme of recruitment enabled teaching strengths to be augmented and a wider range of academic skills and levels of competence to be brought to bear. But very much had to be achieved by the existing lecturers. The latter had to accept quite rigorous personal development programmes, in many cases having considerably to enhance their own qualifications, and they had to learn complex new skills of course formation, reaching a quality of output which not only satisfied themselves, but which was acceptable to external assessors who often seemed very hard to please. The truth is it was a difficult, uncomfortable, if sometimes very rewarding process, and it quickly became clear that the College's future depended not just on a handful of leading individuals, but on the staff as a whole being willing to make the required individual and collective effort. There were many defeats, checks and knock-backs, but gradually the campaign was won and the main landmarks are summarised below.

Whatever was achieved within the College there is no question but that a crucial factor in the development was the existence and operation of the Council for National Academic Awards. In its early years inevitably C.N.A.A. was largely preoccupied by the requirements of the large Polytechnics in England and by equivalent institutions such as Napier College or Paisley Technical College in Scotland. However, the rigorous supervision of C.N.A.A. ensured that the degrees produced by such colleges in the late 1960s and early 1970s, obtained 'whole-hearted acceptance by industry'.[38]

By the mid 1970s C.N.A.A.'s procedures were well organised and perhaps there was more scope to give attention to smaller, but ambitious colleges such as Queen Margaret. Miss Morgan had immediately understood the need to develop links with the Council and persuaded officers to consider validation of a degree in Dietetics. In April and June of 1975 various delegations from C.N.A.A., including members of the Life Sciences Board, visited the College and were assured by the Principal, staff and Governors that the necessary resources would be supplied and the staff development and recruitment programmes would be implemented in order to support degree level work. By January of 1976 Governors learned with pleasure that C.N.A.A. was prepared to recognise the College's suitability as an establishment able to offer its degrees. Visiting officers had 'viewed with confidence the academic developments which were taking place in the College, and looked forward to receiving submissions in respect of the further degree courses which the College hoped to introduce in the near future'. Permission was granted to proceed with the Dietetics degree.[39]

While these moves were going on work had also been in hand to develop a Home Economics degree and a BA in the subject was approved from 1977. Two key traditional areas of interest to the College, therefore, had successfully been moved up to degree level, and the progress of similar development elsewhere in the College gradually picked up momentum. As far as Institutional Management was concerned, the ordinary Diploma was withdrawn in 1976 and concentration was devoted to expanding the Higher Diploma and in developing a one-year HCIMA course.

Meanwhile, the broadening process had also moved ahead. In 1972 a Life Sciences Nursing course was commenced and this eventually led, in 1979, to the establishment of a BA Degree in Nursing. Earlier, however, this activity enabled a platform to be established within the College in the training of nurses, and post qualification training courses were introduced in Occupational Health Nursing, Community Psychiatric Nursing, and District Nursing as well as a course for Enrolled Nurses. These, taken together with the Health Visitors course and some other short professional studies, enabled a strong Department of Health and Nursing to develop through the 1970s.

The general health 'interest' was typically approved by the Scottish Office and considerable efforts were made to assist and augment the broadening process within this area. Helpful assistance was given to bring into the College appropriate training programmes from the Health Service and elsewhere and once in residence the latter were quickly developed in academic terms. For example, in Session 1975-76 the Edinburgh School of Speech Therapy, headed by Miss Moira McGovern, moved in, and a B.Sc in Speech Pathology and Therapy was swiftly organised and commenced from 1978. Similarly professional training units in Physiotherapy and Occupational Therapy transferred from the Health Service and their diplomas were replaced by degrees by the mid 1980s. The last acquisitions of this type came when room was found for the Edinburgh School of Chiropody in 1985 and when the classes of the Edinburgh Schools of Radiography were taken over in 1992.

These changes sound straightforward, but in fact the processes were often far from simple since not only C.N.A.A. and S.E.D. had to be satisfied, but also the relevant professional bodies. Sometimes meeting all the requirements involved a development procedure not unlike solving a 'Rubic's' cube, for often no sooner was one condition resolved than it was seen to be in conflict with the wishes of another authority. Gradually, however, the College's internal monitoring and development mechanisms became more effective and skilful and all the various additions steadily added to the reservoir of ability and competence on which the institution was able to draw. Over time, therefore, the processes became swifter and less painful.

Some absolutely new developments had their roots not so much in existing work, but in the effort to keep pace with appropriate technological change and as a consequence of the incidental accumulation of a pool of suitable academic skills. Into this 'second generation' category would fall the BA Degree in Communication Studies, introduced from 1981 and the subsequent Higher Diploma in Information Studies.

Similarly, as staff development continued and as newcomers arrived, so research activities were encouraged. To begin with, this was a fairly ad hoc activity and a few (sometimes) odd initiatives set the pace. Gradually, however, formal College assistance in this area became more organised although, for a time, still at a fairly low level. Nevertheless, it enabled some significant growth towards higher degree work.

In writing of these years one is conscious of failing to set out the previous histories of some of the tributaries which now blended into the main flow of the College and it is hoped that, at some stage, others with more specific interests may provide some of the details elsewhere.[40] Meanwhile, perhaps the reader will accept and forgive the decision to focus here purely on the themes of mainstream College development.

The transformation which commenced throughout the 1970s was not accomplished entirely peacefully and one incident which, in retrospect, seems somehow redolent of the background ambience of that decade occurred in the early summer of 1976. In May of that year the sharp cut-back in school teaching career opportunites resulted in a strike by students at Moray House College and on Monday, 17th the Queen Margaret students - also deeply concerned about the falling numbers who would be accepted for teacher training - decided to join the campaign. They occupied the teaching and administrative parts of the College and for the next three weeks declined to allow staff to pursue their normal work. In fact the occupation was conducted on a reasonably civilised basis, in that the examination programme went ahead and certain administration tasks continued, but although some of the students may have enjoyed the initial excitement, it was a very unfortunate episode. From the voting figures at one or two student meetings, it is clear that despite a student body by then numbering nearly 900, a minority of about 250 were able to exploit the apathy or indifference of the others to prolong the action. Ultimately this support dwindled rapidly and in the face of an increasingly irritated Principal and staff the occupation was abandoned on June 8th having achieved absolutely nothing.

Throughout the 'sit-in' Miss Morgan had retained much of her characteristic good humour and patience, but the 1970s were indeed a strange time in terms of attitudes to 'industrial action'. Perhaps the star of the whole incident was the local post-man who, coming to empty the mail box on the first day, found his way barred by a crowd of students who informed him that no-one was being allowed into the College. 'Going very red in the face he drew himself up and bellowed, 'I am the Queen's messenger and no-one prevents me from collecting the post'. At that the pickets drew back and let him get on with it.'

By the time of her retirement in 1985, the goals set by Miss Morgan had been substantially achieved. The College had reached her target of full-time students and it now had a range of degrees or higher diploma courses operating over a reasonable and interesting field of studies. Moreover, its reputation in the community seemed good and there was no lack of students applying for admission. Indeed, in some cases the problem was a shortage of places for all the students who wanted to obtain a particular qualification and what was obvious to many of the staff was the excellence of the undergraduate performance. As courses were upgraded so it became clear that students were more than willing to accept increasingly demanding intellectual challenges.

The key to Miss Morgan's success was perhaps her ability to persuade and lead her staff through a tricky transitional phase with the minimum of fuss and the maximum of co-operation. Her petite stature and soft north country accent belied

Claudine L. Morgan, Principal of the College, 1971-1985.

a sharp incisive mind and a clear sense of priorities and she departed not only with a distinguished record of accomplishment, but leaving behind many friends and admirers.

The appointment of Donald Leach to the Principalship marked a significant milestone for the College, for not only was he the first male holder of the office, but he was the first to come from a background outwith the general field of domestic science. In a very real sense, therefore, he represented the College's future as an institution of higher learning with a range of interest extending well beyond its traditional compass. Mr Leach is a mathematician and physicist who followed national service in the RAF by a period in industry, before rising through Napier College (now University) to become Assistant Principal/Dean of the Faculty of Science from 1974 to 1985.

Bernard Doherty retired in 1983 to be replaced for a time by Dr Chris Maddox (currently Principal at the Scottish College of Textiles, Galashiels). The present

Professor Donald Leach, Vice-Patron and Principal of the College.

Vice-Principal is Scott Allan, formerly the Head of Department of Communication and Information Studies.

Notwithstanding the major progress which had been accomplished under Miss Morgan's leadership it is true to say that by the mid 1980s there were still areas of obvious weakness to be found in the College. When Mr Leach assumed office he experienced something akin to a culture shock at some of the attitudes which he encountered. While some of the more civilised customary practices inherited from the old college may have provided a pleasant contrast with life elsewhere, inefficiencies in the management structure, the lack of genuine debate in decision making, and the comparatively weak and underdeveloped academic culture were areas of concern. The new Principal recognised that the College was functioning fairly well despite such problems, but part of the reason for this could be attributed to the advantages of surplus capacity and a favourable staff/student ratio. If these were in themselves indications of inefficiency, they also suggested that there were real possibilities for further rapid growth and achievement. Accordingly, he set about upgrading the management structure, stimulating a major improvement in academic procedures and in fully exploiting the available accommodation.[41]

Throughout the later 1980s and early years of the present decade, therefore, the pace of activity quickened as the College matured into its modern identity as an authentic higher education or university level institution. In particular, the procedures for developing and monitoring degrees became much more sophisticated and assured and at the time of writing students are following study on no less than seventeen first degree courses and several other degrees are currently under preparation. Not surprisingly, therefore, the College was well able to accept the full degree awarding powers bestowed on it by the Privy Council in the autumn of 1992.

As the process of development continued so it may be said that the role of C.N.A.A. became somewhat less important as the College's own techniques and levels of competence reached the stage where external supervision was less and less necessary. No doubt this experience was shared in many other contemporary institutions and contributed to the Government's decision effectively to end the binary system of higher education which had obtained since 1965, by permitting many of the polytechnics to become universities under the Higher Education Funding Councils and thereby rendering the Council for National Academic Awards surplus to requirement. However, its demise in 1992 should not be noted without due tribute. As Harold Silver pointed out, throughout the lifetime of C.N.A.A. polytechnics and colleges 'had to establish, explain and justify their roles and objectives in ways that the universities and colleges of the nineteenth and twentieth centuries rarely, if at all, had to do'. Within and under pressure from C.N.A.A. the higher education colleges 'had persistently to explain or debate their roles in relation to research or industry and the professions, non-traditional students or "peer-review".'[42] There can be no question, but that a great improvement was brought about in terms of the quality and relevance of higher education courses and the sector as a whole was able to expand and develop so that many more people were able to enjoy the advantages of a rapidly widening spread of higher education with consequent benefits to the national economy. If the experience of Queen Margaret College in the 1970s and 1980s reflects well on those directly concerned, so does it testify greatly to the credit of the College's indispensable partner over these years. On the other hand, if proper tribute is due to C.N.A.A., there can be few regrets at the ending of the binary system, since many of the relevant institutions were, by the 1990s, well able to enter the university sector. The boundary always had been a nonsense since there never was a good reason for preventing mature institutions, when they were ready, from becoming universities, and arguably the maintenance of an arbitrary and unnecessary division somewhat weakened and reduced the stimulus to progressive growth and improvement at the university level.

Within the College as the degree programme expanded, so the numbers of students seeking places increased and in the past eight years the full time population has more than doubled to presently stand at approximately 2,500.

Similarly, the research effort has increased both in real and in organisational terms. In 1985 the first graduate to be awarded a higher degree was Marjory

Webster who received the C.N.A.A. degree of Master of Philosophy. In 1989 Sarah Whiteley, a nurse whose studies were supervised within the Department of Management and Social Sciences, became the first College-registered student to be awarded a Doctorate of Philosophy. And a year later there was great delight in the Department of Applied Consumer Studies (formerly the Department of Home Economics) when Alice Tam, the brilliant daughter of illiterate Chinese parents, also obtained her Doctorate within the College. Dr Tam's success gave particular pleasure not only because she had also studied for her first degree at the College, but because, as a home economist, her personal attainment demonstrated some of the development which had been achieved in the traditional area.

Meanwhile, and to support higher degree study, staff research activities had also been progressing with the result that in the spring of 1993 and at the first time of asking, the College was able to satisfy the requirements of the University Funding Council's Research Assessment Exercise sufficiently well to secure half a million pounds of research funding. It was a worthy initial effort and the likelihood must be that further significant advance can be expected in the immediate future.

This accelerating growth, of course, has strained the resources of the existing campus close to its limits and moves to develop some of the activities at another location are already in hand.

Such an expansion was partly possible as a direct consequence of Principal Leach's initiative to establish 'Capital Campus' as a method of exploiting fully the College facilities. In particular College residences and other buildings have been used outwith the period of the normal academic calendar for tourist, conference and other commercial purposes. A result was that when, in the autumn of 1993, the need for new premises became urgent, the College was able to obtain the old Leith Academy building in Duke Street and embark on a £2 million modernisation of the premises. The intention is that further expansion of the College will take place at Leith with the Departments of Podiatry and Radiography and Physiotherapy moving there during 1994.

In the context of the time span covered by this history it is remarkable to reflect that the Clermiston campus should have been developed close to its full potential in not much more than twenty years. So delighted was the College's governing body that in April of 1993 it decided to mark the achievement secured under Principal Leach by conferring on him an Honorary Professorship. At the time Professor Leslie Rodger, current Chairman of the Board of Governors, said, 'as we move forward with our plans for a second campus and towards 'university' status, it is very appropriate that we mark the Principal's significant role in this way.'[43]

Through the passage of time since the College moved from Atholl Crescent naturally many changes of personnel have occurred and the establishment has now grown to become much larger and more complex than in the past. Only a tiny handful of the participants in that transfer are still on the staff, but from time to time they regale their colleagues with memories of Atholl Crescent and of the great 'characters' who seemed to fill the building in these days. Moreover, strange echoes of the old College survive even if they are barely comprehended, still less understood by the modern generation. For example, staff still sometimes refer to one of the ladies' rooms as the 'pink parlour', but few of them realise that the expression derives from the name given to the Principal's powder room at Atholl Crescent after one particularly spectacular redecoration. No wonder Mrs King would gleefully murmur to her guests, 'would you like to see my room?'

One truly remarkable continuity is represented by the College patron, Her Royal Highness Princess Alice, Duchess of Gloucester. In the years since she laid its foundation stone she has attended various College functions and in 1988 she conferred its first honorary degree on Dr Margaret Auld, Chief Nursing Officer of the Scottish Home and Health Department. In 1990 her fiftieth anniversary as College patron was celebrated by various activities, but particularly through gathering the funds to endow an annual travelling scholarship which carries her name. The campaign to raise the money on that occasion was led by Mrs N Mansbridge, a distinguished former student who had served as Chairman of the Board of Governors from 1976 to 1979. Amazingly, the ongoing link with Princess Alice means that the College's entire one hundred and eighteen year history is spanned under the continuous patronage of just two Royal Princesses.

In view of her advancing years, in the summer of 1993 HRH Princess Alice consented to the appointment of the Rt.Hon. the Countess of Elgin and Kincardine as Pro-Patron and, after installation, the latter's first duties were to confer degrees in the autumn graduation ceremony. When this arrangement was reached Professor Leach was formally appointed Vice-Patron and the two new offices have an approximate equivalence to the positions of Chancellor and Vice-Chancellor in a University.

And so the history of the College has unfolded, and reflecting on the whole story one cannot help being struck by the living, organic nature of the institution. Its existence stemmed from the founders' perceptions of the needs of women in the last quarter of the nineteenth century. Its mature years were as a practical college, self-confidently fulfilling a clear purpose and, under the leadership of individuals such as Lady Leslie Mackenzie and Persis Wingfield, contributing enormously (directly and indirectly) to the lives of women and children all over the country.

Then followed a period of potentially terminal decline, at which point many of its sister colleges succumbed in one way or another and disappeared from existence. Indeed, it is a remarkable fact that of all the former domestic science institutions which were once to be found in many towns and cities over the U.K., Queen Margaret College alone survives with its independence proudly intact. (Its last Scottish counterpart, the Queens College, was absorbed into Glasgow's Caledonian University in 1992). Finally, the period from 1970 is a story of renewal and vigorous growth so that the College's future as a valuable and important contributor to higher education in Scotland now seems assured.

Concentrating the account in this manner focuses attention on the interesting question, why did the College survive when all its peer establishments were passing into history? Part of the answer, of course, is explained by circumstances - the early decision to move to a new campus; the crucial support of the S.E.D. in the 1960s;

the vital role of C.N.A.A. are examples. Again, part of the acknowledgement must also go to individuals such as Miss Grainger Stewart, Lady Hirst, Mrs King, Miss Morgan and the staff at the time of the move to Clermiston. They all can be said to have dug in their heels and worked for continued independence. Similarly, more recently the speed with which the College portfolio of courses was developed and broadened (in a way perhaps that Queens College was unable to achieve) meant that the base of course work offered by the College was sufficiently sound to justify accreditation and, therefore, independence at the time when C.N.A.A.'s existence was being terminated. It is perhaps not too much to suggest that the acceleration in development in the last few years came just in time to secure continued independence.

But in the final analysis, the answer must also lie with the key generations of students. Had the market dried up, or had the College's reputation faltered, then it becomes hard to believe that a take-over or merger could have been resisted. However, the fact is that only for a very short time in the 1960s was student recruitment a problem and typically far more students sought admission to courses than could be accommodated. Ultimately that can only be explained by reputation - reputation among students, parents, school-teachers and employers. Arguably the Edinburgh School/College/Queen Margaret College, has always stood for a particular type and quality of education. Feminist (in the best sense of the word), vocationally directed, practical, rigorous, conscious of its market, and caring in a down to earth manner, are some of the terms which might be used to describe the approach to education which forms the basis of the reputation which has enabled the College not only to survive, but to flourish in the world of modern Edinburgh.

Finally, one returns to the question, what would Christian Guthrie Wright, Louisa Stevenson and their friends and colleagues think of the institution which has developed from the School which they established so long ago in their passion to contribute to the progress of women? There can be no precise answer, of course, and yet one can be confident that they would be over-joyed, and particularly to find the modern students reaching the highest levels of attainment. What can really be said with certainty, however, is that those associated with the College of today can be very proud indeed of its origins and of the valiant women who began its story.

APPENDIX A

Certificates

NATIONAL TRAINING SCHOOL OF COOKERY.

Exhibition Road, South Kensington, S.W.

CERTIFICATE OF LEARNER'S KNOWLEDGE.

It has been reported by the Examiner to the Executive Committee that ___Miss C.E. Guthrie Wright___

of ___6 Lynedoch Street Edinburgh___ *has

attended an Examination by papers, and has obtained* ___965___

marks out of a possible total of 1000 marks for written

answers to questions.

By order of the Committee of Management.

___Francis Hadgett___
Secretary.

___11___ *day of* ___August___ 1875

NATIONAL TRAINING SCHOOL OF COOKERY.

SOUTH KENSINGTON.

EXAMINATION OF LEARNERS, 24th JULY, 1875.

1. What are the four chemical elements which enter into the composition of all flesh and muscle? Which of these is it most important to preserve during the process of cooking? (30 marks.)

2. What kind of fish offers the largest amount of nutriment at the smallest cost? (10 marks.)

3. What are the *principal processes* in use in the preparation of food for the table? In what respect do they materially differ? Which process is best calculated to retain the nutritious principles? (30 marks.)

4. If *potatoes* form the principal diet of a family, what other kinds of food should be taken with them, and why? (20 marks.)

5. What general principle is it requisite to observe in the management of fuel, etc., in order, without waste, to have always at command a clear and bright fire? (30 marks.)

6. What general rules ought to be observed with respect to roasting meat—describe the process, as shortly as possible, and the time you would allow for roasting a leg of mutton weighing—say 9 lb. 10 oz. How much might a joint of that weight be expected to lose while roasting. (80 marks.)

7. What difference would you observe in boiling meat intended to be eaten, and in boiling it merely for the purpose of extracting soup from it? To what degree of heat would you allow the water to rise in either case? What should be done, to get the scum to rise, and how should the scum be removed? (50 marks.)

8. Describe the process of trussing a fowl for *roasting*. In what respect does it differ from trussing a fowl for *boiling*? (40 marks.)

9. How would you prepare a MUTTON BROTH, say for six persons—what quantity and quality of meat and what other ingredients should you require? (35 marks.)

10. How would you prepare jelly from calves' feet? (30 marks.)

11. How would you make a savoury *omelette* (say, with three eggs,) and what other ingredients would you use? (35 marks.)

12. Describe the preparation of *lobster cutlets.* (40 marks.)

13. How would you prepare puff paste? (60 marks.)

14. What is the difference between an open and close range? (20 marks.)

15. How would you clean a copper stewpan? and what materials would you use for the purpose? (20 marks.)

16. When would you use a copper saucepan in preference to an iron one? and why? (20 marks.)

17. What is dripping? and how is it clarified? (20 marks.)

National Training School for Cookery.

EXAMINATION OF LEARNERS, JULY 24TH, 1875.

FIRST GRADE

To rank in the first grade, a Student must obtain over 800 marks out of a total of 1000 marks, given for correct answers to the examination questions.

Order of Merit.	NAME.				Marks.
1.	Miss C. E. Guthrie Wright...	...	...		965
2.	Miss Julia Vincent ...	...	...	...	930
3.	Miss Marian Smithard	...	...	...	815

SECOND GRADE

To rank in the second grade, a Student must obtain over 600 marks.

4.	Miss Isobel D. Middleton ...	...	...		750
5.	Miss Laura Wand ...	...	...	...	745

THIRD GRADE

To rank in the third grade, a Student must obtain over 400 marks.

6.	Mrs. F. Clark	...	...	...	...	575
7.	Mrs. Deacon	...	...	...	...	500
8.	Mrs. Gothard	...	...	...	...	480

If a Student wishes to be re-examined in Theory, to obtain a higher position, she can do so on paying a fee of ten shillings.

NATIONAL TRAINING SCHOOL OF COOKERY.

Exhibition Road, South Kensington, S.W.

PRACTICE CERTIFICATE FOR ARTIZAN COOKERY.

Families spending from 7s. to 20s. weekly in the purchase of food to be cooked.

It has been reported to the Executive Committee of the School that _Miss C.S. Guthrie Wright_

of _6 Lynedoch Place, Edinburgh_

having attended the Course in the Artizan Kitchen, has obtained

_670_ marks out of a possible total of 800 marks.

Frances Hadgate,
Secretary.

NATIONAL TRAINING SCHOOL OF COOKERY.

Exhibition Road, South Kensington, S.W.

CERTIFICATE FOR PRELIMINARY PRACTICE IN CLEANING.

It has been reported to the Executive Committee

that _Miss C.S. Guthrie Wright_

of _6 Lynedoch Place, Edinburgh_ having

attended a Course of Preliminary Practice in Cleaning, has

obtained _600_ marks out of a possible total of _600_ marks.

By order of the Committee of Management.

Frances Hadgate,
Secretary.

_20_ day of _July_ 1875

APPENDIX B

Syllabuses

Edinburgh School of Cookery.

ALBERT BUILDINGS, SHANDWICK PLACE.

SESSION 1877-78. COMMENCING JANUARY 3.

I.—DEMONSTRATION LESSONS.

1. HIGH-CLASS COOKERY.—On Tuesdays and Fridays, from 2.30 to 4.30 p.m. Ticket for Course of Twelve Lessons, 15s; Single Admission, 1s 6d.

2. PLAIN COOKERY.—On Mondays and Thursdays, from 2.30 to 4.30 p.m. Ticket for Course of Twelve Lessons, 10s 6d; Single Admission, 1s.

3. CHEAP COOKERY.—On Saturdays, at 4 p.m. Ticket for Course of Twelve Lessons, 5s; Single Admission, 6d.

4. CHEAP COOKERY.—On Mondays at 7 o'clock; Single Admission, 2d. One Lesson in each Course will be on Sick-Room Cookery. Courses of Lessons on Cheap Cookery will be given in various Districts of the Town during the Winter Months.

Tickets for Cheap Cookery Lessons, for distribution, in packets of not fewer than Six, may be purchased at any of the above Classes.

II.—PRACTICE LESSONS.

1. HIGH CLASS COOKERY.—(a.) On Mondays and Tuesdays, from 10 to 12.30. (b.) On Thursdays and Fridays, from 10 to 12.30. Ticket for Course of Twelve Lessons, £2, 2s—with admission to the corresponding Demonstration Class. (c.) On Wednesdays, from 7 to 9 p.m. Ticket for Course of Twelve Lessons, £1, 10s.

2. PLAIN COOKERY.—(a.) On Mondays and Tuesdays, from 10 to 12.30. (b.) On Thursdays and Fridays, from 10 to 12.30—with admission to the corresponding Demonstration Class. (c.) On Wednesdays, from 7 to 9 p.m. Ticket for Course of Twelve Lessons, £1, 1s.

3. SINGLE LESSONS on Special Dishes, on Wednesdays, from 2.30 to 5 p.m.; 5s each Lesson.

4. CHEAP COOKERY.—A Class will be formed, on Saturdays, at 10 a.m., if a sufficient number of pupils enrol themselves.

III.—LESSONS IN CLEANING AND SCULLERY WORK.

On Wednesdays, from 10 to 12 noon. Ticket for Course of Six Lessons, 3s; Single Lesson, 1s.

Information regarding Certificates for Learners and for Cooks may be obtained at the School. At the close of each Lesson, the dishes not sold to Pupils will be sold to the Public at a moderate price.

Edinburgh School of Cookery.

ALBERT BUILDINGS, SHANDWICK PLACE.

SESSION 1878-79. COMMENCING OCTOBER 21.

I.—DEMONSTRATION LESSONS.

1. HIGH-CLASS COOKERY.—On Tuesdays, from 2.30 to 4.30 p.m. Ticket for Course of Twelve Lessons, 15s; Single Admission 1s 6d.

2. PLAIN COOKERY.—On Mondays and Thursdays, from 2.30 to 4.30 p.m. Ticket for Course of Twelve Lessons, 10s 6d; Single Admission, 1s.

3. CHEAP COOKERY.—On Mondays, at 7 o'clock; Single Admission, 2d. Courses of 12 Lessons on Cheap Cookery will be given in the Dalry and Fountainbridge Public Schools, on Fridays, at 7, commencing Nov. 1st, and at their close Courses will be given in the Causewayside and Canongate Schools. Admission, 2d.

One Lesson in each Course will be given on Sick-Room Cookery. Tickets for Cheap Cookery Lessons, for distribution, in packets of not fewer than Six, may be purchased at the SCHOOL OF COOKERY.

II.—PRACTICE LESSONS.

1. HIGH-CLASS COOKERY.—(*Class A.*) On Mondays and Tuesdays, from 10 to 12.30. (*Class B.*) On Wednesdays and Thursdays, from 10 to 12.30. Ticket for Course of Twelve Lessons, £2, 2s—with admission to the corresponding Demonstration Class. (*Class C.*) On Wednesdays, from 7 to 9.30 p.m. Ticket for Course of Twelve Lessons, £1, 10s.

2. PLAIN COOKERY.—(*Class A.*) On Mondays and Tuesdays, from 10 to 12.30. (*Class B.*) On Wednesdays and Thursdays, from 10 to 12.30. Ticket for Course of Twelve Lessons, £1, 10s—with admission to the corresponding Demonstration Class. (*Class C.*) On Wednesdays, from 7 to 9.30. Ticket for Course of Twelve Lessons, £1, 1s.

3. SINGLE LESSONS on Special Dishes, 5s each lesson; to former practice pupils, 4s (High Class), and 3s (Plain Cookery) when the dishes cooked are purchased by them.

4. CHEAP COOKERY.—On Saturdays, from 10 to 12.30. Ticket for Course of Twelve Lessons, £1, 1s—with admission to the corresponding Demonstration Class.

III.—LESSONS IN CLEANING AND SCULLERY WORK.

On Saturdays, from 10 to 12 noon. Ticket for Course of Six Lessons, 3s; Single Lesson, 1s.

APPENDIX C

Patrons

Edinburgh School of Cookery 1875-1891

H.R. & I.H. The Duchess of Edinburgh

H.R.H. The Princess Louise, Marchioness of Lorne

Her Grace the Duchess of Buccleuch

The Dowager Lady Ruthven

Edinburgh School/College of Domestic Science/Queen Margaret College

H.R.H. The Princess Louise, Marchioness of Lorne, Duchess of Argyll - 1891-1939

H.R.H. The Princess Alice, Duchess of Gloucester - 1940 to the present time

Pro-Patron, The Rt.Hon. The Countess of Elgin and Kincardine - 1993

Vice Patron, Professor Donald Leach - 1993 -

APPENDIX D

Leaders

The Edinburgh School of Cookery 1875-1891

Miss Louisa Stevenson, Honorary Treasurer

Miss C.E. Guthrie Wright, Honorary Secretary

The Edinburgh School of Cookery and Domestic Economy Limited 1891-1909, Chairmen and Hon. Secretaries of the Board of Directors

Chairmen

Miss Louisa Stevenson, 1892-1905

Miss C.E. Guthrie Wright, 1905-1907

Miss E.G.Dalmahoy, 1907-1909

Honorary Secretaries

Miss C.E.Guthrie Wright, 1892-1905

Miss J.C.Melvin, 1905-1909

The Edinburgh School/College of Domestic Science/Queen Margaret College 1909-1993

Chairmen of the School/College Council/Board of Governors

Professor A. Darroch, 1909-1924

Sir Malcolm Smith, KBE, 1924-1929

T.G. Nasmyth, MD, DSc, 1930-1931

C.W.Allan, JP, 1931-1935

Sheriff E.W. Neish, 1935-1938

Lady Haldane, 1938-1943

Lady Leslie Mackenzie, CBE, LLD, 1943-1945

J.R.Peddie, CBE,D.Litt, 1945-1947

Lady Darling, 1947-1949

Lady Gray, 1949-1954

Lady Henderson, 1954-1957

Miss K. Grainger-Stewart, 1958-1970

Lady Hirst, 1970-1974

J.S.Brunton, 1974-1976

Mrs N. Mansbridge, 1976-1979

Professor D.J. Manners, 1979-1983

M.Orde, 1983-1988

Professor L. Rodger, 1989-

Principals of the School/College

Miss Ethel de la Cour, 1909-1930

Miss G.M. Croft, 1930-1931

Miss Persis L. Wingfield, 1932-1960

Miss Bertha Danielli, 1960-1962

Mrs Aileen King, 1963-1971

Miss Claudine L. Morgan, 1971-1984

Professor Donald Leach, 1985-

Vice Principals

Miss Jean B. Cunningham, 1931-1943

Miss Marjorie H. Craig, 1943-1945

Miss Isobel E. Nettleship, 1945-1962

Dr Barbara M. Henderson, 1962-1973

Mr Bernard Doherty, 1973-1983

Dr Christopher E.R.Maddox, 1983-1988

Dr Vivienne Wylie, 1989

Mr Scott B. Allan, 1989-

References

Chapter 1

1. There are many excellent works, but see, for example, Olive and Sydney Checkland, *Industry and Ethos, Scotland 1832-1914* (1984); or W Hamish Fraser and R J Morris (eds) *People and Society in Scotland, Vol ll, 1830-1914,* (1990). R.K.Webb, *Modern England* (1980) provides a good standard guide to the general social history of the period, although, of course, it includes nothing specifically on Scotland.

2. O and S Checkland, op cit, (1989 ed) p36

3. Eleanor Gordon, essay on *Women's Spheres* in Fraser and Morris, op cit, p209

4. Caroline Davidson, *A Woman's Work is Never Done* (1982), p16

5. Ibid, p20, (quoting Browne and Balfour, *Water Supply* London 1880, pp48-51) J.F.Birrell, *An Edinburgh Alphabet,* (1980), p252

6. O and S Checkland, op cit, p109

7. Margaret Bryant, *The Unexpected Revolution* (1979), p29

8. L Strachey, *Eminent Victorians* (1926 ed), p120

9. Josephine Butler, *The Education and Employment of Women* (1868), reproduced in Dale Spender (ed) *The Education Papers: Women's Quest for Equality in Britain 1850-1912,* (1987), p73

10. M Bryant, op cit, p35

11. J Butler, in D Spender, op cit, p70

12. Ibid, p79

13. A notable exception is the interesting unpublished PhD thesis by Helen Corr, *The Gender Division of Labour in the Scottish Teaching Profession 1872-1914, with Particular Reference to Elementary School Teaching,* Edinburgh University (1984). The best general account of the movement is perhaps Margaret Bryant's *The Unexpected Revolution.* Although she pays little attention to events in Scotland, for example, Bryant does clearly recognise the requirement for local studies to develop a more balanced perspective. (p106)

14. Ibid, p100

15. E Gordon, op cit, p226

16. Sheila Hamilton, *The First Generation of University Women, 1869-1930,* in G Donaldson (ed), *Four Centuries: Edinburgh University Life 1583-1983,* (1983), p102

17. Ibid, p100

18. Lady Frances Balfour, *Ne Obliviscaris,* Vol ll (1930), p120 quoted in E Gordon, op cit, p226

19. Mary Cathcart Borer, *Willingly to School,* (1978), pp278-9

20. Norman L Walker, *Chapters from the History of the Free Church of Scotland,* (Edinburgh,1895), pp119-120

21. For an account of the Argyll Report see R D Anderson, *Education and Opportunity in Victorian Scotland; Schools and Universities* (1983)

22. S Hamilton in G Donaldson, op cit, p102, quoting *MacMillan's Magazine,* xvi (1867), p432

23. S.E.S. Mair, An Appreciation of Christian Eddington Guthrie Wright in *The Edinburgh School of Cookery Magazine,* (1925), p23

24. quoted in M Bryant, op cit, p87

25. Emily Davies, *Home and the Higher Education* (1878), in D Spender, op cit, p111

26. See Sara Delamont, *The Domestic Ideology and Women's Education,* in Sara Delamont and Lorna Duffin (eds), *The Nineteenth Century Woman: Her Culture and Physical World,* (1978), for a discussion of this subject.

27. J Butler, in D Spender, op cit, pp79-83

28. Elizabeth Wolstenholme-Elmy, *The Education of Girls, its Present and its Future* (1869), in D Spender, op cit, pp158-159

29. Maria Grey, *On the Special Requirements for Improving the Education of Girls,* (1871), in D Spender, op cit, p180

30. Emily A E Shirreff, *The Work of the National Union* (1873), in D Spender, op cit, p212

31. Ibid, pp 215-223

32. Jehanne Wake, *Princess Louise: Queen Victoria's Unconventional Daughter* (1988), p96

33. M C Borer, op cit, p287

34. Sir Wyndham Dunston, *The Times,* 8 December 1939, p11

35. See, for example, D Spender, op cit, p187 or p199, and J Wake, op cit, p170

36. See, for example, in the appreciation of Louisa Stevenson by Mary Kerr in *The Edinburgh School of Cookery Magazine 1925,* p24

37. M Bryant, op cit, pp72-73

38. S Smiles, *Character,* (1890), quoted in Carol Dyhouse, *Girls Growing Up in Late-Victorian and Edwardian England* (1981). Dyhouse presents an interesting discussion of gender roles, as does, for example, Joan N Burstyn, *Victorian Education and the Ideal of Womanhood,* (1980)

39. C Davidson, op cit, p20

40. Ibid, p34

41. W.H.Court, *A Concise Economic History of Britain* (1954), p201

42. Webb, op cit, p376

43. Court, op cit

Chapter 2

1. Dorothy Stone, *The National,* (1976), p8

2. Ibid, p10

3. Ibid, pp11-14

4. *The Times,* 7 July,1875; Scrap Book

5. Neville Marsh, *The History of Queen Elizabeth College,* p215

6. E.S.C. Magazine, 1925 p22

7. Ibid p20

8. See Lettice Milne Rae, *Ladies in Debate 1865-1935,* (1936)

9. Ibid, p37

10. *E.S.C. Magazine,* 1925, p10

11. James Barr, *The United Free Church of Scotland* (1934), p265

12. Reports of *The Scotsman, The Edinburgh Courant* and *The Daily Review,* 22 April, 1875, Scrap Book

13. Minute dated 24 April, 1875

14. *Edinburgh Courant* 22 April, 1875

15. Handbill dated 28 June, 1875

16. Letter to the Duchess of Ruthven, 26 October, 1875, Letter Book 1

17. *The Scotsman,* 19 October, 1875, Scrap Book

18. *The Edinburgh Daily Review,* 10 November, 1875, Scrap Book

19. *Dunfermline Saturday Press,* 13 November, 1875, Scrap Book

20. *The Edinburgh Daily Review, The Edinburgh Courant, The Scotsman,* 10 November, 1875, Scrap Book

21. Letters to J C Buckmaster, 29 October, 1875 and 3 November, 1875, Letter Book 1

22. *The Scotsman, The Edinburgh Courant,* 16 November, 1875, Scrap Book

23. *The Scotsman,* 18 November, 1875

24. Letter to A Hoggan, 20 November, 1875, Letter Book 1

25. *The Scotsman,* 2 December, 1875, Scrap Book

26. *The Edinburgh Courant,* 5 June, 1876, Scrap Book

27. Letter to the Secretary, School of Arts, 21 December, 1875, Letter Book 1

28. *Perthshire Advertiser,* 5 May, 1876; *Alloa Advertiser,* 20 May, 1876; *Fife News,* 5 June, 1876, Scrap Book

29. Letters to Miss Middleton, 15 June; to Mrs Robertson, 7 July; to Miss Middleton 8 July; 15 July; and 18 July; all 1876. Letter Book 1

30. Letter to Miss Middleton, 1 June, 1876. Letter Book 1

31. Letter to Miss Dod(d)s, 15 June, 1876. Letter Book 1

32. Letter to Mrs MacPherson, 27 October, 1876. Letter Book 1

33. Daphne Bennett, *Emily Davies and the Liberation of Women,* (1989), for an account of Emily Davies's life at Gateshead.

34. M Bryant, op cit, p61

35. *The E.S.C. Magazine* (1925), p24, Appreciation by Mary Kerr. (Mary Kerr joined the 'Ladies' Edinburgh Debating Society in 1881 and was, therefore, very much in touch with events at the time when the Stevenson sisters were most active.)

36. Edythe Lutzker, *Women Gain a Place in Medicine,* (1969), p94

37. *The E.S.C. Magazine* (1925), p25

38. Lettice Milne Rae, op cit, p37

39. Ibid, p42

40. Anon. *Recollections of the Public Work and Home Life of Louisa and Flora Stevenson* (printed for private circulation at the behest of their neices and with an after-thought by their life long friend, Miss E.T. McLaren) (written 1914)

41. Letter to Rev H Calderwood 23 June, 1876, and *The Scotsman*, 15 July, 1876. Letter Book 1

42. *The Scotsman*, 28 September, 1876. Scrap Book

43. *The Scotsman*, 30 September, 1876. Scrap Book

44. Helen Corr, (1984), op cit, p212

45. Letter to Thos. Gray of School Board, Leith, 13 October, 1876, in which she states, 'I go to Liverpool on Monday for a few days ..' Letter Book 1

46. Margaret E Scott, *History of Fanny Calder College of Domestic Science*, Appendix 11

47. First Annual Report, 1876

48. *The Scotsman*, 3 November, 1876. Scrap Book

49. Letter to James Nairn, Esq., 2 November, 1876. Letter Book 1

50. *Fifeshire Journal*, 14 September, 1876. Scrap Book

51. *The Edinburgh Daily Review*, 18 September, 1876. Scrap Book

52. *The Aberdeen Free Press*, 24 October 1876, and 27 October 1876. Scrap Book

53. *Dundee Advertiser*, 27 October, 1876. Scrap Book

54. *Dunfermline Press*, 11 November, 1876. Scrap Book

55. *The Scotsman*, 28 November, 1876. Scrap Book

56. Letters to Mrs Reid and Mrs Geddes, 3 October 1876 and 8 November, 1876. Letter Book 1

57. Letter to Mrs Geddes, 2 December, 1876. Letter Book 1

58. Letter to Mr Dick, 13 December, 1876. Letter Book 1

59. Letter to Madame Guillaume, 27 November, 1876. Letter Book 1

60. Letters concerning Miss Middleton, 23 December and 29 December, 1876, and 3 January, 17 January, 8 February, 15 February, 16 February, and 22 February,1877. Letter Book 1

61. Letters to Miss Dodds, 2 October, ? October and 30 October, 1877. Letter Book 1

62. Annual Report, 1876-77

63. Letters to Mrs Edmonds, 31 December, 1877 and 22 January, 1878. Letter Book 1

64. Letter to Mr Moncur, 13 December, 1876 Letter Book 1

65. Letter of ? February, 1877. Letter Book 1

66. Letter to M Paterson, 27 October, 1877. Letter Book 1

67. Annual Report, 1876-77

68. *Elgin Courant*, 9 January, 1877 and *Banffshire Journal*, 11 January, 1877. Scrap Book

69. *Newcastle Chronicle*, 9 January, 1877. Scrap Book

70. Letter to Mrs Fenwick, 24 January, 1878. Letter Book 1

71. M E Scott, op cit, p101

72. Letter to Miss F Calder, 5 March, 1878. Letter Book 1

73. Report on talk by Miss de la Cour, 10 June, 1955

74. Annual Report, 1876-77

75. Letter to B P Walker, ? October 1877. Letter Book 1

76. Letter to Wolf and Co, 19 January, 1878. Letter Book 1

77. Annual Report 1877-78

78. Ibid, and Annual Report 1878-79

79. Annual Report 1877-78

80. Annual Report 1878-79

81. Ibid

82. Letter to the Edinburgh School Board, 7 November, 1879. Letter Book 1

83. Diploma Speech by Miss de la Cour, 1955

84. *Manchester Guardian*, 9 November, 1880. Scrap Book 1

85. Some of this information is based on a note on Manchester, probably prepared by or for Miss C L Morgan in 1975.

86. Letters to Mr Broadflower of the Manchester Committee, dated 3 June, 20 September and 13 October, 1890. Letter Book 2

87. Letter to A Hodgson, 30 September, 1889. Letter Book 2

88. Letters from Miss Scott to Mrs Wagstaffe and Miss Flemming, 4 July, 14 September and 21 September, 1887. Letter Book 2

89. Testimonial to Miss D M Scott, 8 September, 1889. Letter Book 2

90. Letters to R & A Mair, October, 1888, Letter Book 2

91. Letters of 7 and 8 June, 4 July and 27 August,1887 and letter to Miss Musgrove, 22 December, 1887. Letter Book 2

92. Monica E Baly, *A History of the Queen's Nursing Institute*, (1987), p43, quoting Dr Hurry, *District Nursing on a Provident Basis*, (1898)

93. Ibid, quoting the Royal Charter

94. Ibid, quoting Report of the Sub-Committee for the National association for Providing Trained Nurses for the Sick Poor, GLRO NC/15/13b, June 1875.

95. Ibid, p37

96. *The Scotsman*, 25 February, 1907. Scrap Book

97. Culled from M E Baly, op cit, pp30-38 and Miss Guthrie Wright's obituary notice in *The Scotsman*, 25 February, 1907.

98. Handbill

99. Memorial to the Lords of the Scotch Education Department, December, 1887.

100. Regulations Concerning Elementary School Teachers' Cookery Diploma.

Chapter 3

1. Private Memorandum by the Executie Committee, December 1890

2. *E.S.C. Magazine*, (1925), p16, article by H F Cadell, Financial Development of the School.

3. Letter to W F Pollock, 9 February, 1891. Letter Book 2

4. Letter of 13 February, 1891. Letter Book 2

5. H F Cadell, op cit, p17

6. *E.S.C. Magazine*, (1925), p29, article by A Pearce, Recollections of the School.

7. Notice advertising the new School and Housewife's Diploma, 1891.

8. Letter to Miss Leith, 14 April, 1891. Letter Book 2

9. Notice advertising the new School and Housewife's Diploma, 1891.

10. Regulations for Boarders, July 1892.

11. A Pearce, op cit, p29.

12. *The Lady, The Christian World, The Truth*, all 27 August, 1891. Scrap Book

13. *The Queen*, 10 October, 1891. Scrap Book

14. Handbill, and *The Court Journal*, 3 September, 1892. Scrap Book

15. *The Baltimore Daily*, 1893 (article by-line date 30 July). Scrap Book

16. Letter concerning Miss Jack, 5 July, 1888. Letter Book 2

17. Letter to Miss Jack, 13 April, 1891. Letter Book 2

18. Letter of re-engagement, 7 May, 1892. Letter Book 2

19. Letter to Town Clerk, 28 July, 1892; letters to Miss Crawford, 6 and 8 May, 1893. Letter Book 2. Talk by Miss de la Cour, 10 June, 1955 and H F Cadell, op cit, p17.

20. Talk by Miss de La Cour, and H F Cadell, op cit.

21. Edinburgh School Board, Report of the Committee on Domestic Economy, 8 March, 1898.

22. Talk by Miss de la Cour. *E.S.C. Magazine*, (1925), articles by Miss J C Melvin, *Unofficial Memories*, pp26-28, and A Pearce, p30.

23. Letter to H F Cadell, 1 May, 1907. Letter Book 2

24. *North British Advertiser*, 14 December, 1901. Scrap Book

25. Jehanne Wake, op cit, p363

26. Letter to Mr Watt, 30 November, 1893

27. Letters to Miss Harrison, 28 December, 1893 and 12 October, 1894. Letter Book 2

28. Letters to Miss Rotheram, July-September, 1895. Letter Book 2

29. Letter to Miss Horne, 29 November, 1900. Letter Book 2

30. Letter to Miss Horne, 6 June, 1901. Letter Book 2

31. Letter for Mr Calderwood, 8 July, 1906. Letter Book 2

32. Memo for Miss Guthrie Wright, 26 October, 1905. Letter Book 2

33. Letter to Miss Mcleish, July 1910. Letter Book 2. And letter from Miss Mcleish (undated).

34. Annual Report, 28 November, 1901.

35. The best discussion of this subject is contained in the thesis by Helen Corr, (1984) op cit.

36. C Dyhouse, op cit, p95.

37. For a discussion of infant mortality rates in Scotland see R Mitchison, *British Population Change Since 1860. Studies in Economic and Social History*, Macmillan series, 1977, p50.

38. PP1903 Cmnd. 1507 Vol xxx, *Report of the Royal Commission on Physical Training* (Scotland).

39. C Dyhouse, op cit, p92.

40. Ibid, pp93-95.

41. Ibid, for a discussion of this question.

42. A M Mackenzie, *Scotland in Modern Times* (1941), p332.

43. Anon *(Recollections etc)* op cit, quoting *The Scotsman*, 19th April 1906, and for Miss McLaren's comments, pp16-22 44. *E.S.C.Magazine*, (1925). op cit, p10.

45. *The Scotsman*, 25 February, 1907. Scrap Book.

46. *The Scotsman*, 1 March, 1907. Scrap Book.

47. Edinburgh Provisional Committee for the Training of Teachers - Report of Conference with the Edinburgh School of Cookery and Domestic Economy, 27 November, 1907.

48. Elizabeth Wolstenholme-Elmy, in D. Spender, op cit, p157.

49. Dundee Institute of Technology, *The First Hundred Years 1888-1988*, (1989), p1.

50. Letter to shareholders, 4 June, 1909; Notice of Extraordinary General Meeting of the Edinburgh School of Cookery, 24 June, 1909; Report of the Interim Council of the New Edinburgh School of Cookery and Domestic Economy, to the new School Council, 2 December, 1907. *The Scotsman,* 9 July, 13 and 16 October, 1909. Scrap Book.

51. *The Scotsman,* undated, but about December, 1910. Scrap Book.

52. Appeal for Extension Fund, 1912 and Annual Report, 1911.

53. Report by Sub-Committee of the Finance Committee,16 February, 1910.

54. *E.S.C. Magazine* (1925), p13. Proposals regarding the Appointment of District Superintendents in Domestic Science; and Regulations for the Training of Teachers 1912.

55. Helen Corr, in W H Fraser and R J Morris, op cit, pp307-308.

56. Civic and Social Course Syllabus, 1913-1914. And unidentified newspaper cutting c1910. Scrap Book.

57. *E.S.C.Magazine,* (1925) pp31-32.

58. Visitors Book

59. Letter to Miss Whitaker, 27 July, 1911. Letter Book 2.

60. Letter to Miss Turnbull, 12 February, 1915. Letter Book 2.

61. Letter to Miss Allan, 18 April, 1914; and to Mr Watson, 26 March, 1913. Letter Book 2.

62. Extract of letter from Mrs Agnes Forbes (no date).

63. Report of Miss de la Cour's Talk, 10 June, 1955.

64. Posters dated 14 January and 17 June, 1915; and 28 March and 24 April, 1917.

65. Letter from Miss de la Cour, July 1915.

66. Voluntary Scheme of Rations.

67. *The Scottish Gentlewomen*, 9 February, 1918. Scrap Book.

68. The Edinburgh and Glasgow Joint Committee for the Training of Munitions Welfare Supervisors, Syllabus of lectures.

69. Extract of letters from Martha E R Coggins and S Jessica Clarke. (undated).

70. E.S.C. Magazine (1925), H F Cadell, op cit, p18

71. Ibid, pp12-13 and pp18-20.
72. Ibid, p34.
73. Extracts of letters from Maragret Gardiner and Mrs Isabel Merrill (undated).
74. Lettice Milne Rae, op cit, Foreword by Sarah Siddons Mair.

Chapter 4

1. *E.S.C. Magazine,* (June, 1925), pp3-4.
2. *E.S.C. Magazine,* (Dec, 1925), pp3-5.
3. *E.S.C. Magazine,* (July, 1929), pp5-6.
4. Minutes of the Meetings of Council, 13/1/1931, 7/4/1931, 17/4/1931, 6/5/1931. 12/5/1931.
5. Minutes of the Meetings of Council, 7/10/1931, 19/11/1931 and 30/11/1931.
6. *Edinburgh College of Domestic Science Magazine,* 1942-43, p6
7. Report of Miss de la Cour's talk, 10 June, 1955.
8. Report on College, 1932 (typescript).
9. Report on the College, 1925-1932 (typescript p2).
10. Interview with J MacDougall, 1990.
11. Sea-Cooks, Miss P L Wingfield, (typescript).
12. Extract of letter from Mrs R M Marshall (undated)
13. *E.C.D.S. Magazine,* 1934, p7
14. Ibid, p5
15. *E.C.D.S. Magazine,* 1940; also Miss P L Wingfield, 'Atholl Crescent in the Second World War', (typescript p5).
16. *E.C.D.S. Magazine,* 1940, pp9-10
17. Ibid, 1940-1941
18. Ibid, 1941, p14
19. Ibid, 1944, p23
20. Ibid, 1945, p6
21. Ibid.
22. Ibid, 1947, p28
23. *The Scotsman,* (undated) 1950, Scrap Book.
24. Minutes of College Committee 1/11/49, 6/12/49, 7/2/50, 7/3/50 and 2/5/50.
25. Marjorie East, *Home Economics, Past, Present and Future,* Boston (1980), p10.
26. *The Scotsman,* 18 and 19 August, 1953. Scrap Book.
27. Note on College 1952-1960, dated 9 October, 1964. (typescript).
28. Minutes of College Committee, 1/3/1960.
29. Minutes of College and Hostels Committee, 4/10/1966
30. Minutes of College and Finance Committees, 1/10/1957, 8/10/1957 and 3/12/1957.
31. Minutes of College Committee, 3/12/1957.
32. Minutes of College Council, 13/10/1959 and 26/1/1960.
33. Ibid, 10/2/1960 and 3/5/1960.

34. Ibid, 23/1/1962.

35. Ibid, 10/7/1962.

36. Ibid, 23/1/1962.

37. For example, Ibid, 2/2/1961 and 4/7/1961.

38. For example, Ibid, 2/10/1962.

39. Ibid, 28/7/1961 and 20/2/1962.

Chapter 5

1. J.R.Peddie, *Education*, in Henry W. Meikle (ed) *Scotland*, (1947), pp128-137.

2. H.Silver, *A Higher Education: The Council for National Academic Awards and British Higher Education 1964-1989*, (1990), p24.

3. J. Gibson, *The Thistle and The Crown: A History of the Scottish Office*, (1985), p147.

4. James Scotland, *The History of Scottish Education*, Vol 2., p180, pp192-193.

5. Ibid, pp246-247.

6. *Report of the Committee on Higher Education*, (1963), p146.

7. Ibid, pp142-143.

8. Lord Robbins, *Higher Education Revisited*, (1980), p99.

9. See Silver, op cit, Chapter 4, for a full discussion of this subject.

10. Ibid, pp68-69.

11. *E.S.C.Magazine*, (1925), p33.

12. Minutes of College Council, 6/2/1962, 25/10/1962, and 26/1/1965.

13. Minutes of College Committee, 5/2/1963.

14. Minutes of College Council, 7/7/1964, 6/10/1964, and 12/7/1966.

15. Ibid, 11/10/1966.

16. Ibid, 28/1/1964, 3/5/1966.

17. Minutes of Finance Committee, 17/3/1964 and of College Council 7/7/1964.

18. Minutes of College Council, 3/12/1963.

19. Ibid, 28/1/1964.

20. See Ibid, 3/12/1963, 5/5/1964, 4/5/1965, 1/3/1966, and 3/5/1966 for some of the discussions on the development of the Dietetics Diploma.

21. Ibid, 1/5/1962.

22. Extraordinary Meeting of College Council, 13/4/65.

23. Minutes of College Council, 9/7/1963 and 8/10/1963.

24. *Scottish Field*, June 1971.

25. *Home Economics*, August 1971.

26. Minutes of Finance Committee, 20/10/70 and 10/2/71.

27. Minutes of College and Hostels Committee 1/12/70.

28. Eileen M Byrne, *Women in Education* (1978), p147, pp254-257.

29. Minutes of College Council, 26/10/71.

30. Minute of Extraordinary Meeting of Members of the College, 22/3/1972.

31. College and Hostels Committee, 5/12/72.

32. Ibid, 6/11/73.

33. Minutes of Governing Body, 11/6/74.

34. Ibid, 29/10/74.

35. Minutes of College Council, 24/4/73 and Chairman's Committee, 1/2/73.

36. Minutes of Finance and General Purposes Committee, 19/11/74.

37. Interview with Dr B. Henderson, 24/9/93.

38. H.Silver, op cit, p97.

39. Minutes of Governing Body, 27/1/76.

40. See, for example, Professor McGovern's interesting article, *Speech & Language Therapy Education in Edinburgh 1764-1993* in *History of Education Society Bulletin*, 54 (1994)

41. Interview with Principal Leach, 23/9/93.

42. H.Silver, op cit, p2.

43. Q.M. Newsletter, Issue 29, May 1993, p12.

Index